Superheroes and Philosophy

Popular Culture and Philosophy™
Series Editor: George A. Reisch
(Series Editor for this volume was William Irwin)

Superheroes and Philosophy

Truth, Justice, and the Socratic Way

Edited by
TOM MORRIS
and
MATT MORRIS

OPEN COURT
Chicago and La Salle, Illinois

Volume 13 in the series, Popular Culture and Philosophy™

Front cover art: conceived and drawn by Craig Rousseau, colored by J.D. Smith.

To order books from Open Court, call toll-free 1-800-815-2280, or visit our website at www.opencourtbooks.com.

Open Court Publishing Company is a division of Carus Publishing Company.

Library of Congress Cataloging-in-Publication Data

Superheroes and philosophy / edited by Tom Morris and Matt Morris.
     p. cm.—(Popular culture and philosophy ; v. 13)
    Includes bibliographical references and index.
    ISBN-13: 978-0-8126-9573-1 (alk. paper)
    ISBN-10: 0-8126-9573-9 (alk. paper)
    1. Comic books, strips, etc.—Moral and ethical aspects.
  2. Heroes in literature. I. Morris, Thomas V. II. Morris, Matt, 1983- III. Series.
    PN6712.S86 2005
    741.5'09—dc22

                                       2005005935

Contents

Part Three

Superheroes and Moral Duty   145

Part Four

Identity and Superhero Metaphysics   221

Men in Bright Tights and Wild Fights, Often at Great Heights, and, of Course, Some Amazing Women, Too!

Look! Up on the screen! Or, over there, in the bookstore! It's a superhero! It's—lots and lots of superheroes! Holy Pop Culture! What's going on?

The whole country is learning the secret that's been kept alive for years by a core group of comic-book fans—the classic superhero stories, as they continue to be produced by some of the best writers and artists alive, can be wildly fun, suspenseful, exciting, and even profoundly thought-provoking. Like Plato and Aristotle, Superman and Batman are here to stay. So are Spider-Man, Daredevil, the Fantastic Four, and the Uncanny X-Men, among many other mythic heroes in tights.

One of the most striking pop culture developments of the present day is the strong resurgence of the costumed super-hero as an entertainment and cultural icon. A recent, nationally syndicated newspaper article on this turn of events began with the sweeping sentence, "It's become a comic-book world." The global reference is appropriate. Not many fictional characters in history have attained anything like the international recog-nition of Superman and Batman. These two titans of the comics have inspired radio, television, film, and musical depic-tions since their first appearances in the late 1930s. You can see someone wearing a Superman or Batman T-shirt in almost any part of the world, and under some of the most extraordi-nary circumstances. Now, many of their junior colleagues are being featured on the big screen, and some of them are becoming huge film and merchandising franchises themselves. The first Spider-Man movie surprised the film community with the single largest U.S. opening weekend gross revenues in his-tory. And *Spider-Man 2* topped even that in worldwide box office receipts. Over the next few years, this trend is predicted to continue, with sequels, long-awaited launches, and films being made on lesser-known superhero characters as well as all the major icons.

Superheroes have become a part of our cultural language. Perpetually popular *Seinfeld* reruns often showcase esoteric discussions between Jerry and George over some bit of superhero trivia. The theme song for the popular NBC comedy *Scrubs* casually references Superman. Contemporary rock, rap, and pop music all contain allusions to the spandex crowd. Comic-book shops dot the landscapes of big cities, suburbs, and small town strip malls, bringing together an amazing array of fans. And the larger comic-book conventions held around the country annually, once hosting hundreds of participants, have in the past few years reached an all-time peak attendance, with the flagship San Diego convention recently enjoying a crowd of 87,000 fans over three or four days.

What's even more important is that current aficionados of the comic-book superheroes include some of the hottest opinion makers and trend setters of the day, with top box office megastars vying to be cast as their superhero favorites, respected novelists sprinkling their narratives with superhero references, and at least one celebrated film director, the ever-inventive Kevin Smith, actually writing some very popular superhero comic books himself.

Philosophy in the Superhero Stories

The superhero comics constitute one of those original American art forms like jazz, blues, muscle cars, and *Krispy Kreme* doughnuts that have reached out to the world and have made a distinctive impact across cultures. Even the most casual observer knows that these stories are full of action, adventure, suspense, and incredible artwork. But what too few people realize is that they also deserve serious intellectual attention for their fascinating presentations of deep philosophical themes and ideas. Really. We're not kidding.

The best superhero comics, in addition to being tremendously entertaining, introduce and treat in vivid ways some of the most interesting and important questions facing all human beings—questions regarding ethics, personal and social responsibility, justice, crime and punishment, the mind and human emotions, personal identity, the soul, the notion of destiny, the meaning of our lives, how we think about science and nature, the role of faith in the rough and tumble of this world, the importance of friendship, what love really means, the nature of a family, the classic virtues like courage, and many other important issues. It's about time that, in particular, the best comic books got their due and were more widely recognized for their innovative and intriguing ways of raising and wrestling with these pressing human concerns.

The classic and current comic books on superheroes, for all their immense popularity among young people up into their early thirties, deserve an even broader audience of adult readers. Most adults will admit to having read and enjoyed superhero comics in their youth, but they eventually allowed other forms of entertainment, as well as the demands of formal education, work, and family life to push this distinctive experience out of their lives. This is a modern aesthetic tragedy. Comic books and graphic novels occupy a unique artistic space along the spectrum of fictional narrative. Like movies and television shows, they make powerful use of visual imagery. But like novels and short stories, they allow us to pace our own experience of their presentations. Their weave of prose and art is powerful, and their vivid presentations of ideas can echo long after we've closed their colorful pages.

The best superhero stories raise issues that human beings have always faced, but some of them are questions we all may confront in striking new ways in the very near future. If there actually were people in our world with dramatic superpowers, how would you react to them? How do you think they would affect your life and attitudes? But we can make it even more personal. What would you do if you found yourself one day with incredibly enhanced powers? How would you react if you were offered the opportunity to genetically alter and supercharge your baby in its early embryonic stages, in such a way as to make it capable of doing great good, or terrible harm? Genetic research and nanotechnology may soon bring into the real world some core issues that the superhero comics have been grappling with for a long time. Are we philosophically prepared for such a radically augmented future? Can we handle the choices we are likely some day to face? We may need to ponder the lessons of the superheroes a bit more.

The contributors to this volume appreciate the power of the superheroes both to delight us and to make us think. You'll find in these pages some provocative essays by some of the brightest comic book fans to be found in the halls of academia and some striking contributions by some of the best thinkers to be found in the world of comic books. Philosophy professors, great comic-book editors, insightful superhero writers, historians, and fans have come together in this book to wrestle with some of the most pressing issues raised in the pages of the superhero comic books as well as in their recent films. We hope that these forays into superhero philosophy will contribute to your own reflections as you enjoy the escapades of these remarkable men and women in their bright tights and wild fights, often at great heights.

Acknowledgments

The editors have many people to thank for helping make this project possible. First, we want to thank Dr. Jennifer Baker for sponsoring Matt's research into Aristotle and Batman. In the comic-book world, Chris Ryall at IDW Publishing is Plato's ideal of the philosopher-king, transposed into the Editor-in-Chief mode. He has helped us throughout the project in so many ways. We super-appreciate it. And Scott Tipton, Professor and Exalted Emperor of *Comics 101* at the popular website *MoviePoopShoot.com*, has done more to help us than we can even remember, typically reading drafts of chapters and commenting on them so fast that he made Flash look slow. Thomas, John, Jim, and Mac at Fanboy Comics in Wilmington, NC have assisted us with expert advice every step of the way, telling us what we just *had* to read. They are walking encyclopedias of the esoteric and arcane within the world of comics. Our comic-book writers, Jeph Loeb, Dennis O'Neil, and Mark Waid, have also helped us in many ways far beyond their written contributions.

We want to thank Bill Irwin and Open Court's Editorial Director David Ramsay Steele for launching the great series of books on pop culture and philosophy in which the present volume has found its perfect home. Thanks also to Troy Marzziotti for reading some of the drafts for us. Our family—Mary, Sara, little Gracie, and the dogs—have all been very understanding and supportive as we got out of all kinds of actual work because we were too busy reading comic books.

Finally, we thank all the comic-book writers, artists, and editors of the past and present who have created this amazing art form where great entertainment and profound ideas can meet.

Part One

The Image of the Superhero

1

The Real Truth about Superman: And the Rest of Us, Too

MARK WAID

Superman, the grandfather of all superheroes, is a cultural institution. Even the most elite and insulated intellectuals have been exposed to enough pop culture to be familiar with the Man of Steel and what he stands for. He fights a "never-ending battle" for truth, for justice, and—still enthusiastically after all these years, despite the fact that no one can define it any more—for "the American Way." Consequently, he is as close as contemporary Western culture has yet come to envisioning a champion who is the epitome of unselfishness. The truest moral statement that can be made of Superman is that he invariably puts the needs of others first.

Or does he?

Preparation for a Surprise

Some people adopt astronomy or entomology as their life's study and can identify the most prominent Magellanic nebulae in the cosmos or the least visible aphid in the garden. Others devote their time and energy to analyzing and cataloguing, in excruciating detail, anything from Welsh folk tales to the box scores of the 1969 Mets. Me, ever since I was a boy, I've been fascinated by the mythology of Superman. Though it's not my day job (not exactly), that's my field of focused expertise. I freely admit that it's—to put it charitably—rather "specialized," but for all my other wide and varied interests, nothing in this world has ever held quite the same fascination for me as has the Man of Steel.

At a time in my emotionally tumultuous teenage years when I most needed guidance and inspiration, I found a father figure in Superman. Fictional or not, the power of his spirit quite literally saved my life, and ever since, I have done what I can to return the favor by investing in his legend. In the process, and without design, I became one of the world's leading authorities on the Last Son of Krypton. Over the years, I've retained the dubious distinction of being the only man alive to have read every Superman story, watched every cartoon, and TV show, and movie, listened to every radio drama, and unearthed every unpublished manuscript about him. I've so thoroughly immersed myself in every aspect of the Superman lore—and, along the way, absorbed such minutiae as Clark Kent's Social Security number and his boyhood sweetheart's mother's maiden name—that I regularly field queries from sources as varied as *Time* magazine, *The History Channel*, and the *Smallville* television producers. Long before now, I thought I knew Superman inside and out. But I was wrong.

The One Question I Could Not Answer

Up until the spring of 2002, it had been a good, long while since anyone had stumped me with a Superman question. That changed the day I had to face one that, oddly, it had never even occurred to me to ask:

"Why does he do what he does?"

The man who confronted me with those words and got to savor watching a lifetime of smugness evaporate from my face as I flailed for an answer was Dan Didio, Executive Editor of DC Comics, the publishers of Superman's exploits. Again, being a Superman expert is not my day job, though it's certainly a pertinent sideline. For most of my adult life, I've enjoyed a career as a reasonably successful comic book writer, and my boss had just approached me about creating a new Superman series called *Superman: Birthright* that would, as he put it, "re-imagine Superman for the twenty-first century." Understandably, he wanted to get my take on Superman's basic motivation. Why does Superman do what he does? What are his reasons? What moves him to take on the role of everyone's protector and defender? Why does he invariably seek to do the right thing?

"Why? Because," I responded with a telling stammer,

"because doing the right thing is . . . is . . . is the right thing to do . . ."

"I'm hiring you to re-imagine harder than *that*," my boss insisted, and he had a point. Because I grew up with Superman, because I took his fictional presence for granted, I was falling back on an easy, childlike—and knee-jerk—answer. The truth of the matter was, I hadn't any real clue, and if I was going to do my part to revitalize the character's impact on a post-9/11 world . . . well, Superman deserved more than that from me.

Comic book superheroes were created as, and always have been at root, an adolescent power fantasy. As literary constructs go, they don't need to be terribly complex; in their primary-colored costumes, fighting gaudy villains and hyper-dramatic menaces that aren't terribly subtle, they're intended to excite the imaginations of children with the same fire and energy as the myths and fairy tales of years past. But, to kids today, as the stars and profiles of Batman, Spider-Man, and Wolverine have risen, Superman has become increasingly irrelevant. As a pop-culture force, he enjoyed his greatest impact nearly a half-century ago, and today there are entire generations to whom Superman is about as meaningful and significant as Woody Woodpecker or Amos 'n' Andy. And, speaking as a man in his early forties, it's tempting to simply assume that "kids today don't know what's good." But that ignores the undeniable fact that the Gen-X and Gen-Next audience I cater to as a comics writer perceive the world around them as far more dangerous, far more unfair, and far more screwed up than my generation ever did. To them, and probably more accurately so than the child in me would like to believe, their world is one where unrestrained capitalism always wins, where politicians always lie, where sports idols take drugs and beat their wives, and where white picket fences are suspect because they hide dark things.

And Superman, the ultraconservative Big, Blue Boy Scout, actively *protects* that status quo. No wonder he's lost his sheen.

How relevant is a man who flies and wears a red cape to kids who have to pass through metal detectors at school? How inspirational is an invulnerable alien to young people who are taught that the moral visionaries and inspirational figures of history—from Bobby Kennedy to Martin Luther King to Mohandas Gandhi—got the same reward for their efforts: a bullet and a burial?[1] Modern times have created a new distance between Superman and his intended audience, because now they can't help but ask "why?" If this "Man of Tomorrow"—a.k.a. Kal-El, the Last Son of the planet Krypton—grew up in today's world, with anything even remotely resembling a contemporary point of view on heroism, why on Earth would he even consider embracing a path of selflessness? What possible reward could public service hold for a Superman who could, if he so desired, remain out of the public eye and media scrutiny? What would a full-time career of doing good for others offer a man who could, comfortably and safely cloaked in a T-shirt and jeans, make a very good living by wringing a diamond out of the occasional lump of coal? Or, to put it another way, this is a unique individual who could have anything he wanted for himself, so why does he spend nearly all his time taking care of others?

Yes. I know. It's a little weird to be asking such intense questions about someone who's, oh, *not real*. But that's the job of a comics writer—to give life to these heroes in ways that make them believable and keep them relevant. I was convinced that good answers could be mined from the character—provided I was willing to first forget everything I'd spent a lifetime knowing about him. The great philosopher Socrates (469–399 B.C.) believed that any genuine search for wisdom begins when we first admit that we do not really know. Only then can we truly learn. Socrates should have written comics.

A big part of retelling the Superman myth for a modern audience came in finding some distance, in allowing myself the perspective necessary to separate its timeless elements from the details that could be updated. There was no reason, for instance, that the *Daily Planet*—reporter Clark Kent's traditional employer of choice—couldn't be a World Wide Web news service instead of a print broadsheet. Or, for example, in our privacy-conscious day and age, in this retelling, a man with x-ray vision and super-hearing would have to earn the trust of the citizens of Metropolis rather than just assume it was his for the asking. Still, most of the Superman lore that I took for granted continued to hold up under scrutiny. Rocketed as an infant from a doomed

---

[1] Gandhi was cremated and his ashes, mixed with milk, were scattered in the Ganges River—a form of burial akin to burial at sea but especially holy for Hindus.

planet orbiting a dying, red star? Check—although his rocket ship would now have to be equipped with all manner of detection-cloaking devices to keep it hidden from NORAD. Adopted by a kindly Midwestern farming couple and named Clark Kent? Certainly—but I wanted to position the Kent family as a little younger, and therefore a little more energetically invested in Clark's upbringing. Disguised as a mild-mannered citizen? Absolutely. In fact, this aspect of his character, upon renewed scrutiny, made more sense to me than ever. Of course, Kal-El is going to want to sport a low profile. How would you react if someone you thought you knew suddenly revealed that he was freakishly strong or could melt your car with an angry glance? People get seriously weirded-out when they see this man use his powers openly. It makes them retroactively paranoid. He has superhuman powers *and* he's been keeping them a secret? That's a *big* secret. What else has he been keeping from them, they'd wonder. The possibilities would be endless, and some of them sinister.

Who is he, *really?*

We know the answer to that one, as does Kal-El. He has vague, dreamlike memories of his lost home world, particularly every evening at dusk, when he feels an inexplicable sadness and longing in watching the setting sun turn red on the horizon. And every time, in his Clark identity, that he has to politely forego a pickup touch-football game for fear of crippling the opposing line, every time he hears the splash of an Antarctic penguin while trying to relax on a Hawaiian beach, every time he surrenders himself to a moment of unbridled joy and looks down to see that he's quite literally walking on air, he gets the message loud and clear: He's not from around here. He doesn't belong here. He was raised as one of us, but he's really not one of us. Superman is the sole survivor of his race. He is an alien being, and he is probably more alone in this world than anyone else ever has been.

And that's the key.

The Need to Belong

The basic desire to belong is a fundamental aspect of human nature. As defined by psychologist Abraham Maslow (1908–1970), our need to connect to others is paramount to our well-being, prioritized just below our physiological needs (which have virtually no significance to Kal-El, whose cellular structure derives its nourishment not from food but from solar energy) and our need for safety (an instinct that is also likely to be slightly foreign to a man who can survive a direct nuclear blast). It's fair to presume that, despite his extraterrestrial origins, Kal-El feels the same basic need for community that is shared by all the human beings around him; if not, he most likely wouldn't bother being Clark Kent at all and would just as soon soar off to explore the greater solar system and galaxies beyond than work a nine-to-five in Metropolis.

Building from this assumption, I began to examine some theories as to how Kal-El might meet this need for community, but it wasn't until I came across a specific passage on the Internet by an author named Marianne Williamson that everything crystallized for me:

> Our deepest fear is not that we are inadequate. Our deepest fear is that we are powerful beyond measure. It is our light, not our darkness that most frightens us. We ask ourselves, Who am I to be brilliant, gorgeous, talented, fabulous? Actually, who are you *not* to be? You are a child of God. Your playing small does not serve the world. There is nothing enlightened about shrinking so that other people won't feel insecure around you. We are all meant to shine, as children do. We were born to make manifest the glory of God that is within us. It is not just in some of us; it is in everyone. And as we let our own light shine, we unconsciously give other people permission to do the same. As we are liberated from our own fear, our presence automatically liberates others.[2]

How does Kal-El connect with the world around him? Not by turning his back on his alien heritage, though that was certainly his instinct while he was growing up in a small town. No, he ultimately connects by *embracing* that heritage—by creating as an adult a new identity for himself that is as Kryptonian as Clark Kent is human. Kal-El knows instinctively that it is only when he puts his gifts to use that he truly feels alive and engaged. Only by acting to his fullest potential, rather than hiding on the sidelines behind a pair of fake eyeglasses, can he genuinely partic-

---

[2] Marianne Williamson, *A Return to Love: Reflections on the Principles of* A Course in Miracles (New York: Harper Collins, 1992).

ipate in the world around him. Only by being openly Kryptonian can he also be an Earthman with exuberance and excellence. When he lives as who he really is, in full authenticity to his nature and gifts, and then brings his distinctive strengths into the service of others, he takes his rightful place in the larger community, in which he now genuinely belongs and can feel fulfilled. It is no coincidence that, when the philosopher Aristotle (384–322 B.C.) wanted to understand the roots of happiness, he began to explore what it takes to live with excellence. Superman, in his own way, discovered the same connection.

Kal-El, it occurred to me as I began to formulate *Superman: Birthright*, would have only some passing familiarity with his origins, but that would be enough. There were two artifacts left to him by his birth parents, both of which accompanied him on his journey. The first was a Kryptonian "e-book" of sorts—an electronic tablet chronicling in comic-book-style illustrations a history of Krypton, and while the accompanying language in it was foreign to him, Kal-El still gleaned from its pictures that his was a race of adventurers and explorers eager to plant their banner to mark the victory of their survival. His birth race were people of accomplishment and great deeds. The second artifact he had was the banner itself: a red-and-blue flag centered around an alien glyph that, had the Kryptonians spoken an Earth language, might have borne a more-than-coincidental similarity to our letter "S." A flag always signals a sense of distinctiveness, achievement, and pride. It roots any individual who embraces it in a past, and in a people, while at the same time preparing him to live in the present and launch out into the prospect of a meaningful future with a sense of tradition, direction, and value.

Basing his own design on what he knew about the historical fashions of his Kryptonian "tribe," Kal-El used that flag and created a colorful garment that would resonate with their image, and yet still be unique to himself, a caped uniform that proudly celebrated and honored his race. Then, wearing it, he took to the skies boldly and unashamedly, using his superpowers to save lives and maintain the peace. It was during his very first public appearance that a fellow reporter named Lois Lane decided that the symbol emblazoned on this hero's chest stood for "Superman," and so the name stuck, as did the mission.

The Great Paradox

The resultant paradox brought me up short. Superman has, since his creation, been a shining example to readers everywhere of the virtue of selfless heroism—but he has accomplished this *by acting in his own self-interest*. Yes, Superman aids those in peril because he senses a higher moral obligation, and yes, he does it because his natural instincts and his Midwestern upbringing drive him towards acts of morality—but along with that genuine altruism is a healthy amount of self-awareness and a surprisingly enviable ability on his part to balance his own internal needs with the needs of others in a way that most benefits everyone. In helping others, Superman helps himself. In helping himself, he helps others. When he comes to the aid of other people, he is exercising his distinctive powers and fulfilling his authentic destiny. That, of course, benefits him. When he embraces his history and nature and launches out in the one set of activities that will most fulfill and satisfy him, he is helping others. There is no exclusive, blanket choice to be made between the needs of the individual and the needs of the larger community. There is no contradiction here between self and society. But it's a bit paradoxical in a very inspirational way. Superman properly fulfills his own nature, and his destiny, and the result is that many others are better off as well.

The man really does have a secret identity, and it's one that's been clever enough to fool me since I was a child. I don't think he'd discourage me from exposing this one, however. Superman is really the authentic individual accepting who he most deeply is, celebrating that true self, and then using all his powers for the good of others as well as himself.

Long past the point where I believed I had anything left to learn from a simple hero of my childhood, Superman stands revealed to me as a tool through which I can examine the balance of selflessness and self-interest in my own life, which is every bit as valuable a lesson as the ones he taught me years ago. He really does fight a never-ending battle.

2
Heroes and Superheroes

JEPH LOEB and TOM MORRIS

Many writers, artists, and other people who are in the superhero business have taken up this interesting task because we believe that the stories of these characters embody our deepest hopes and fears, as well as our highest aspirations, and that they can help us deal with our worst nightmares. They chart out questions we'll all have to face in the future. And they shed new light on our present condition. In addition, they do all this in such a way as to give us a new sense of direction and resolve as we live our own lives.

Defining a Hero and a Superhero

Let's start with a simple question. What is a superhero? What sets a superhero apart from a normal person? Well, first of all, they tend to look a bit different. Some wear capes and, since the time of Count Dracula, very few other people have donned this particular garb. Some of them have cool gadgets they keep in utility belts. One has metal claws that pop out of his hands. Another is very green and you wouldn't want to be around him when he's angry. There's a lot of spandex involved, and movement high above the ground is common. Hyphenated or compound names ending in "man" or "woman" or "boy" or "girl" tend to be a dead giveaway as well. As a rule, superheroes have powers and abilities far beyond those of ordinary mortals. And to a person they pursue justice, defending the defenseless, helping those who cannot help themselves, and overcoming evil with the force of good.

Some people think that the concept of a superhero is problematic. Understanding a hero as a person who risks life and limb for the sake of others, and taking the prefix "super" to indicate the possession of superpowers, they reason that the more super an individual might be, the less heroic he or she could possibly be, and conversely, the more heroic a person is, the less super they'd have to be. The reasoning is simple. The more powerful a person is, the less he or she would risk in fighting evil or helping someone else. What's so heroic about stopping an armed robbery if your skin is bullet proof and your strength is irresistible by any ordinary, or even extraordinary, street thug? On the other hand, if you're actually heroic in your actions, it must be because you did indeed have a lot to lose, if things had gone badly, which can't be true unless you lack the typical powers that are distinctive of superheroes. If this argument is right, then, at worst, the concept of a superhero, in it's extreme idealism, is an oxymoron, which means that it's literally incoherent, a contradiction in terms. At best, it would follow that the only super-powered individuals fighting evil and working for the good of others who normally could be considered heroic would have to be those on the low end of the power spectrum, with few protections and many vulnerabilities. Superman, for example, would be disqualified from counting as heroic in his normal actions, except perhaps when he faced Kryptonite.

As tempting as this reasoning might seem, it's just based on a simple misunderstanding of the heroic. The Oxford English Dictionary defines "hero" as a term coming down to us from Greek antiquity, and as meaning "man of super-human qualities, favored by the gods." The second definition given is "illustrious warrior," and the third is "man admired for achievements and noble qualities." This third definition is of particular interest.

No level of achievements alone is enough to make someone a hero. That person must embody noble qualities as well. Go look up the word "noble" and you'll find phrases like "of lofty character or ideals" and "morally elevated." The concept of a hero is a moral category. The idea of a superhero is not an oxymoron—a composite concept composed of two incompatible notions: that of an utterly invulnerable being risking personal vulnerabilities (which of course he can't have since he's invulnerable) for the sake of a greater good. That's not the idea of a superhero at all. A superhero is an extraordinarily powerful per-

son, with weaknesses as well as strengths, whose noble character guides him or her into worthy achievements.

But let's back up a moment and look at the fundamental
idea of a hero a bit more. There are many heroes in works of
fiction, and in the real world, who don't have superpowers at
all. The heroes who live and work around us every day include
firemen, police officers, doctors, nurses, and teachers. People
in these jobs are often able to rise above the universal and altogether natural concern for the self, with its interests, and put
the needs of others first on their list of priorities. They fight for
human health, safety, growth, and excellence. They are the
warriors of everyday life whose sacrifices and noble deeds benefit us all.

But we don't often think of these people as heroes. And
that's too bad. Their contributions are so common, and so regular to our experience, that we can easily overlook their distinctive character. We notice such people and recognize them
as heroic only when they go far beyond the range of their normally heroic activities and catch our attention in a particularly
dramatic way. But if we only understood things more deeply,
we would see their normal activity for the drama and true heroism that it often is. In a culture of pervasive self-interest and
self-indulgent passivity, where people are often more inclined
to be spectators than participants, and typically embrace easy
comfort rather than initiating needed change, we can forget the
relative rarity of the motivation behind what is actually heroic
activity. We like to think about such people and their jobs that,
"They do it because they like to do it." And we comfort ourselves that, because of this, "They're really no better than the
rest of us."

One of the problems that J. Jonah Jamison, Editor-in-Chief of
the New York tabloid, the *Daily Bugle,* has with Spider-Man is
that the mere existence of a man who lives for others, who sacrifices important aspects of his private life in an ongoing effort
to help and save people he doesn't even know is something like
a standing rebuke to the rest of us for our unconcerned inertia,
and thus complicity, in the face of the many evils of the world.
In some prominent comic-book stories, ordinary people first
welcome superheroes as needed saviors, then come to take
them for granted, and finally begin to resent them for their heroically never-ending efforts to do what the rest of the population

ought to be doing, too. The superheroes stand out, not just because of their outfits and powers, but because of their altruistic activism and dedication to what is good.

In an interesting way, we can and should extend our concept of the heroic beyond those occupations that obviously require facing personal danger for the good of others, or that involve financial sacrifice in the service of what is socially needed. We should realize that a stay-at-home mother can be a hero, as can a public servant, an engineer, a musician, or an artist. Anyone who stands for the good and the right, and does so against the pull of forces that would defeat their effort can be seen as heroic. A person can make a heroic struggle against cancer, or some other terrible disease. A young man or woman can fight heroically for their own education, against all odds and expectations. Heroism as a concept should never be diminished by over-application, but at the same time, we do not properly understand it unless we see its application wherever it is appropriate.

This insight can help us to address another worry about the term "superhero." Since the original Greek definition of a hero involved the attribution of "super-human qualities," we might be tempted to think that the word "superhero" intrinsically involves a clumsy redundancy. But as the core concept of a hero has morphed over time from the ancient idea that did involve something like superpowers to the more modern notion that focuses mainly on high achievements and moral nobility, there is need for a term that brings the component of superior power back into the balance. And this is how we get our concept of a superhero. A superhero is a hero with superhuman powers, or at least with human abilities that have been developed to a superhuman level. That gets Batman and Green Arrow, among others, into the fray, where they belong. But remembering the "super," we can never allow ourselves to forget the "hero" element as well. There are limits to the development of superhero psychology on the part of comic-book writers and film writers. There can be darkness in a character as well as light, as there is in any human life, but that darkness must ultimately be constrained by the good and noble, or we have left the realm of the properly superheroic. Not every costumed crime-fighter is necessarily a hero, and not every one with superhuman powers is necessarily a superhero.

How to Be a Hero

In *Superman for All Seasons*, it was important to represent the true nature of the heroic choice that Clark Kent made, and had to continue to make, in order to be the superhero we know as Superman. To serve as many people who needed his help as possible, he had to leave the home of his loving family, the hometown where he had grown up, and the girl with whom he shared a special bond, and a secret, and move away, alone, to launch his mission of service. He had to make real sacrifices. And, when you think about it, sacrifice—along with the ability to make sacrifices—is something like a forgotten virtue in much of modern life. Or at least, it's under-appreciated. We tend to think of it in almost wholly negative terms, focusing on what we're being asked to give up, and losing sight of the value of the goal that cannot be attained without the sacrifice. A sacrifice is always a down payment, or an up-front cost. It's both rational and beneficial when what is being purchased by that cost is of great good, and can't be attained in any other way.

Superman sacrifices a lot in order to be able to do the heroic things he does. So does Peter Parker, in order to serve as Spider-Man. Matt Murdock gives up his nights, and much of his time off, in order to protect the innocent people of Hell's Kitchen and beyond. And all this sacrifice takes self-discipline, which is just about as far off the radar screen as sacrifice is for many people these days, as something good, valuable, and important in the arsenal of human qualities that are desirable to have. Power without self-discipline is either just wasted, or it's dangerous. Self-discipline is a form of focus that helps make the greatest goods possible.

In the *Superman for All Seasons* narrative, Lois Lane is so taken aback by how someone with Superman's powers could use them the way he does precisely because it's so relatively uncommon to see such a thing. The more power we get, the more avidly we tend to serve ourselves, and our own interests. But this is where the superheroes stand apart. They realize that there is no real self-fulfillment without self-giving. They understand that we have our talents and powers in order to use them, and that to use them for the good of others as well as ourselves is the highest use we can make of them.

The concept of a hero is what philosophers call a normative concept. It doesn't just characterize what is, it offers us a glimpse of what ought to be. It has a claim on us. It presents us with something to aspire to in our own lives. The superheroes provide great, fictionally vivid images of the heroic, and are both inspirational and aspirational. When they are developed properly and portrayed well, they present us with something to which we all should aspire. Plato believed that the good is inherently attractive. Unless we are blocked from seeing it and appreciating it for what it is, what is good will draw us in its direction. It will motivate us and direct our steps. That's why the depiction of the heroic in superhero stories is of moral force. From our childhoods and on into adulthood, the superheroes can remind us of the importance of self-discipline, self-sacrifice, and expending ourselves for something good, noble, and important. They can broaden our mental horizons and support our moral determination, while also entertaining us.

We don't necessarily have to say that superhero comics are intentionally instructional, or moralistic in nature. Sometimes, they're just fun. But it's very reasonable to suggest that the superheroes have been around for so long, and have continued to be so popular, in part, because they speak to our nature, as well as to both our aspirations and our fears. We all aspire to make a difference, to have an impact in this world, and to be acknowledged for that impact. The superheroes can keep that flame alive in our hearts as we ponder their sense of mission, and as we see them live it. But their stories can also speak to our fears, and in equally important ways.

Fear and the Superhero Stories

We all fear harm. That's just part of what it is to be human. The superhero stories portray vividly many forms of harm that can conceivably enter into our lives. The mad scientists, the power-hungry politicians, the disaffected loners with a grudge, the organized crime, the terrorism, the businessmen with nothing but profit on their minds, all remind us of the many sources of danger in our world. And, in addition, we are often both fascinated and a little worried about what is out there in the larger universe. Many superhero stories address these fears as well. The superheroes show us that all these dangers can be confronted and overcome. They display the power of character and courage over adversity. And so, even in dealing with our fears, they can be inspirational.

We will all confront adversity in our lives. And that can be dispiriting. We are often inclined to just give up and find an easier path. But the superheroes show us that nothing worth doing is easy. Even with their superpowers, the greatest of the superheroes often prevail against adversity only because of what philosophers know of as the classic virtues, and some neo-classic ones as well, like courage, determination, persistence, teamwork, and creativity. They don't accept defeat. They won't ever give up. They believe in themselves, and in their cause, and they go all-out to achieve their goals. By showing us how even very powerful people have to fight and struggle and stick to that fight in order to prevail, they help us deal with the fears that we all face concerning our own prospects in the world. So, it will be tough. So what? We can do it.

There is even another sort of fear, less obvious, but perhaps just as important, that many superhero narratives bring to our attention. Many of us fear what we may have to do to stand up to the evil in the world. Will we have to resort to force and violence in order to contain or defeat the forces that threaten us and those we love? The superheroes often do, but they know where to draw the line. Will we?

Many great philosophers have understood that we human beings are creatures of habit. Once we resort to violence to solve a problem, we are a bit more likely to do the same thing again on a future occasion—whether that future occasion really requires it or not. We are inclined to do what we have become accustomed to doing, and any single act can begin to accustom us to something new. If we are sent to war in a foreign land, will we return as more violent people? Will it ruin our lives? Will we be forever changed in detrimental ways? That's a real fear for any good person living in the modern world.

Along with our tendency to form habits, we all have something like an ever-rising threshold of expectations that plays out in many dimensions of our lives. The rising threshold phenomenon is a very general thing. The more money people make, the more they want, and the more they think is necessary for a comfortable life. A glass of wine with dinner can over time very easily become two glasses, and then three. The use of force and violence works the same way. What once was completely unacceptable can quickly come to seem unfortunately necessary, however regrettable, and ultimately even perfectly fine, as you move forward more deeply into new territory. We see this in wartime when accepted forms of violence can give rise over time to terrible atrocities. Good people rightly fear the effects that a use of force or violence could have on their own souls. If it comes to resisting evil with violence, what will that do to me? In violently defeating evil, will I actually have allowed evil to win after all, but in a different form, in my own soul?

The superheroes give us examples of good people who are able to use force when it's necessary, even sometimes taking violent actions, within limits, to defeat and subdue otherwise unstoppable evil, but without letting that get out of hand or rebound in self-defeating ways on their own characters. Batman, Spider-Man, and Daredevil, along with Superman and many others, exercise a great deal of self-restraint, and are careful to draw a line they will not cross. They are able to fight evil without becoming evil. In doing so, they address our common fear that it can't be done. They show us that we can do whatever we have to do, in the face of evil, if we stay firmly in touch with our noblest motivations and our most cherished values. But that doesn't mean that this is not dangerous. It's very dangerous. But good can still prevail.

The Example of the Superhero

Whether he's stopping a purse snatcher, foiling one of Lex Luthor's evil plots, or even deflecting an asteroid from its collision course with Earth, Superman gives us an ongoing example of what a commitment to truth, justice, and not just the American way, but the genuinely *human* way should look like. Many other superheroes show us this as well. We're all meant to be active in our creation of good lives, for ourselves, and for the other people around us. We're supposed to be concerned about our communities and our greater world. There is evil to be resisted and great good to be done. Life awaits our best contributions. The superheroes work for not just people who appreciate their efforts, but often for people who criticize and revile them. They don't do what they do because it's popular. They do it because it's right.

The superheroes are obviously very gifted individuals. In the ancient world, the prominent, and very practical Roman philosopher Seneca once said, "No man of exalted gifts is pleased with anything low and inferior. A vision of great achievement calls out to him and lifts him up."[1] This is literally true of Superman and many others. But all of us are gifted in some way. All of us have talents and powers. If we can follow the superheroes in not allowing what is low and inferior to interfere with our development and use of those gifts, we can bring a little of the superhero mindset into our own lives.

The philosopher Seneca also gave us all a great piece of advice when he wrote:

> Choose for yourself a moral hero whose life, conversation, and expressive face all please you, then picture him to yourself at all times as your protector, and as your ethical pattern. We all need someone whose example can regulate our characters.[2]

And then, again:

> Cherish some man of great character, and keep him always in mind. Then live as if he were watching you, and order all your actions as if he saw them.[3]

Many other ancient philosophers also urged us to do this. And it's very effective. People may carry around in their heads the image of a good parent, an admired sibling, a great teacher, a wise older friend or mentor, or even a noble moral leader like Gandhi, as a touchstone for their decisions and actions. What would my father do? What would my mother do? Would I act like this if my best teacher, or my spouse were watching me? And, as funny as it might seem, the best of the superheroes can function for us in precisely the same way. They are moral examples. Superman can inspire us. Batman can keep us going even when the going is very tough. Spider-Man can help us understand that the voice of conscience is always more important than

---

[1] Translation by Tom Morris, in Tom Morris, *The Stoic Art of Living* (Chicago: Open Court, 2004), p. 21.
[2] *The Stoic Art of Living*, p. 55.
[3] *The Stoic Art of Living*, p. 56

the cacophony of voices around us, who may be condemning us, belittling us, or just dismissing what we think of as so important. Daredevil can remind us that our limitations need not hold us back, and that we all have hidden strengths we can draw on when circumstances are especially challenging.

The heroic path is sometimes lonely, but it's always right. With an image of the superheroes in mind, we may find it a bit easier to stay true to the high moral road that alone will satisfy us in the end. What would Superman do? Go do your version of it. The world always needs one more hero.

3

The Crimson Viper versus the Maniacal Morphing Meme

DENNIS O'NEIL

You're staring at the pavement, muttering about The Crimson Viper. I think I know what's bothering you. "The new Viper sucks," you mumble, and I sigh, and ask you to elaborate, to give me the whole story, chapter and verse, though I already know pretty much what you'll say. You're aching to tell it . . . you *have* to tell it to *someone*. You don't get along with your mother, you fired your therapist, and I'm standing here.

What the Problem Seems to Be

What you say is: When you were a big comics reader, all through high school and well into college, you had a favorite superhero, The Crimson Viper. He was an important part of your life. Then real life took you away from comics. You met the person you refer to as "Her," your own personal soul mate and nemesis, and married Her, and fought with Her every night and most mornings, and finally moved out and, seeking solace, visited the nearest comic book shop. When you saw a whole section of a rack devoted to The Crimson Viper, you did something you hadn't done in months: you smiled. You blew some significant money buying all the back issues you missed, sped back to your (dreary) motel, flopped onto the (lumpy) mattress, opened a comic book and . . .

Five minutes later, you flung it across the—dingy—room. This was *wrong*! This was not *your* Viper!

No, it wasn't. The Viper had changed significantly in the four years you'd been away from him. You're outraged. You feel as betrayed as you did when you learned the real reason for all those visits to Her sister.

What the Problem Is

"Your problem is," I say, "that you're trying to do what Heraclitus said couldn't be done."

You're still looking at the pavement.

"Remember that summer course you took when you learned that you needed another credit to get your degree?" I ask. "What was it called . . . ? 'An In-Depth Look At the Great Philosophers From Parmenides to Foucault?' Something like that . . . Anyway, you remember it?"

You raise your eyes and nod.

"Okay, then you might also remember reading about Heraclitus. Greek, lived about 2,500 years ago."

Your expression tells me, eloquently, that thinking about Heraclitus is not at the very top of your priorities.

I blunder on: "Heraclitus said that we can never step into the same river twice. What he meant was, things are constantly in flux. Pretty much what modern physicists say."

I'm not sure I have your attention, but at least you haven't returned your gaze to the asphalt

"Now, some time before Heraclitus, around 2900 B.C.E.," I continue, "over in China a guy named Fu Hsi was writing the *I Ching*, also known as the book of changes."

You want to know if this is the same *I Ching* that your hippie cousin uses to predict the future, or so he imagines.

"The very same," I say. "A lot of people, not just hippies, use it as an oracle. I don't have an opinion about that and, to tell the truth, I'm not much interested in it. What concerns us is that one of the lessons the book teaches is that things and situations are constantly changing. In fact, the *Ching* says that things eventually become their opposites. Yin eventually becomes yang. Light becomes darkness. Heat becomes cold. Health becomes illness. The Republican Party of the mid-nineteenth century became its opposite in the twenty-first century, as did its rival, the Democratic Party."

Your body language tells me that you've settled into the conversation. You'll hear me out, unless I bore you absolutely to death. So I change my focus from ancient sages to a man who lived a lot more recently, though he's hardly contemporary. I remind you that Charles Darwin introduced to the world the term "Evolution," by which he meant the principle of change in the realm of biology—of plants and animals.

"The new Viper sucks," you say, and I'm speechless, which probably does not cause you to grieve. Have you been listening to anything I've been saying? *Anything?*

Let me continue trying.

The One Constant Is Change

First, you have to realize that *everything*, every single thing in the universe, changes if it persists—that is, if it lasts any length of time. Remember old Heraclitus? Fu Hsi? And be aware that the Crimson Viper has been continuously published for more than thirty years. Now, there may be a dozen ways of looking at superheroes like the Crimson Viper, maybe even more, but we'll restrict ourselves to just two—as archetypes and as memes. Your puzzled expression cues me to your need for a definition. Okay, we'll begin with "archetype." (Pay attention, we may have a quiz . . .)

An archetype, according to Carl Gustav Jung (1875–1961), who was a major-league psychologist, is an inherited memory represented in the mind by a universal symbol and observed in dreams and myths. In other words, it's an image that's hard-wired into our mental computers.

Now, let's consider where comic book . . . no, where all fiction comes from. I'm talking historically here, not psychologically; I'm asking, I guess, where the first stories were told. The answer is lost to antiquity. But, probably, the first stories were told by weary hunters gathered around campfires. The first recorded stories were in the form of drama and they were presented at the Festivals of Dionysius in Greece, about 600 B.C.E. Which means that they were part of the local religion and allied to mythology; after all, mythology is just other people's religion, no? The plays themselves didn't change much, as far as we know, but the myths did.

Want a few examples? Okay, try these: Nemesis, whose name is now synonymous with villain, began life as an idea of moral equilibrium. Odysseus was a hero to the Greeks, a creep to the Romans. Hades wore two hats: he was a god of wealth and a god of the dead. And to bring the discussion closer to our own culture, Satan went from being an early Egyptian god of immortality, to a judge, to an angel of light, to the source of everything rotten in the world. The guy who was originally Santa Claus wasn't a right jolly old elf with reindeer and sleigh full of toys. Want more? The library and the Internet can probably supply it.

Can we agree that comic-book superheroes are modern incarnations of some of the archetypes the good Dr. Jung mentioned? I mean, think about it for a second. Isn't Superman a science-fictiony version of Hercules and Samson? You look doubtful. Okay, let me quote something that Supes's creator, Jerry Siegel, actually *said* when describing how he came up with the world's most iconic cape-wearer: "All of a sudden it hits me. I conceive of a character like Samson, Hercules, and all the strong men I ever heard of rolled into one—*only more so.*"

We can go on. The Flash is a recasting of Mercury, the messenger of the Roman gods. Wonder Woman is actually *presented* as one of the bad-ass ladies in the Greek myths, the Amazons. The Marvel Comics character Thor is pretty much lifted whole from Norse mythology. Hawkman bears a strong resemblance to a couple of other mythic Greeks, Daedalus and Icarus.

Convinced? Then onward! Earlier, we agreed that the myths changed. Here, from George Lucas, the Star Wars honcho, is a description of the process:

> Mythology is a performance piece that gets acted out over hundreds of years before it actually becomes embedded in clay on a tablet or is put down on a piece of paper to be codified as a fixed thing. But originally it was performed for a group of people in a way in which the psychological feedback would tell the narrator which way to go. Mythology was created out of what emotionally worked as a story.

So, in days of yore—way, *way* yore—bards or minstrels or whatever the entertainers of the era were called went from place to place, telling their tales and changing the material as they saw what pleased the crowds. That's probably how Homer operated. But of course, he *heard* what pleased the crowds. And that worked just as well.

Today, things are different . . . well, not so much *different* as *faster*. The feedback that Homer got from one group of villagers at a time over years we get in a few weeks or even quicker. Readers either read or do not read your comic book. Audiences either watch or do not watch your TV show. Or listen to your music. Or buy tickets to your movie. Or play your video game or go to your amusement park, or . . .

You get the idea. Within a couple of months, at most, a purveyor of entertainment usually knows if his product has hit or missed. And that's if he waits for the money or the ratings to be counted. If he fires up the ol' computer, he can log onto an appropriate Web site and get a response virtually immediately, and if he's selling comic books, that response can be pretty vehement!

Of course, there are exceptions. Sometimes, something that isn't an immediate success finds patrons gradually and eventually triumphs. But it doesn't happen often, not in twenty-first-century America. The days when a media magnate like William Randolph Hearst would keep a comic strip like *Krazy Kat* going for decades just because he, personally, *liked* it are pretty much history. Mostly, the storyteller knows pretty quickly if he's succeeding and, if he's permitted to, begins making alterations accordingly.

The Scheme of the Meme

You ask what all this has to do with the Viper; actually, you don't ask, you grumble a question.

To answer, I'm afraid I'll have to talk about the other way we said we'd consider superheroes, as memes, and that, of course, requires another definition. Here goes. A *meme* is, according to the unimpeachably authoritative Oxford English Dictionary, "an element of a culture that may be considered to be passed on by non-genetic means, especially imitation." According to Richard Dawkins, the guy who made up the word, memes behave like biological genes; they're cultural parallels to Darwinian natural selection. (It won't astonish you to learn that Dawkins is a geneticist.) And, like genes, memes change as they pass from generation to generation. On the one hand, a meme is propagated into the future because it captures something that works. On the other hand, as it's passed on, it changes under new pressures. That happens . . . well, for a lot of reasons. The creators get new ideas, or are *forced* to get new ideas because a hungry market demands new stories. (I suspect that was the case with Jerry Siegel and Joe Shuster, of Superman fame.) Or the creators age and gradually begin to think about the world differently, and these changes are subtly reflected in their work. Or new creators with their own ideas begin working with the character. Or new creators arrive at a fresh synthesis of the ideas of their predecessors. Or a character's popularity wanes and innovations are introduced to rescue him. Or some fellow in a big, corner office near the top of a Manhattan office building has a brainstorm and everyone agrees with him because they have bills to pay and the job market's tight. Or a witches brew of all of the above occurs and . . . *voilà*!—a transformation!

Examples? Okay, some quick, easy ones. Superman went from merely being faster than a speeding bullet, more powerful than a locomotive and able to leap tall buildings in a single bound to moving at near-light speed and blowing out stars as if they were birthday candles. Batman began as one of those gentlemen crime fighters so abundant in the pop culture of the 1930s and 1940s, and then became, in turn, a father figure, a cop, a leading citizen, a comedian, and a dark avenger. Spider-Man lost a lot of his nerdiness. The Fantastic Four acquired superhero costumes—in their first appearance, they wore civvies. The Hulk changed color, from grey to green, and at times preserved his civilized ways when those devilish gamma rays transformed him from gentle Bruce Banner to the high-jumping giant, while at other times he seemed to be a king-sized stalk of unbridled id. Green Arrow started his career as an arrow-shooting Batman and grew into an arrow-shooting activist, though his political orientation swung from right to left, depending on who was writing his scripts. Another greenie, Green Lantern, even changed who he *was*: in the 1940s, he was a radio announcer, Alan Scott; in the 1960s and 1970s, he was Hal Jordan, a test pilot, and currently he's a freelance artist, Kyle Rayner . . . Then there's Nick Fury . . .

But you're fidgeting. Clearly, you've had enough examples. So I return to my main point: If you've been faithful to the character who's transformed and the changes have happened gradually, you might not be terribly offended by them; they might seem natural and organic. But to leave a beloved hero and come back and find him unrecognizable . . . well, as a former president might have said, I feel your pain.

If a character jumps from one *medium* to another, the process can accelerate. When Superman first moved from the comics pages to the radio waves in the early 1940s, he acquired a young pal, Jimmy Olsen, and something that could lay him low, Kryptonite. So, although Supes himself didn't change much on the radio, his milieu certainly did. A lot of people probably knew Batman from his various television incarnations, especially the live-action laff-riot that starred Adam West and later, some of them picked up the comic books and there was this gloomy, obsessed, *dark* dude skulking around the shadows with nary a *bam* or *pow* in sight. The Caped Crusader morphed from comedian to avenger because, suddenly, nobody was finding the comedian funny anymore, but there was still profit to be made from the Batman franchise. When Captain Marvel moved to Saturday-morning television, he acquired a fifty-something mentor and traveling companion, catchily called "Mr. Mentor," and a snazzy RV to cruise around the back roads of Southern California in—another case of a character's milieu altering to accommodate the notions of new bosses. And when Wonder Woman first made the jump to video . . . well, fans of the Amazon Princess barely recognized her. (I'm referring to the TV movie aired in 1974, the one that starred Cathy Lee Crosby, not the later, much better Lynda Carter version.) I could go on . . . the movies gave Captain America a gun. Radio made the Shadow invisible. Television reduced Sky King's sleek jet to a modest, single engine prop plane. Et cetera, et cetera, et cetera . . .

What We Want and What We Get

It's probably fair to say that every one of these changes, whether they stunk up the character or greatly improved him, caused somebody woe. Every fictional hero is *somebody's* favorite, and if the hero was your favorite when you were seeking escape from boring classrooms, bullying siblings, and that cruel bastard in the seventh grade who gave you a wedgie whenever the playground monitor wasn't looking, you have a special feeling for him. He was part of your childhood, a part that wasn't rotten.

A few years ago, I spoke about comics to a class at a seriously major university, and at a reception after my talk, I asked a bunch of grad students what they thought comic book fans *wanted*. An extremely bright young man named Paul Dworkin had this opinion: *Fans want comics writers, artists and editors to preserve a part of their childhood.*

I think Mr. Dworkin was right. But comics creators simply *can't* comply with these fans' wishes, not without reprinting the same story month after month, year after year, decade after decade . . . which would eventually bore even the most dedicated devotee and cause him to look for amusement elsewhere. If new stories are written, the meme-archetype will evolve, for all the reasons already cited. And somebody will be outraged.

Something just occurred to me. The changes in Heraclitus's river aren't the only reason you can't step into it twice. *You're* another reason. *You've* changed. Okay, the current version of the Crimson Viper isn't your Crimson Viper, but maybe you're not his reader, either. You've aged and grown and done some tough living and maybe what was once an escape and an entertainment for you simply isn't anymore.

And finally . . . Why should comic book heroes be the only things that don't change? Consider the Crimson Viper a part of the vast, timeless dance of Being, one with the whole pulsing cosmos—shrinking, swelling, spinning, ever becoming Other, ever becoming Next, dying, becoming reborn, presenting myriad aspects of the eternal All . . .

"Still sucks," you say.

4

Superhero Revisionism in *Watchmen* and *The Dark Knight Returns*

AEON J. SKOBLE

The two graphic novels, *The Dark Knight Returns* and *Watchmen*, invite us to completely rethink our conception of the superhero, and press us to reconsider some of the funda-mental moral principles that have traditionally underwritten our appreciation of superheroes. Just as *Unforgiven* is generally thought of as a "revisionist" western, presenting somewhat familiar themes and characters in a very different light, *The Dark Knight Returns*[1] does a revisionist job by re-inventing two of the oldest comic book superheroes, and *Watchmen*[2] does so by pre-senting an entirely new superhero world, complete with its own back-story.

These two graphic novels have been enormously influential in terms of how superheroes have been presented and thought of since the mid-to-late 1980s. Many sophisticated elements of comics today that we now take as givens—the way they raise questions of justice and vengeance, their exploration of the ethics of vigilantism, and their depiction of ambivalent and even hostile reactions toward superheroes from the general public as well as from government—are largely traceable to these works. So let's take a look at some of the more important ways in which they re-conceive the superhero.

---

[1] Frank Miller, Klaus Janson, and Lynn Varley, *The Dark Knight Returns* (New York: DC Comics/Warner Books, 1986).
[2] Alan Moore and Dave Gibbons, *Watchmen* (New York: DC Comics/Warner Books, 1986).

Crime-Fighters and Vigilantes

In one sense, independent costumed crime-fighters are by definition vigilantes—they take the law into their own hands. In the
real world, this is generally regarded as, at best, problematic. For
example, the influential British philosopher John Locke
(1632–1704) long ago persuasively argued that an important element of the defining conditions of civil society is that each of us
gives up his right to private vengeance, delegating it to a legiti-
mately formed government, for the purposes of objective judgment and sentencing.[3] It makes us all more secure, on this
theory, to have the pursuit and punishment of wrongdoers be
the delegated task of some agency of the state. On this view, it's
wrong for me to try to apprehend or punish robbers, as this is
the properly assigned function of the state's police force and
court system.

Even on this standard account, though, there are exceptions.
For example, I may defend myself against an attacker, and I may
come to the aid of a third-party suffering an attack. But in most
jurisdictions, there are stringent rules and guidelines to which
this sort of "private justice" is subject, and among them, typically, is a rule that says I may not go out of my way to look for
trouble and then defend against it. In the 1974 movie *Death
Wish*, architect Paul Kersey (played by Charles Bronson) clearly
defends himself and others against attackers, but the problematic aspect of his behavior is that he goes out at night looking
for attackers to neutralize.[4] As a result, the police label him a
vigilante. But this is precisely what superheroes do: they don't
merely engage in self-defense against imminent threats, they go
out looking for the bad guys. In some story lines, of course, the
classic superheroes engage in purely defensive action: Galactus
comes to destroy Earth, so the Fantastic Four fight back. But
more often, superheroes function as a sort of unauthorized
police auxiliary unit—Paul Kersey with a mask and, usually,
with superpowers. For most of the history of comics, the moral
status of this sort of vigilantism wasn't addressed as a serious
topic of consideration. We welcomed and applauded our crime-

---

[3] See his *Second Treatise* (Cambridge: Cambridge University Press, 1960),
Chapter VIII.

[4] His primary motivation is responding to brutal attacks on his wife and daughter, the former of which was fatal.

fighting superiors. We were just glad to see the bad guys get what was coming to them. But this all changed in 1986.

In his 1939 origin story, we learned that Batman was prompted to devote his life to fighting crime by the murder of his parents. As a costumed crime-fighter, he was therefore a vigilante, but he enjoyed close relations with the local authorities, who not only appreciated his help but came to depend on it. Frank Miller's 1986 story about Batman, *The Dark Knight Returns*,[5] explicitly examines the moral issues surrounding superhero vigilantism by re-imagining the Batman's psyche as much more deeply traumatized by his parents' murder. Batman here acknowledges the vigilante nature of the costumed crime-fighter, telling a congressional committee, "Sure we're criminals, we've always been criminals. We have to be criminals."[6] Of course, this is completely accurate only in a technical way, and Batman means it ironically. He breaks some of the laws of Gotham in order to pursue the real criminals who are violating more important laws, and to protect the law-abiding citizens of the city from these thugs and murderers. To the extent that any laws on the books protect criminals and impede the pursuit of justice, Batman will be a lawbreaker.

In Miller's retelling, Batman had once enjoyed a close relationship with the police, but was obliged to "retire" after public anti-vigilante pressure, and when he returns a decade later, he soon finds a new police commissioner issuing a warrant for his arrest. Miller also shows TV talking heads and members of the general public debating the moral status of Batman's vigilantism. Some view him as a dangerous and possibly fascist reactionary, while others see him as true champion of justice. Miller goes so far as to satirize the "expert opinion" emanating from academics by having a leading criminal psychiatrist argue that Batman is actually responsible for the crimes committed by The Joker and Two-Face.

---

[5] I don't mean to show less than great respect to the artists with whom the writers collaborate to make these *graphic* novels: Miller here collaborates with Klaus Janson and Lynn Varley, and Alan Moore's collaborator on *Watchmen* was Dave Gibbons. Without the visual art, the stories would be far less effective, but inasmuch as my discussion concerns plot, theme, and dialogue, I'll be referring to Miller and Moore.

[6] *The Dark Knight Returns*, Book 3, p. 31.

Truth, Justice, and the American Way

By way of contrast, Miller has Superman respond to the same social and political pressures that mount against free agent vigilantes by becoming a government operative who works in secret. Miller's Superman understands the resentment that at least partially fuels the anti-superhero movement: "The rest of us recognized the danger—of the endless envy of those not blessed. . . . We must not remind them that giants walk the Earth."[7]

Batman regards Superman as having allowed himself to be co-opted, but Superman sees his decision to work for the government as justified in utilitarian terms, directed to the greater good: "I gave them my obedience and my invisibility. They gave me a license and let us live. No, I don't like it. But I get to save lives—and the media stays quiet."[8] Both recognize that the nature of their distinctive activities makes them "outlaws," regardless of the fact that their motivation is to fight crime and keep innocent people safe. For Superman, this can only mean going to work for the government, more as a soldier in the Cold War than in the War on Crime. Batman's interpretation of this is telling:

> You always say yes—to anyone with a badge—or a *flag* . . . You sold us out, Clark. You gave them—the *power*—that should have been *ours*. Just like your parents taught you to. My parents taught me a *different* lesson—lying on this street—shaking in deep shock—dying for no reason at all—they showed me that the world only makes sense when you *force* it to.[9]

For Batman, the presence of a badge or a flag is neither necessary nor sufficient for justice. Laws may be unjust, politicians may be corrupt, and the legal system may actually protect the wicked, but none of this will deter Batman from his mission. The crime-fighting vigilante superhero does not let anything stand between him and the attainment of what he sees as real justice. Why should well-meaning social structures be allowed to stand in the way of what is objectively right?

---

[7] *The Dark Knight Returns*, Book 3, pp. 16–26.
[8] *The Dark Knight Returns*, Book 3, p. 35.
[9] *The Dark Knight Returns*, Book 4, pp. 38–40.

This can all seem to make some degree of sense, provided that the vigilante is in fact doing good, but it would be far more troubling if vigilantes lack a clear perception of right and wrong. For example, the return of the Batman inspires some members of a large and powerful street gang that he vanquishes to themselves become crime-fighting vigilantes—the "Sons of the Batman"—but they kill, and they maim far more indiscriminately than their namesake ever would. Indeed, Batman has always carefully avoided killing his adversaries, preferring to deliver apprehended criminals to the police alive, if somewhat damaged. He comes to regret this for the first time only toward the end of the story, when it occurs to him that by not killing the Joker long ago, there is a sense in which he bears some responsibility for the hundreds of people the Joker subsequently murdered.

Despite Batman's willingness to break rules, he has always been cautious and measured in his use of violence, he has refused to cross certain lines, and he has consistently interfered with and apprehended only criminals. His customary use of physical violence in the service of basic justice can come to seem appropriate to the context of the sociopathic street gangs and homicidal masterminds in which he finds himself, and while this may be at some level immensely disquieting, it raises the question of who is the more honest—the vigilante who understands the trade-off necessary for the protection of the innocent in such circumstances, or those vocal critics of the superhero who deplore the methods of social protection on which they themselves have come to depend.

A Whole New World

By bringing into clearer view the reality of the ethical dimensions of vigilantism, and by exploring the underlying psychological context within which superheroes operate, Miller's story forces us to rethink our understanding of Batman and Superman, and thus to re-examine our related notions of right and wrong.

Alan Moore's original single-issue series, and now prominent graphic novel, *Watchmen*[10] also leads us to rethink our funda-

---

[10] See Note 5 above.

mental moral ideas and our attitudes toward the concept of a superhero, but it does so through a more wholesale re-imagining of the world of superheroes. In this case, we are given a critical distance on the phenomenon by being presented with a different fictional world. It's not the DC Comics world of Batman, Superman, Green Arrow, and the rest of the Justice League, and neither is it the Marvel Comics world of Spider-Man, X-Men, and the Fantastic Four—Moore creates an entirely new and different collection of masked crime-fighters, along with one clearly superhuman superhero. The world of Moore's story begins by asking the question of what would happen if the 1938 release of the first "Superman" comic book story had inspired some real people to become masked crime-fighters. He then recapitulates comic book history by inventing a "golden age" collection of superheroes and various costumed vigilantes, as well as a later generation following in their footsteps. The narrative of *Watchmen* uses them to delve into the psychology as well as the ethical and political ramifications of vigilantism.

One way that *Watchmen* forces us to rethink the superhero is by portraying several costumed crime-fighters as at least to some extent psychologically troubled. Moore's character Rorschach, for example, has been traumatized by an abusive childhood, and is in many ways emotionally and psychologically maladjusted. He is absolutely ruthless in his willingness to use violence to fight crime, yet his commitment to justice seems real and uncompromising. While the earlier generation of Moore's superheroes was inspired by the "Superman" comic book character, Rorschach was spurred into action by another event from the real world: the 1964 murder of Kitty Genovese. Newspaper accounts of the time were unsparing in their revelation that thirty-eight witnesses had watched and had done nothing while she was being stabbed to death in an urban public space.[11]

In the real world, the advent of the Superman comics did not bring about a wave of masked crime-fighters, and neither did the murder of Kitty Genovese. But in *Watchmen*, the reports of this murder made the man who became Rorschach "ashamed for humanity," and inspired him to don a grotesque ink-blot mask,

---

[11] Martin Gansburg, "Thirty-Eight Who Saw Murder Didn't Call Police," *New York Times* (March 27th, 1964).

"a face that I could bear to look at in the mirror,"[12] and go out to fight crime. One thing that is a bit disquieting about Moore's retelling of the story is that the presumably "normal" people who actually witnessed the famous murder did nothing, but the one person who took action because of it, launching in response a life-long campaign against crime, is an individual any of us would consider a deeply damaged and disturbed man.

Unlike Superman and Spider-Man, neither Rorschach nor Batman possesses any superpowers. Yet they choose to devote their lives to fighting crime. Are they "revenge-driven psychopaths," or should any of us who recoil from them be considered like the ordinary monsters from Kitty Genovese's neighborhood, whose complicity in horror consists in utter inaction? Or could both these things be true? One of Moore's epigraphs is the famous aphorism penned by the philosopher Friedrich Nietzsche (1844–1900), "Whoever fights monsters should see to it that in the process he does not become a monster. And when you look long into an abyss, the abyss also looks into you."[13] Has Rorschach (or Batman) failed to heed this advice? Or is it the rest of us who are too conservative, too frightened, or too weak to take a noble risk and engage the monsters?

The superhero's most fundamental attitude seems to be that, contrary to Locke, it's everyone's right, if not duty, to fight crime, and to do whatever we can to seek justice for ourselves and for our communities. Spider-Man famously realized that "with great power comes great responsibility,"[14] but Rorschach shows us that the "power" to fight crime is largely a matter of will, or choice, which seems to create a greater responsibility for all of us.

Look On My Works, Ye Mighty

Some of Moore's other characters are more psychologically stable than Rorschach. Both the original Nite Owl and his successor seem entirely sane and emotionally well adjusted in at least most respects, sincerely motivated by a desire to help others,

---

[12] *Watchmen*, Chapter VI, p. 10.

[13] Epigraph to *Watchmen*, Chapter VI; from Friedrich Nietzsche, *Beyond Good and Evil* (New York: Vintage, 1989), p. 89.

[14] Stan Lee and Steve Ditko, *Amazing Fantasy* #15, 1962.

and convinced that they can make a difference. But even the current Nite Owl has his secrets, and perhaps private fetishes tied up with his costuming. Most of the costumed crime-fighters in *Watchmen* seem to be psychologically unhealthy in one way or another. The Comedian is thuggish and sadistic. The super-powered Doctor Manhattan is so detached from the human world as to be emotionally uncomprehending. They all seem as inclined to argue with each other as to pursue criminals. And Ozymandias, the man who is by far the most intelligent of the merely human vigilantes, as well as being immensely successful by normal worldly standards, is a clearly megalomaniacal individual, taking no less than Alexander the Great as his personal role model.

Ozymandias is a particularly interesting case. He accurately predicts that the world is moving toward nuclear holocaust, and then both creates and successfully executes an elaborate plan to stop this likely annihilation of all life. Using the talents of some of the most creative people on the planet, whom he kills when their work is complete to keep it secret, he sets up a fake alien intrusion into New York City involving an explosion that he knows will kill millions of people. His expectation is that the sudden appearance of an alien foe threatening human life will bring together all the otherwise warring nations in peaceful collaboration against this new common enemy. Before they can ever conclude that there is no more of a threat from beyond forthcoming, new habits of harmonious co-operation will have changed the face of the Earth into a peaceful environment that subsequently will support human fulfillment and happiness.

The plan hatched by Ozymandias succeeds, at the expense of three million lives. Is he insane? Is he evil? On the one hand, he was able to analyze accurately a growing threat of nuclear war, sparked and exacerbated by international gamesmanship. And the drastic solution he concocts to save the world and restore peace seems to be successful. Yet, that solution is in itself utterly repellent, since it entails intentionally killing millions of people and deceiving all the others still living. Can the end justify the means?

To the way of thinking employed by Ozymandias, the deaths of even many more people could be justified in the name of saving billions of other lives and ending war between nations. If this brings about the "stronger, loving world" he intends, then he is completely convinced it is the right thing to do. Is his action just tremendously effective? Or is it utterly mad? Is it sadly necessary? Or is it irredeemably evil? We can't avoid confronting the issues. And these questions lead us back to our understanding of superheroes.

Ironically, the arch-villain in Moore's story turns out to be one of its brightly costumed public heroes, and even more ironically, it is precisely the one who is by far the most popular with the general public, Ozymandias. This erstwhile hero arrogantly explains to his shocked vigilante peers, after his horrific deed has been accomplished, that their greatest achievement as heroes has been their failure to stop him from saving the planet. They immediately want to tell the world the truth about what he has done. But he reasons with them that if they do, they will eliminate the one benefit that could have justified all the deaths, and they will make the situation as a result much worse.

The most serious moral judgment on all the rest of the costumed crime-fighters then comes in their acquiescing to his argument and agreeing to remain complicit in the secret of what has transpired, in order not to disrupt the fragile peace that it has accomplished. The only one of them with superpowers, and yet the one of them utterly devoid of human feelings, Dr. Manhattan, even seems persuaded by the overall logic Ozymandias has used to justify his actions, and a short time later leaves the Earth, apparently satisfied with the resulting state of things. The only person who will not be co-opted and refuses to keep silent about the scheme is Rorschach. He rejects the utilitarian reasoning applied in this way, with its implication that it can be right to inflict such widespread pain, suffering, and death on innocent people so that a greater good might possibly result. He vows to tell the world the whole truth about what has just happened and, before he is killed by Dr. Manhattan to ensure his silence, he exclaims: "Never compromise. . . . Evil must be punished."[15]

The questions that force themselves on us are not just whether Ozymandias has gone insane, or has descended into evil, or both. We are forced to ask whether anyone in his position could ever be right in doing something like he did. We are

---

[15] *Watchmen*, Chapter XII, pp. 20–23.

then necessarily confronted with the further question of whether we who absolutely recoil from such an action could in any way ourselves be blameworthy for being too weak to do whatever might be necessary to save the planet. This cluster of questions can be asked in different ways. Has this man, this intelligent and popular superhero, "become a monster,"[16] or is he just a misunderstood savior? Is the scrappy and scruffy Rorschach being stubborn, due to his obsessive fixation with what he considers to be justice, or is he right to reject the utilitarian ethic that has been used to rationalize the murder of millions? Moore's requiring us to take up these questions, like Miller's questions about the nature of vigilantism, forces us to confront fundamental issues of ethics, law, and psychology in considering how we regard superheroes, and then ultimately in considering how we regard ourselves in our own roles in the world.

Rethinking the Superhero Concept

There are many important ways in which we can be led by *Watchmen* to rethink the superhero concept: Could anyone ever be trusted to occupy the position of a watchman over the world? In the effort "to save the world," or most of the world, could a person in the position of a superhero be tempted to do what is in itself actually and deeply evil, so that good may result? Is the Olympian perspective, whereby a person places himself above all others as a judge concerning how and whether they should live, a good and sensible perspective for initiating action in a world of uncertainty? That is to say, could anyone whose power, knowledge, and position might incline them to be grandiosely concerned about "the world" be trusted to do the right thing for individuals in the world? Or is the savior mindset inherently dangerous for any human being to adopt?

In many panels that snake through sections of *Watchmen*, there is a strange parallel story about a man lost at sea who is intent on enacting revenge against the pirates he holds responsible for the destruction of his ship and the deaths of his shipmates. The story is conveyed in the panels of a comic book being read by a young man sitting near a newsstand in New York as the greater action of the real story plays out around him.

---

[16] He did literally *create* a monster.

The connection between this bizarre and grotesque pirate tale and the main narrative of the novel is never made explicitly clear by the author, but one point of contact is obvious. The "hero" of the seafaring yarn, in his attempts to see that justice is done, runs squarely into what is often called "the law of unintended consequences" and ends up committing horrendous evil, to his own surprise, and against the very people he was aiming to help, or at least avenge. The knowledge that he thought was sufficient to guide him as he sought his own justice outside the law ended up being a tissue of fantasy and falsehood, and it led to tragedy. One of the main dangers faced by any superhero would consist in just that—the limitations of any perspective in an immensely complex world, the potential inaccuracy of even the most carefully formed beliefs, and the law of unintended consequences could easily doom rogue vigilante efforts to the perpetration of tremendous harm rather than the attainment of cosmic justice, and thus undermine the whole concept of the superhero.

Questioning the concept of the superhero ultimately involves questioning ourselves. And the main question is not whether we as ordinary people would be prepared to do what a superhero might have to do under the most extraordinary circumstances, but rather whether we are in fact prepared to do whatever we can do in ordinary ways to make the world such that it doesn't require extraordinary salvation from a superhero acting outside the bounds of what we might otherwise think is morally acceptable. Against the backdrop of some bleak and nihilistic statements about meaning in the universe and in life, Alan Moore seems to be making the classic existentialist move of throwing the responsibility of meaning and justice onto us all, and showing us what can result if we abdicate that responsibility, leaving it to a few, or to any one person who would usurp the right to decide for the rest of us how we are to be protected and kept safe. Whatever we make of the nihilism, we can take the lesson to heart. If normal human beings had been doing what they should be doing, in normal human ways, a person like Ozymandias most likely would never have gotten into a position where he could reasonably come to believe that he had to take drastic action to save us from ourselves. We would have been doing that all along.

Who Watches the Watchmen?

An interesting commonality of *The Dark Knight Returns* and *Watchmen* is that, in both stories, public sentiment has turned against the superheroes, and their activities are explicitly criminalized, unless they officially work for the government. Like Miller's Superman, Moore's Doctor Manhattan and The Comedian are co-opted by the state, allowed to function as paramilitary government operatives, and the rest are forced into retirement (if they hadn't quit already), except for the fringe-dwelling Rorschach, who continued to terrorize the criminal underworld but because of that became himself a wanted criminal. Whether emotionally disturbed or not, the costumed crime-fighters had chosen to help people, yet the prevailing public sentiment became antagonistic. The referent of Moore's title, and a common graffiti slogan in the New York of his story, is a famous line from the ancient writer Juvenal (*ca.* 55–*ca.* 130), "Who Watches the Watchmen?"[17] The costumed crime-fighters— the "superheroes" here—are in one sense protecting the people from themselves, as The Comedian notes, and in turn the people don't trust them.[18] Is the resentment of the general population based on fear, as The Comedian suggests, or is their animosity based on the envy suggested by Superman in *The Dark Knight Returns*? Or could it be based on guilt?

One further question is raised by both these stories: would we have more to fear from costumed superheroes operating as vigilante crime-fighters outside officially sanctioned authority, or as covert operatives of the government? Part of the significance of this superhero revisionism is in the way it makes us think about the nature of authority, just as it makes us think about the ethics of vigilantism and the relationship between law and morality. Certainly a criminal has more to fear from Rorschach or Batman than from Doctor Manhattan or Superman, although political enemies of the United States would need to be more fearful of the latter.

One colloquial argument against vigilantism is sometimes invoked against government power itself: how do you know

---

[17] "Quis custodiet ipsos custodies," Juvenal, *Satires*, VI, 347

[18] The Comedian makes this observation to Nite Owl while pacifying mass riots during the police strike. *Watchmen*, Chapter II, p. 18.

you're right? Batman harms only wrongdoers, but the Sons of the Batman are less well grounded in both detective skills and ethics. Nevertheless, the U.S. Government orders Superman to put a stop to Batman's activities. Doctor Manhattan kills Rorschach. The question of who watches the watchmen is of course an issue in political theory, not just a question about costumed crime-fighters. But if earlier generations first came to understand ethics, law and order, and political authority by way of the older portrayals of superheroes, the superhero revisionism in the works of Moore and Miller forces us also to rethink our ethics, our roles in the broader world, and our views about law and social order. Moore and Miller are asking us to look into the abyss, and then to use it as a mirror for seeing ourselves more clearly.[19]

---

[19] I am grateful to Tom Morris for many helpful suggestions.

Part Two

The Existential World of the Superhero

5

God, the Devil, and Matt Murdock

TOM MORRIS

There aren't many references to God in the mainline superhero stories. Religious activities hardly ever figure into these narratives. We don't see Superman sitting in church or Bruce Wayne poring over a Bat-Bible for inspiration and guidance. The Fantastic Four don't have prayer times together to discern the direction their work should take. The world of the superheroes is for the most part a pretty secular place. The only Preacher who serves as a prominent character in the world of popular comics at all isn't a very typical example of the life of faith.

Some of the superheroes, like Thor and Wonder Woman, are presented as minor deities themselves, but otherwise there is very little mention in any mainstream comics of a Creator, any sort of divine plan for humanity, or even a role for anything like a personal faith in God throughout the course of anyone's life. The superhero comics don't typically take religious institutions as part of the normal backdrop for their narratives, and they don't usually represent their characters as having any distinctively theological concerns. It's almost as if this whole side of ordinary life doesn't exist.

One of the few minor exceptions to this involves the life and faith of Matt Murdock, at least as he has been represented in a few of the more prominent Daredevil stories over the years. It's not that Matt is depicted in normal religious settings or as engaged in typical religious activities—for the most part, he isn't. But there are just enough hints in the neo-classic Daredevil origin story, as conceived by Frank Miller, and in many of the more interesting developments of his ongoing life as a costumed crime fighter, especially at the hands of the very philosophical Kevin Smith, that we can be led to ask some compelling questions about him as a man of faith.

The Man and His Faith

Matt Murdock was raised in a poor neighborhood blighted with crime—Hell's Kitchen, in New York City. At the time we get to know him, his father is a washed-up prizefighter. His mother is absent from the home, and we learn only later that, at some point very early in Matt's life, she left the family. We also eventually find out that, at a later time, she became a nun. We can reasonably infer from this that there is likely some form of a Catholic background to his family life, and it's plausible that he learned at least the rudiments of the faith perhaps from his mother, before she left home, and also from his father. In one story, Matt's mother says this to her grown, crime-fighting son: "I know your father raised you in the faith. I also know after reading about your two lives over the years that you work on the side of the just. You're an angel, Matthew—not one of the heavenly host, granted, but a servant of God nonetheless" (*Guardian Devil #4*, "The Devil's Distaff").

Matt Murdock certainly has his doubts about religion, about divine providence, about the love and care of a benevolent Creator, and occasionally, even about whether there really is any sort of God at all. But these spiritual weeds seem to spring up now and then in the basic soil of a religious soul. Daredevil's later religious musings, occasional prayers, and use of religious categories as well as religious language all seem to reflect the sensibilities of a man who grew up in a household of at least nominal religiosity, if not genuine faith, rather than displaying the usually more articulate and bold perspectives of an adult convert to a religious worldview. His faith is an often unspoken, deeper part of his mindset that seems to influence his beliefs, attitudes, and actions in a subtle way, rather than forming an explicit part of his daily, conscious thinking. It's also a side of Daredevil that we don't really see in the early years of the comics. It first begins to come to light under the storytelling power of Frank Miller and, much later, takes on added depth in the stories penned by film director and lifetime comics fan Kevin Smith. From the image they build up, it's clear that Matt

Murdock is a Catholic, although a troubled and often conflicted one, and that this is in some way relevant to what he does as the costumed superhero, Daredevil.

This brings up a number of interesting philosophical questions. What is the relation between a life of religious faith and a sense of mission as a costumed vigilante? Does a deep religious sensibility, or even a real faith, help a superhero like Daredevil, or somehow set him up for harm? Is religious faith a form of strength, or is it a source of weakness for a person in his position? Is it a good thing or a bad thing?

There is an important philosophical principle I first articulated many years ago in the book *Making Sense of It All*—a crucial cosmic truth that I like to call "The Double Power Principle." This principle specifies that, typically, the more power something has for good, the more it correspondingly has for ill, and vice versa—it's up to us how we use it. This one simple principle explains both the promise and threat of nuclear power, technology of all sorts (think of the Internet, genetic engineering, and nanotechnology), and religion, among many other things. All have great power for good and correspondingly great power for ill. Many people strongly denounce genetic engineering or institutionalized religion, because either can potentially be a source of great harm in human life. But the fact that something can be a source of great harm just shows, in accordance with The Double Power Principle, that it also can be a source of great good as well. The actual results are up to us.

According to The Double Power Principle, the role of religion in a person's life could conceivably go in either of the two directions. It could be a source of good or ill—perhaps of great good or terrible harm. In connection with this insight, we can then ask a more specific philosophical question: What could possibly be the role of traditional religious faith in the life of a costumed vigilante superhero? In particular, is Daredevil's Catholicism a source of inner strength and guidance for him, or is it rather a cause of weakness and confusion? Does it help him or hurt him?

These issues are related to a broader question that philosophers ask and that's also worth some reflection: Is religious faith generally a source of blindness to the harsher realities of the world, or could it be more like Daredevil's radar sense, allowing any of us at least the possibility of discerning realities that other people who go through life without it are likely to miss? Is faith blind, like Matt Murdock, or does it have its own distinctive forms of perception, again, like our hero? That will determine, in part, whether it's a source of strength or of weakness.

But before we plunge into questions that will help us clarify the role of religious faith in the life of Daredevil, we should back up a step and get clear on a preliminary issue. Is Matt Murdock, or Daredevil, really a man of genuine faith at all? We need to draw a careful distinction between religiosity as an outward form of behavior and perhaps even an inner pattern of thought that might be based on nothing more than habit or superstition, and authentic faith, which is a much deeper inner commitment and disposition of the soul. Not everything that quacks like a duck is a duck.

In at least the well-known Miller and Smith storylines, Matt comes from a nominally religious home and carries into his adulthood a distinctive religious sensibility. He sometimes thinks in terms of religious categories. He talks to God, even when expressing doubts about his existence. He even complains to God like another famous warrior and defender of the oppressed, King David, in the *Psalms*. "Why do the wicked prosper?" "Why do the righteous suffer?" Daredevil resents the evil in the world—he takes it personally—and he deplores the pain and suffering that have come into his own life. He seems to be sensitive to evil in the way that a genuinely spiritual person tends to be—viewing it not as just an unavoidable and disagreeable fact of life, but as somehow a blight, a departure from how things are supposed to be. He personally suffers when the innocent suffer and feels great satisfaction—with at least a temporary sense of rightness and closure—when justice is done.

This is all positive evidence that he may indeed be, in some important sense, a man of faith, however complex and ambivalent his inner life is. In fact, it is precisely this inner complexity that, in part, makes him so interesting as a superhero and as a person. He is a dedicated man of the law who acts as a vigilante. He is a sensitive person of compassion who seems to enjoy pounding on his enemies. If he is a man of faith, it often looks more like the "eye for an eye" faith of the Old Testament than the "Blessed are the meek" and "Turn the other cheek" faith of the New Testament.

But is he indeed, in any substantive sense, a man of faith? Even limiting our question to the content of the Miller and Smith narratives, it may not be so clear. Religiosity isn't the same thing as faith. But it's sometimes not easy to tell the two apart. Religiosity is superficial, real faith is deeper. Religiosity is, typically, just a matter of habit. Faith is normally something much more all-involving. We can't make a good judgment about Matt Murdock's deepest inner life without looking at all the evidence. So let's consider for at least a moment the negative side of the case. As a good attorney, Matt himself would surely approve.

Faith and Fear

Daredevil is described universally as "The Man Without Fear." An adversary of his in the story, "The Devil's Distaff"—a villain named "Quentin Beck"—states without any sort of further explanation that a man without fear is a man without faith. Why? Is faith necessarily—or at least most often—a bridge over fear? That's certainly the way many outsiders seem to picture faith, and so it's no surprise that a man like Quentin Beck would think of it in this way. The view is simple: Fearful people cling onto religious faith to keep their emotions under control. Religion is a coping mechanism used to block out all the terrors of life. The most extreme version of this perspective says that human beings invented religious faith precisely because of their fear. Many people would rather deceive themselves with the unfounded platitudes of religion than face up to the horrific realities of life and death in a hostile, uncaring universe. If this view were right, then being a man without fear would then indeed presumably make Matt Murdock a man without faith. There would be no role for this religious attitude to play in his life, no real function for it in his mindset. It couldn't get any hold on him, or take root in his life.

The problem is that this view isn't even close to being right. What Quentin Beck says merely expresses a common misunderstanding of faith. As many of the best philosophers of religion have realized, faith is not just the knee-jerk reaction of fearful people, a crutch and defense against a frightening world. Freud thought so. But Freud was wrong about a lot of things. This is actually a fairly good characterization of superstition, and perhaps shallow religiosity, but not genuine faith. Superstition is a fearful and desperate effort to manipulate reality into conformity with our needs. Authentic faith is more like a personal yielding of the ego, along with its demands, to something greater than the self. It involves a deep embracing of some positive values and realities that we are completely free to ignore and deny—ultimate realities that are perhaps vastly more important than the superficial ones so much more obvious to us.

This common misunderstanding of faith and its relation to fear is even more completely wrong than this point alone would indicate. Some of the greatest, most extreme examples of fearless heroism in all of human history have involved people with an unusually strong religious faith. Consider the prophets, apostles, missionaries, and ordinary believers over the centuries who have gladly gone to their deaths rather than repudiate and abandon their beliefs. It could very well be that only a person of strong faith can rationally live without fear. So when Beck said that a man without fear is a man without faith, he got it backwards. Perhaps it's closer to the truth to say that a man without fear is, most likely, a man of strong faith.

Even sincere religious people sometimes misunderstand what faith is. A careful philosophical analysis will show that genuine religious faith is not so much an intellectual certitude about theological matters as it is a total commitment to certain absolute cosmic values, and an allegiance—however halting or imperfect—to an unseen Source of all good. We wrongly think of faith as mostly a matter of theoretical belief and religious talk, when it's actually more about practical commitment and courageous action, on however large or small a scale. Matt Murdock commits to the eternal realities he can understand—truth, justice, hope, and love. And he clearly commits his life to the good of other people. These commitments may spring from, and in turn prepare him for, a deeper commitment to other eternal realities and, in particular, that central commitment of love between the Creator and the created person that is properly reflected back. Matt's not a paradigm of saintliness, by any means. But there is evidence he's moving in the direction of real faith. Like all the rest of us, he is a work in progress. And so is his faith.

Before moving on, let's linger a moment on something. Is the tagline "The Man Without Fear" a literally accurate description of Daredevil, or is it just a great example of classic comic book hyperbole? Daredevil clearly seems to be a man utterly devoid of the normal catalogue of human fears, and of the most common neurotic ones as well. He is completely without a fear of heights, a fear of falling, a fear of open spaces, a fear of crowds, a fear of physical pain, a fear of dying, and the quite peculiar fear that recent surveys have shown to be, oddly, the most commonly acknowledged contemporary aversion—a fear of public speaking. Matt Murdock is a very good trial attorney, after all.

But, in another sense, couldn't it be said that Daredevil often fears that a particular criminal will harm or kill an innocent victim in a specific set of circumstances? Doesn't he sometimes fear that his friend Foggy will be harmed, or that his true love, Karen Page, will be hurt? Isn't this sort of fear precisely what sets him into action? It's surely not just a belief that someone is about to be injured that propels him to leap off a building and intervene in a situation where he is likely to incur physical harm—he couldn't be motivated to this extent by a mere factual belief alone. The source of such an intense impulse is likely a deep aversion to the potential realization of the negative possibility that he envisions. And what is this sort of deep aversion but a form of fear? He fears that, apart from his intervention, an innocent person will suffer harm. He is usually motivated by a fear that someone will be the unnecessary victim of an evil act and wrongly endure pain or loss if he doesn't personally, and forcefully, take action.

This can lead us to an important philosophical distinction. Daredevil seems to have no self-referential "fear of"—a terror that involves the thought of harm to oneself—the powerful emotion that, at a certain level, can shut down thought and block action, rendering an ordinary person, in effect, paralyzed. He shows no evidence of that knot in the gut, tightness of the throat, trembling of the hands, dizziness, queasiness, mental panic, or dry mouth and hesitation that normal people feel in situations of sudden danger. Daredevil seems to experience only the sort of "fear that" which can motivate courageous and decisive action. When we say that he is "The Man Without Fear," this is surely all we mean. He is without the distinctive emotion that we paradigmatically understand as fear—the aversive, visceral reaction that tends to interfere with proper action. Perhaps, in the light of this distinction, we should more accurately use the concept of "concern" for what we have just called "fear that" and reserve the simple term 'fear' for what is normally denoted

by the phrase 'fear of.' In that case, we could say straightfor-
wardly that Daredevil is "The Man Without Fear."

We have seen that, contrary to the claim of Quentin Beck,
this would not imply at all that Daredevil is "a man without
faith." We are probably hitting closer to the mark by invoking
his degree of deep-down faithfulness to explain his evident fearlessness. The Bible at one point describes true believers as living "by faith and not by sight." This is a characterization that
captures Matt Murdock unusually well.

Daredevil clearly has times of doubt and crises of faith. That's
the nature of faith for most of us in the world in which we actually live. It isn't a form of untroubled, self-assured, intellectual
certainty. It isn't essentially a calm and peaceful assurance of the
mind at all. It is a commitment of the heart. And theologians
have suggested for thousands of years that faith may ultimately
be more about the hold God has on us than the hold we have
on God. That's why we can wiggle on the hook with all our
might and still be people of faith. Faith is ultimately a connection that not even our most troubling doubts can break, however thin and fragile it often might seem to be. Even when Matt
is about to lose his grip on faith, the object of his faith never
loses its grip on him.

Daredevil's Faith as a Source of Strength

A superhero needs various forms of strength. He first must have,
most obviously, some form of great physical power. He has to
be able to overcome the bad guys in a fight, or save the good
guys in a disaster. But he also needs mental strength, the ability
to think on his feet, or off his feet, sometimes high in the air. He
has to be able to remember accurately, envision creatively, reason well, deduce, and infer. Batman is perhaps the best example
of a superhero with tremendous mental, or intellectual, prowess.
Without any actual superpowers, his extremely well developed
body, incredible skills of combat, and finely honed intellectual
abilities give him an edge in any confrontation. But a superhero
also needs one further form of strength, a firmness of character,
as this has been understood since at least the times of the ancient
Greek philosophers. A strong character includes such qualities as
courage, resilience, persistence, integrity, and a concern for other
people that is firm and overriding in its motivational impact.

Could there also be yet another form of strength that a super-hero might benefit from having? The case of Daredevil and his religious sensibilities can lead us to ask whether there is such a thing as spiritual strength, and whether this is something that could help a superhero in his mission or in his life. We may find it helpful to approach this question by asking another one, regarding an issue that may shed some light on what it is for anything to count as a strength or as a weakness for a person.

Let's consider again, but in a slightly different way, the issue of Daredevil's fearlessness. Is fearlessness a source of strength, as we might ordinarily tend to assume, or could it rather end up being a surprising source of weakness? If fearlessness is in fact in some way a source of weakness, and religious faith encourages fearlessness, then faith would indirectly, and perhaps in a surprising way, be a source of weakness as well.

The crucial question is this: Is a man without fear simply insensible to the realities of danger and possible loss in the world? Is fearlessness like color-blindness or tone-deafness? Is it just an inability to perceive and feel in a certain way? The great philosopher Aristotle believed that every virtue, or human strength, is a mid-point between two vices—an extreme of too little would constitute one vice, and an extreme of too much would count as the other vice. He saw the virtue of true courage as occupying a mid-point between the two extremes of cowardice, on the one hand (the "too little" in response to danger), and rashness or foolhardiness on the other hand (the "too much" in the face of danger). The classic virtue of courage is not at all understood as requiring an absence of fear, but it is thought of rather as the ability to act in support of great values, despite any fear we might experience. A brave man isn't necessarily someone who doesn't feel fear at all, he is most often just a person who does what he thinks is right, despite any fears that might threaten to hold him back.

This simple conceptual clarification can underscore the importance of our question as to whether a man without fear is in the end just a man blind to risk and thereby prone to the self-destructive extreme of rashness, or foolhardiness. If that's so, and Matt Murdock's religious faith ultimately generates his fearlessness, as I have suggested it might, then his faith could be seen as a source of dangerous vulnerability, or weakness, in so far as it might encourage imprudent, self-destructive actions.

There's an interesting scene in Frank Miller's graphic novel _Daredevil: The Man Without Fear_ that pointedly raises this issue. After Matt first meets the young and wild rich girl, Elektra, she takes him for an insanely fast ride in her red convertible. They get out of the sports car and stand on the edge of a cliff. Elektra says: "This is where we belong. Always on the brink. The rest lead safe, numb lives. But you—when I saw you on the rooftops, I knew—we're two of a kind. Drawn to the edge—and past it."

Is Elektra right? Is Daredevil just like her? Is his fearlessness necessarily a source of irresponsible and self-destructively irrational action, "beyond the edge"? If so, it doesn't look like a source of strength for the long-term, but rather like a personal quality that might well prevent there being any "long-term," at least, in this world.

Our concern can be blocked quite easily. An absence of fear need not encourage rashness and crazy behavior. And that's because fear is not the only thing that can preclude foolhardiness. Common sense can, too—what philosophers call prudence, or practical rationality. Guided by the right values concerning his own life as well as the lives of others, Matt Murdock, or Daredevil, knows—more or less well—when to act and when to pull back. Even if he never experiences fear, he may still be able to tell perfectly well where to draw the line.

Consider a situation in _Daredevil_ #233, "Armageddon": Daredevil is fighting a super-powered soldier who has been sent by a crime boss to destroy Hell's Kitchen. After a difficult battle, he is finally poised to stop this adversary. Several other powerful individuals suddenly appear on the scene, including Captain America and Thor. The armored superhero known as Iron Man then confronts Daredevil, holds his upraised palm toward him, and says: "Daredevil—that man is ours. On federal authority, stand back. You have five seconds." We're then told, "There is a soft hum as computer circuitry generates enough power to level a building—and holds it, waiting. Not being stupid, Matt backs away" (Miller and Mazzucchelli, _Born Again_, p. 155).

It didn't take an emotional experience of fear to generate prudent action on Matt's part, only a full understanding of the situation, and the right beliefs and values to guide him. Despite his frequently extreme actions, Daredevil is normally a man of practical rationality underneath it all. His religious sensibilities arguably do nothing to undercut this. In fact, to the contrary, it could be that some of the values he learned in church as a youth, or from his religious parents in his earliest years, provide at least a part of this prudential guidance.

The most fundamental religious values Matt likely absorbed embrace a love of neighbor, a respect for truth, a concern for justice, a compassion for the oppressed, and a proper valuing of external and internal realities. If Matt Murdock is to any extent a good Catholic, or even a bad Catholic with moderately good leanings, then he will have at least some of the right values and beliefs that can provide useful, reliable guidance in difficult circumstances. And this is a large part of what it takes for practical rationality or prudence, one of the qualities that ultimately contributes to personal strength for any of us, superhero or not. If his religious faith gives Daredevil good guidance in the realm of values, good insight into the world of facts, and a source of both encouragement and restraint as he seeks to uphold justice for those who are not strong enough to secure it for themselves, then it's safe to say that this is a distinctive form of spiritual strength that would benefit any superhero, or any ordinary human being.

The Catholic in Spandex

Supposing that Matt Murdock is indeed a Catholic and that he has some measure of authentic personal faith, we still can't shake the question: To what extent can he even possibly be considered a "good Catholic"? He's certainly no altar-boy, as even his mother seems to admit. But Matt does pretty well with at least most of the Ten Commandments—he doesn't indulge in idolatry, covet other people's stuff, or bear false witness against others; he honors his father and mother as much as most good people, and more than some; he works hard to restrain but not to kill bad guys, regardless of what they do; and he may even usually take it easy on the Sabbath, when the law office of Nelson and Murdock isn't open.

However, his conduct in many other ways violates various Biblical prescriptions and church requirements. First, he is not often seen in a church, and when he is, it's not to attend a religious service. And his sexual history alone seems more than sufficient to build up a need to visit the confessional on a fairly frequent basis. Nonetheless, it's still possible that in some way he is, and seeks to be, a good Catholic, by his own lights. In other words, he may have dismissed certain demands of the church as outmoded, old-fashioned, and not really relevant to modern life, and yet at the same time he may still have embraced other more fundamental requirements as universal, beneficial, and right for him. Of course, many traditional Catholics may be thinking at this point: If Matt Murdock wants to pick his theological and moral commitments to suit his interests, perhaps he should be a Methodist, or an Episcopalian. But Frank Miller has commented that the level of guilt he displays in various circumstances indicates clearly that Catholicism is his proper home. His life of faith is very imperfect, but that's not so different from the life of many basically decent Catholics these days.

Matt's Catholic faith is just one thread in a much broader fabric of religious community through whose efforts he has received whatever measure he has. We often tend to think of Daredevil as the ultimate example of working without a net. But perhaps his personal safety net is ultimately his mother and her faith, a faith that has been passed on to him. Like a lively, intimate experience of God, his mother Maggie is largely absent from his life. Yet, also a bit like divine providence, she appears when he most needs her. Consider for example the anguished prayer she makes for him while he lies in a bed, broken, desperately ill, and nearly dead, in Frank Miller's powerful story, "Born Again" (*Daredevil* #230):

> The fever grows in him. No Earthly force can stop it. He has lost too much blood. His body cannot fight. He will die. But he has so very much to do, my Lord. His soul is troubled. But it is a good man's soul, my Lord. He needs only to be shown your way. Then he will rise as your own and bring light to this poisoned city. He will be as a spear of lightning in your hand, my Lord.
>
> If I am to be punished for past sins, so be it. If I am to be cast into Hell, so be it. But spare him. So many need him. Hear my plea. (*Legends* 2, page 95)

Maggie's spiritual faith is the force behind what in this story is considered Matt's physical rebirth. It most likely is behind his ongoing spiritual impulses as well.

In modern times, we may have far too individualistic a conception of religious faith. More ancient religious traditions have a more communitarian view of the human person and our condition, and not in the sense that our individuality is lost in a larger collectivity, but in the sense that the individual person and the larger community are understood as existing in deep forms of dynamic interdependence. In line with this, the New Testament presents the faith of one person as somehow benefiting or covering others in the same family. Perhaps Maggie's faith is Matt's ultimate support, and the source of whatever measure of faith and fearlessness he does have. He is at least some sort of Catholic—good or bad, strong or weak—because she is now a strong person of faith.

When Matt experiences a crisis of faith, and expresses it to his mother, as recounted by Kevin Smith in "The Devil's Distaff," it's her powerful example and simple, profound reasoning that together turn him around. She tells him a story that presents something like a version of "Pascal's Wager"—an engaging argument for religious belief and the life of faith that was constructed by the great mathematician, scientist, and philosopher of the seventeenth century, Blaise Pascal. In the story Maggie tells, a skeptical, worldly knight is explaining to a simple religious peasant that he doesn't believe in God, and seeks instead to suck the marrow out of life in this world. He challenges the peasant, who is giving up so much worldly pleasure for the sake of heaven, to consider how sad it will be if he dies and has been wrong, and there is no heaven or God. The peasant replies by suggesting that it would be so much worse to live as if there is no God and then discover you were wrong.

Pascal long ago claimed that in a world such as ours, which is sufficiently ambiguous as to allow people, on the basis of theoretical argument and the available evidence alone, either to believe there is a God or to believe there is no God, another line of practical reasoning should come into our thinking. We should ask ourselves what we gain or lose by either belief. If we believe there is no God and live consistently as atheists, and then turn out to be right, we gain only the few finite pleasures of this world that would be forbidden to the believer, as well as one truth we otherwise would have missed. If we are atheists and are wrong, we will die to discover that we have aligned ourselves on this Earth with a way of life that has diminished and perhaps even extirpated any spiritual qualities we might have had that would have allowed us an eternal relationship of bliss with our Creator. We thus presumably lose an infinite good.

If, by contrast, we believe that there is a God and live in accordance with this belief in the best possible ways, giving up whatever few pleasures would be incompatible with our convictions, and yet cultivating other pleasures and enjoying everything else in a deeper and broader perspective, and we're right, we have positioned ourselves for the infinite gain of eternal joy in the presence and embrace of God. If, on the other hand, we believe in God and are wrong, Pascal thought, we will have lost whatever finite pleasures we could otherwise have experienced, but we can still live a full and bountiful life of virtue, peace, joy, and love, in companionship with others who similarly seek to rise to their highest spiritual aspirations.

To sum up this line of thinking, atheism carries with it the possibility of small finite gain if it's right, or a terrible infinite loss, if it's wrong. Theism carries with it the possibility of a wonderful infinite gain if it's right, or a small finite loss, if it's wrong. Assuming that a rational person seeks to avoid the worst possible losses and to maximize his chance of the best possible gains, compatible with the evidence that exists, then Pascal concluded that a rational person should bet his life on God. When Matt Murdock hears even a small reflection of this philosophical reasoning in his mother's simple fable, he is moved, and somehow calmed in his formerly troubled and doubtful spirit.

Pascal also famously wrote about "the greatness and wretchedness of man"—how we human beings are in some ways great like gods and are in other ways unbelievably small and disappointing. The extremes of good and evil that are wrapped up in our behavior are truly amazing. Matt Murdock seems to recognize this and sense that we are created to be more than the victims and victimizers of Hell's Kitchen. We are here for something more, something truly great. And yet, we are fallen—far from our potential and created intent. Echoing Pascal's ruminations in the story, "And a Child Shall Lead Them All," Daredevil speaks in his heart to God, saying:

> Every night, you put on an immorality play for me . . . You show me the disparity of man's magnificence to his actions, eons of evolvement, and we're still seeking the darkened corners to sate

our lowest impulses. How disappointing it must be for you to see us at our worst . . . if you even exist." (*Daredevil: Guardian Devil*)

The Psalmist wrote long ago, "The fool has said in his heart 'There is no God.'" Matt Murdock wonders about it in his mind, but in his heart, he prays, he complains, and he objects. Great people of faith in Biblical times interrogated God, reasoned with God, negotiated, implored, and occasionally doubted God. That didn't mean they didn't have faith. It just meant they were fully human people of faith—which is what we get with Matt.

The Vigilante Man of Faith: Hero or Tragic Figure?

Is Daredevil a hero, or a tragic figure, or both? He certainly is heroic in his defense of otherwise defenseless people. And he is heroic in his customary—and often extraordinary—efforts not to kill those he seeks to restrain from committing acts of terrible evil. He seems to want very badly not to break the classic religious commandment against killing. Villains may die by accident as a result of their own efforts to eliminate Daredevil. But even when he considers killing the most evil and murderous of them, he chooses not to. In *Daredevil* issue #165, he says to Doctor Octopus, who as a result of his own evil actions has ended up in danger of death by electrocution, "I should let you fry, Octopus. But then I'd be no better than you." He goes on to save the villainous man.

Even when villains fighting Daredevil or fleeing from him die by their own foolish actions, our sensitive vigilante seems genuinely sorry, as if a child of God has been lost unnecessarily. In the story "A Grave Mistake," drawn but not written by Frank Miller when he was a young artist first assigned to Daredevil, the evil Death Stalker dies in an effort to kill our hero, and Daredevil simply prays, "may God have mercy on his soul" (*Visionaries,* Volume 1).

Fortunately for superheroes, there is nothing in The Ten Commandments that says, "Thou shalt not kick thy neighbor's butt." And that's a very good thing for Daredevil. In one story, he discovers that one of the worst villains of all, Bullseye, has cancer and is going to die unless he gets medical help. Daredevil pursues him to get him that help, while announcing,

"I am going to save your life, Bullseye . . . even if I have to beat you senseless to do it."

Matt Murdock seems to hold the traditional religious view that it is ultimately not our genetics or our heritage that defines us, but our own choices in the world. In the Marvel Comic, *Daredevil—Dead-pool, '97,* Typhoid Mary Walker is trying to blame an accident that Daredevil once inadvertently caused for her descent into crime and murder. He says, "No, Mary. You are who you are because of the choices you make. Sometimes life is tragedy and pain and accidents! But was I there when you pulled your first trigger? Was I there the first time you took a life? No! You made that choice on your own."

Daredevil's own choices show that he values and cherishes life. He seems to think that where there's life there's hope. But it can certainly look like he morphs from heroic to tragic whenever he extends this conviction to the apparently unredeemable, like his arch-nemesis, Bullseye. By refraining from either killing him or allowing him to die on numerous occasions, our spiritually attuned superhero comes to feel partly responsible for the evil that this man subsequently commits.

In *Daredevil,* issue #169, city detective Nick Manolis goes so far as to suggest that, on one particular occasion, Daredevil should have just let this wicked man die. Daredevil replies: "Nick, men like Bullseye would rule the world—were it not for a structure of laws that society has created to keep such men in check. The moment one man takes another man's life in his own hands, he is rejecting the law—and working to destroy that structure. If Bullseye is a menace to society, it is society that must make him pay the price, not you. And not me. I—I wanted him to die, Nick. I detest what he does . . . what he is. But I'm not God—I'm not the law—and I'm not a murderer." He then silently walks away from the still-objecting detective but, in his heart, Matt prays to God that he was right in what he has done and in what he has said. On this occasion and many others, he seeks to do the right thing, and he ultimately looks to an overarching divine order for the assistance and assurance that he otherwise might never have. He is clearly a hero. But he is also almost certainly a tragic figure to anyone who does not share his conviction that his efforts are countenanced, guided, and ultimately augmented by an overarching divine providence that, alone, is the ultimate source of justice in the world.

We have asked the question of whether Matt Murdock is, in any recognizable sense at all, a man of real faith and a "good Catholic." We've looked at some evidence and arguments on both sides. The final answer may be that he does the best he can with what the New Testament calls "the two great commandments" that sum up the life of faith—the commandment to love God, and the injunction to love our neighbor as we love ourselves. It seems not to be too big a stretch to sum up the hold that God apparently has on Matt's life and the degree to which he tries to enact divine justice by concluding that he loves God, even when he worries about his existence. This is no small thing for a scholar, lawyer, and basically decent, yet deeply troubled blind man living in the middle of all the crime, hate, and abuse to be found in Hell's Kitchen. Daredevil clearly also seeks to love his neighbor as himself. He certainly does more than most to take care of any neighbor he might have. He risks his life almost every night so that others can enjoy some measure of safety and security. He does good things for others whenever he can, and he does so in many ways. He's a good friend. He has noble aspirations. He prays. He defends the weak. And he can't shake the feeling that he lives under the overall guidance of a being he can't see or hear, even with his super-enhanced senses. He seems to be a Catholic of a fairly distinctive sort, one with a measure of real spiritual faith and enough honesty to admit his own doubts, while also having enough persistence never to allow those doubts to completely have the upper hand in his life.

Knowing Matt, however, he probably would not try in the least to make the case that he is, by any stretch of the imagination, a good Catholic. He might even admit quite readily that he is a bad Catholic, perhaps even a very bad one indeed. But I think that, deep in his heart, he may feel that this in the end is much better than not having any sort of faith at all. And I suspect that, all things considered, he believes that his faith is a source of at least some strength and guidance, rather than in any way being a cause of weakness and confusion. Without the measure of faith he does have, he might be far worse off than he is on even his very worst days. And, with the kinds of days he often has, that says a lot.

6
The Power and the Glory

CHARLES TALIAFERRO and
CRAIG LINDAHL-URBEN

A powerful river of narrative flows from our tradition of reflection on virtue and vice in the ancient Greek stories of their gods and heroes, down to the modern world, where we continue to dramatize the battle between good and evil in our tales of heroic adventure and conflict. The morality that we find in the mainstream superhero comic books is very similar to the morality and general wisdom that emerges from ancient philosophical ethics.

There's one set of lessons in particular that we can find in both the ancient stories and the modern comic panels: the pursuit of power and glory is as dangerous as it is seductive. The highest glory that can be attained by human beings must come as a side effect of other, worthy pursuits, and always consists, at least in part, in an understanding that people are more valuable than power.

From Olympus to Galactus

In early Greek myths we are often reminded of the danger of recklessly seeking pre-eminent praise and glory. In the story of Icarus, for example, a young man perishes because of his pursuit of glory. He is given wings that are glued to his body, enabling him to soar over the Mediterranean. Intoxicated by his new superhuman power, he flies too close to the sun; the sun melts his wings, and he falls to his death. Lessons from such stories abound in which a misuse of power reveals to us the great harm that can come from a foolish or malicious pursuit of grandeur.[1] This theme is reflected in many comic book stories about the villains and supervillains with whom the superheroes have to deal. A scientific discovery, or a sudden acquisition of power, sets off a maniacal pursuit of more power and glory that inevitably spirals downward to a crash.

We find a similar revelation in the 1960s Marvel Universe when the Fantastic Four have to contend with an adversary known as "Dr. Doom," as well as with an immense devourer of planets, the being called "Galactus." The formerly normal human beings who became the Fantastic Four got their super-powers from an accident that occurred while they were trying out an experimental rocket. As an unexpected side effect, they were all transformed. The brilliant scientist Reed Richards turned into Mr. Fantastic, with an amazingly elastic body. His girl-friend Sue Storm gained the power to become invisible and extend a mental force field around things. Her younger brother Johnny Storm became a Human Torch. Their tough but lovable friend Ben Grimm became horribly disfigured as the Thing, and yet in the bargain was given tremendous strength.

The Fantastic Four are sometimes celebrated as "the super-heroes with problems." But they all work through or around these problems in order to, in Ben's words, "use their power to help mankind." In the Marvel Universe, that help is definitely needed because bad guys are popping up all the time and threatening the lives of ordinary people. We want to look at two of the major foes the Fantastic Four have had to face, along with an associate of one of those foes, in order to contrast two approaches to living, one operating from a highly ethical perspective and the other led on by the seductive lure of power and glory.

We'll first look at Dr. Doom, who originally met the Fantastic Four in issue #5 and, then, Galactus, who was introduced in issue #48. Doom is an evil megalomaniacal scientific genius, and a former college classmate of Reed Richards. Galactus is a cosmic force almost beyond good and evil, an immense being who must destroy and consume whole worlds in order to survive. A further player in the drama is the advance man for Galactus, his

---

[1] A good overview of early Greek philosophy on pride, wisdom, good and evil, can be found in Raymond Devettere's *Introduction to Virtue Ethics* (Washington: Georgetown University Press, 2002).

scout, or "herald," the Silver Surfer, who travels the universe looking for worlds appropriate for him to consume. Let's look at each of these foes in the order in which they originally approached the Fantastic Four.

A Doomed Pursuit of Power and Glory

Dr. Doom was first on the scene, but it will be useful for us to look in on him right after The Fantastic Four has had to deal with a threat from Galactus. In issues #57–#60, after Galactus has temporarily threatened the existence of the Earth and has departed, we have a good opportunity to view morality in the Marvel Universe. The Silver Surfer is still in the area and Dr. Doom has discovered a way to steal the incredible cosmic power that has been granted to him by his master, Galactus. Doom states his whole philosophy of life when he says, simply, "Power has ever been my God." For a brief time, he is determined to use this stolen power to rule the world.[2] When he succeeds in taking away the power of the Silver Surfer, issue #57 ends with the grand announcement: "The world itself belongs to—Dr. Doom!" Of course, that's the way it is with comic-book supervillains, and villains in the real world—a little power goes right to their heads.

The Silver Surfer had borne his awesome power with a great measure of philosophical equanimity. He was a tranquil, wise, dignified, and calm person, and would never have proclaimed his power and glory the way Doom did immediately upon attaining it. In addition, the Silver Surfer aimed only to serve with his power. Doom aimed only to be served.

When Dr. Doom has just betrayed the trusting, almost innocent, Silver Surfer by using a very scientific and medically advanced-looking machine to steal his power, he preens, "Now, it is I who possess the Cosmic Power which was once his! Never before has any one human being been as totally Supreme—as invincibly superior—as I! Now let mankind beware—for Doctor Doom has attained powers without limit—power enough to chal-

---

[2] In more recent issues of the Fantastic Four—almost forty years after the comics we are examining—Dr. Doom has been reinvented as someone who is focused on protecting his kingdom. But in the 1960s he was the epitome of the evil desire to rule the world and harm the Fantastic Four.

lenge Galactus himself!" It's abundantly clear that the power that had been quietly and humbly contained by the Silver Surfer has been acquired now by someone in a mad pursuit of his own glory as the new "master of all mankind!" The famed historian Lord Acton has often been misquoted as saying that, "Power corrupts, and absolute power corrupts absolutely."[3] From these contrasting examples of the Silver Surfer and Dr. Doom, we can easily infer the more nuanced philosophical conclusion that it is not power itself that is necessarily corrupting; rather it's the interaction of power with the vessel into which it is poured. If a person already has the character flaws to incline him toward corruption, then something like a sudden attainment of power can act on those flaws and send him into a fast downward spiral.

Dr. Doom clearly views the pursuit of power and glory as his right. He also sees it as perfectly permissible to achieve his ends at the expense of the entire world. He views other people as merely means to his ends, or as obstacles to be eliminated. While Doom is busy showing off his new power around the world, his now imprisoned guest, the Silver Surfer, is beaten by his jailer and yet still speaks what could be the words of a Stoic philosopher: "Though bereft of my power—I do not crawl—I do not whimper! I am still the Silver Surfer!" The "vessel" here is still the same, whether it contains power or not. An individual who is not corrupted by the acquisition of power is not destroyed by the loss of it. He is comforted in knowing who he is, with or without power or glory. The Surfer's jailer taunts him with the uselessness of that comfort in light of Doom's power and the Silver Surfer responds, "Your master shall never prevail! Though he possesses Power Absolute—it is power usurped! Somehow, as surely as the cosmos stands, it shall—it must—destroy him!" If we can get beyond the hyper-dramatic prose here, we can glimpse a fundamental belief in an underlying justice in the cosmos.

This is a central point of contact between the Marvel Universe and the best ancient philosophers. They both believe that, like basic physical laws such as gravity, the moral rule of justice will eventually prevail. It's built into the fabric of things. In this particular case of power and its misuse, the laws of

---

[3] What Acton actually wrote was: "Power tends to corrupt, and absolute power corrupts absolutely" (Letter to Bishop Mandell Creighton, April 3rd, 1887).

cosmic justice dictate that if a person who is not able to handle power gains it, especially by unethical means, it will destroy him or her. The real problem with power isn't ever the mere having of it; the problem arises over what kind of person holds and wields it. Power and glory don't exist in a vacuum—they have profound roles to play in the character and actions of people.

The Silver Surfer originally gained his powers when he became the planet spotter and cosmic herald of the immensely powerful and ancient being, Galactus. He volunteered for that role in order to spare his world the fate of being consumed by this voracious entity. The Silver Surfer sacrificed himself, or rather the entirety of his normal life on his world, to serve Galactus with eons of travel alone through the cosmos, finding planets for him to devour. Dr. Doom, by contrast, is quite different. Although his portrayal has become much more sophisticated over the decades in order to appeal more to readers who enjoy his display of ego, power, glory and importance, his ethics haven't changed much. In issue #258, he recalls this early episode with the Silver Surfer and tries again for the "Power Cosmic" using another former herald who had served Galactus. Old habits die hard. As world history shows us, once an urge for power and glory takes control of a person, it's very difficult to break free of it.

Just like readers back at the end of the 1960s, we can be led to wonder how the tremendous power that Dr. Doom took from the Silver Surfer can ever be defeated. The answer ultimately confirms the moral prediction made by the Silver Surfer, and re-establishes the cosmic order that was upset when Doom stole his power, the same moral order that is overturned whenever anyone with bad motives and a corrupt heart uses other people merely as a means to his own selfish ends involving power or glory—or, for that matter, money, status, or fame. Doom's selfish arrogance sets him up for a mistake, and when he makes it, the ultimate source of his power is there to take it away. Galactus in the end strips Doom of what was never rightfully his.

In the Marvel universe, the good bounce back, and the evil are thwarted. The Silver Surfer never embraced power in order to rule over others and enhance his own glory, but rather accepted it because it was the only way he could save his own people. Doom is portrayed as the ultimately self-serving ego, and the Silver Surfer is depicted by contrast as a model of self-giving service.

When we examine Galactus himself, we'll see how a character seemingly beyond good and evil nonetheless cannot escape moral categories, and who, in the end, is won over to the moral point of view.

Galactus: The Power and the Glory

In their search for an ultimate foe for the Fantastic Four to face, Marvel had to move beyond conventional considerations of good and evil. They came up with the extreme being, Galactus, who survives and replenishes his power by consuming entire planets. At one point early in the story arc involving Galactus, the Silver Surfer appears out of the immensities of space and approaches the Earth as possible fodder for his master. This planet is being observed by the Watcher, a member of an immortal race sworn to monitor, but "never to interfere with" the worlds he tracks. Yet despite his vow, the Watcher can't resist wanting to help and save the Earth, because of the human life he sees developing here, and so he tries to cloak the planet from the Silver Surfer. His efforts fail, and the Silver Surfer lands on Earth, signaling Galactus to follow.

When Galactus arrives, he has a conversation with the Watcher. Because of his own power and cosmic status, the Watcher is the only being in the area that Galactus recognizes as capable of having meaningful interaction and dialogue with him. Galactus chides the Watcher for trying to hide the Earth from his herald. And the following conversation takes place:

WATCHER: Heed my words, pillager of the planets! This tiny speck of matter upon which we stand contains intelligent life! You must not destroy it!

GALACTUS: Of what import are brief, nameless lives . . . to Galactus? It is not my intention to injure any living being! I must replenish my energy! If petty creatures are wiped out when I drain a planet, it is regrettable but unavoidable! Watcher, since you seem familiar with those puny creatures, I suggest you advise them to hold their tongues . . . before I erase them in one stroke!

WATCHER: Take warning, Galactus! They are less puny than you think! And the Watcher stands beside them in this fateful hour!

GALACTUS: Then you would violate your pledge never to interfere in cosmic affairs? So be it! Despite your power . . . which I know full well . . . it must not be forgotten . . . I am Supreme unto myself . . . I am Galactus!

The big guy backs down—but not before that last little bit of petulant self-promotion.

Notice in this brief exchange something interesting. Despite the fact that Galactus is depicted overall as existing beyond the reach of good and evil, outside the framework and application of moral categories, he first attempts here to morally justify his planned upcoming actions by making an ethical distinction between what he intends to do, and the unintended, though fully anticipated, consequences of it. He needs to consume a planet in order to maintain his own existence and power. So that is what he intends—a good nurturing meal. He knows now that intelligent, sentient beings will be killed by his action, but protests to the Watcher that this is at worst an unfortunate side effect, but not an intended result, of what he is about to do.

This is a common move often made by much lesser beings than Galactus in the attempt to rationalize doing something that will inevitably result in bad consequences. It's no more convincing here than it is when used by a greedy corporate executive or a corrupt politician. What's especially noteworthy about its appearance in this context is that not even a cosmic being devised to stand beyond good and evil can escape using moral categories, however badly, and for immoral purposes.

But let's get back to the story. After some heroic but ineffectual attempts by the Fantastic Four to challenge Galactus, their only hope for the fate of the Earth rests with a complicated and mysterious plan hatched by the Watcher, along with an unexpected redemption of the Silver Surfer by the blind artist Alicia, the girlfriend of Ben Grimm. Through her beauty, she reaches and enlivens the compassion buried deeply in him during all his time in lonely space. At last, he says that he has "found something worth protecting! Even though it means I must do battle with . . . the Master!" He adds, "It is Galactus who is the Power! I am merely his herald! And yet . . . we are both travelers in the cosmos! My own power has never been fully tested!" This unanticipated resurrection of the Silver Surfer from his emotional death, after ages of not feeling, to a place of compassion for the humans on Earth causes concern with the Watcher, because "without meaning to, the Silver Surfer may himself be the cause of Earth's total destruction!" The Watcher doesn't intend for others to battle with Galactus, because he knows such resistance to be futile. He has a different plan.

In a subsequent confrontation with Galactus, the Silver Surfer reveals that he intends to be his herald no longer. The amount of time this conversation takes inadvertently allows the completion of the Watcher's plan to bring, from "a world so unspeakably distant that it beggars description," a device called the "Ultimate Nullifier," as a real threat against Galactus. The arrival of this one machine that can annihilate everything in the universe surprises and halts Galactus, and the Watcher reasons with him again. In this climactic dialogue, we see some of the insights and virtues that are fundamental in the Marvel Universe. The Watcher begins by referring to the humans who have managed to obtain this terrifying device—the Fantastic Four:

> **WATCHER:** Consider the courage they display! Though they are still in their infancy, you must not disdain them! Did not your race . . . and mine . . . evolve from such humble beginnings? Do they not possess the seed of grandeur within their frail human frames?
>
> **GALACTUS:** But what of Galactus? What of the limitless energy I must absorb if I am to survive?
>
> **WATCHER:** There are other planets! We both know full well that the universe is endless! Destroying a race cannot be the answer!
>
> **GALACTUS:** I grow weary! The prize is not worth the battle! Let the human surrender his weapon, and I shall tarry here no longer!
>
> **WATCHER:** Do as he says, mortal! The promise of Galactus is living Truth itself!

Reed Richards then takes a tremendous risk and hands Galactus the Ultimate Nullifier—the only thing that has prevented him from consuming Earth.

> **GALACTUS:** So! For the first time . . . since the dawn of memory . . . my will has been thwarted! But I bear no malice! Emotion is for lesser beings!

Before he leaves, Galactus proclaims, "The Game is ended! The prize has eluded me! And at last I perceive the glint of Glory within the race of man! Be ever worthy of that glory, humans. . . Be ever mindful of your promise of greatness! . . . for it shall one day lift you beyond the stars . . . or bury you within the ruins of war! The choice is yours!!"

Power and Glory: Tests of Virtue

Galactus may have been meant to hover on the edge of ethics in this drama, but the efforts of human superheroes finally manage to draw him into the arena of the moral. When he leaves the Earth, after the events just reported, he seems to acknowledge the intrinsic value of human beings, but that isn't a realization that stays with him. As in the lives of many people, something extreme has to happen to bring him low before he can fully attain a genuinely ethical mindset.

One of the most interesting aspects of the ethics embedded in the Marvel Universe, and, for that matter, in the DC Universe as well, is that the ethical framework for superheroes has a completely different form or logic than the ethics drawn on to describe the actions of villains. The context in which supervillains are created and judged is a kind of reverse utilitarianism. Utilitarianism, simply and roughly described, is the philosophical view that the right action in any circumstance is the one that produces the greatest good for the greatest number of people. In a perverse counterpoint of this view, a Marvel super-villain typically seeks to create the worst harm for the greatest number of people—as if only this will display properly his triumphant power. Although this "evil twin" of utilitarianism is not a strictly logical negation of its popular conception, it nonetheless seems to be the Marvel guideline for the creation of any truly evil character. But the context that informs the actions of the superheroes is not based on either utilitarianism or this corresponding negative perversion of it.

A superhero acts from the belief that damage to a single person, especially an innocent, cannot be tolerated. Superheroes do not engage in utilitarian thinking by which some harm to an innocent person can be outweighed by creating greater goods for the majority. When presented with the choice between saving an innocent individual and saving a group of people, the typical superhero is incapable of making the choice. Indeed, perhaps even more than the immense powers granted to him or her, the inability to make this choice is what finally defines what it is to be a hero. It is what the hero does next that raises him or her to the superhero status—he or she saves both the innocent individual and the group. The superhero is always focused on the intrinsic value of the individual person and is still able to defeat the evil foe who treats all other entities as expendable. The superhero view of life is not at all utilitarian, but is a form of an alternative ethical viewpoint that has been called "personalism," a philosophy that considers any person to be of fundamental and irreducible value.

Personalism has been developed and expounded by a wide range of philosophers, from Borden Parker Bowne (1847–1910) to Martin Buber (1878–1965). Personalists do not calculate the value of a person in reference to their own self-centered goals, as Dr. Doom would, or in accordance with standard utilitarianism, where the good of the many can outweigh the good of any one individual. Each person is of absolute value. Personalism has roots in both religious ethics and in the work of the great philosopher Immanuel Kant (1724–1804), who contended that every person should be treated as an end in himself or herself and never as merely a means to an independent end.[4] Personalists, as well as Kantians, see the heedless manipulation of persons as a grievous unjustifiable wrong. They are also profoundly committed to the idea of a just community, in which individuals are enabled to flourish with respect and dignity. For Kant and all personalists, the ethics we all use should contribute to a community in which there is both individual and group flourishing. Kant called this a "kingdom of ends" in which each person is free to act in accord with recognizing the value of all other persons. In a personalist ethic, the proper role of power or glory in an individual's life is always judged in connection with how that person respects others and how that power or glory affects the

---

[4] See Kant's *Groundwork for the Metaphysics of Morals*, translated by H.J. Paton (New York: Harper and Row, 1964).

strengthening of the greater community. Neither is to be pursued for its own sake, or for the sake of the individual self.

In the Marvel universe, we constantly see the Fantastic Four and other superheroes displaying personalism, while villains, such as Dr. Doom, employ their perversely selfish stratagems in which great harm for others is either unleashed or threatened in the pursuit of their own individual power and glory. It is the actions of superheroes in accordance with personalism that ultimately wins even Galactus over to the moral point of view.

As we have seen, Galactus hovers on the edge of ethical behavior, and seems to dwell mostly outside the categories of good and evil as an amoral force, for two reasons. The first involves his constitution and the second concerns his ambivalence about being part of any kind of community. First, Galactus must convert animate matter on a massive scale into a form of energy that for him is life-sustaining. His very existence seems to require the death of others. And he just accepts that as a fact, neither good nor bad. This is obviously analogous to the case of ordinary human beings who, typically, without compunction, consume life forms beneath us in the food chain, for the sake of our own preservation. For most of human history, we have also taken this as a fact that is in itself neither good nor bad.

Galactus obviously doesn't consider those he consumes to be part of a mutual moral community. This unfortunately, but also clearly, captures the normal attitude that most of us have toward the rest of the natural world, including most of the animal kingdom. So, the entirety of the Earth and the humans on it are merely so low on the food chain that Galactus not only doesn't respect them, he doesn't even recognize them as fellow moral beings at all. Only through the questions and observations of the Watcher is he able to finally recognize, acknowledge, and even show some respect to us mere mortals—including our superheroes. The appearance of the "Ultimate Nullifier" was likely never intended to harm Galactus, since that obviously would have amounted to a classic case of winning the battle but losing the war. It was intended only as a delay, so that the Watcher could have Galactus's attention and enough time to help him see that humans are capable of amounting to something important in his own eyes. The Watcher hoped that if Galactus could be brought to recognize humans as fellow intelligent beings and find something to respect in them—even that they are a child race with glimmerings of greatness—then perhaps he would take on the crucial stance of an ethical being with regard to us and not just that of a hungry giant looking for his next bowl of Cosmic Cheerios. And of course, the Watcher was right.

Those glimmerings of greatness for humans involve both glory and power. From the histories of individual Marvel superheroes and their supervillains, we are able to see that glory and power can accrue to us in perfectly acceptable ways, but that they are not something we properly can seek to attain for ourselves, for our own selfish benefit. Power and glory can be rightly acquired, but only as a proper consequence of morally appropriate actions. And they can be properly used only for the good of moral communities, and not as tools for the pursuit of self-centered goals. Only the bad guys like Dr. Doom pursue power and glory for their own sake, and then for the sake of further selfish ends. The Fantastic Four, by contrast, use both their power and their glory for the good of other people. They represent the moral point of view and constitute among themselves a moral community that opens itself to broader and broader communities where they can make a difference for good.

Galactus has tremendous power, but he lacks a moral community for using it well. This changes dramatically when he becomes the beneficiary of superhero ethics. Almost two hundred issues after the story arc we've been discussing, in issue #244, Galactus returns to the Earth in pursuit of a former herald, Terrax, who has defied him. After finding and defeating him, Galactus is weakened and must feed to restore his power. Unfortunately—guess what?—we are once again the nearest fast food available. He may have forgotten his previous recognition of human value, but he knows a good meal when he sees it.

This time, when the Fantastic Four come to the rescue, the Avengers and Dr. Strange join forces with them and are able to defeat Galactus in his weakened condition. But, even as he lies dying, the personalist ethics of the superheroes kick in. And, from the mouth of Captain America comes the statement, ". . . but Galactus is a living, sentient being and he does not act out of evil intent. He does what he must, simply to survive, just as we would." To this, Reed Richards replies, "Captain America is right! We are bound to help Galactus."

The cosmic giant is resuscitated and is completely perplexed. He exclaims about himself, in his usual, odd third person way, "Galactus lives! But—Galactus is confused. You had beaten me. A victory so total that Galactus did stand at the very brink of that final abyss to which all that live must someday come. Why have you saved me?" And, expressing precisely the point we want to make about superheroes in the Marvel Universe, Reed Richards replies, "We had no choice, Galactus. We could no more stand by and allow you to die than we could turn our backs on any creature in need."

This has a potent effect. From this point on, Galactus interacts with at least some human beings—prominently featuring the Fantastic Four—as "equals" because of their actions in saving his life. He learns regret for his previous attitudes and true respect for his fellow beings. They are no longer mere tools of his foraging or fodder for his appetite—they are individuals worthy of real moral consideration, demanding his respect and recognition. Galactus has made a move toward the ideal of a personalist moral community. And in his tale of power, fall, restoration, and change, we see in a contemporary story-telling context some of the early Greek philosophical warnings about the ills of *hubris* or vainglory, and the philosophical perspective that any of us will flourish best in a peaceful community of ethical action where the intrinsic value of all persons is recognized and respected. These are lessons from the best of ancient philosophy, and they can be found vividly portrayed in contemporary superhero stories.

7

Myth, Morality, and the Women of the X-Men

REBECCA HOUSEL

> The images of myth are reflections of the spiritual potentialities of every one of us. Through contemplating these, we evoke their powers in our own lives.
>
> —Joseph Campbell, *The Power of Myth*

Since the tragedy of September 11th, 2001, the popularity of films featuring heroes in many forms has soared. Naturally, comic-book superheroes perfectly fit the need, and comic-book based films have set new box-office records. The superhero has become a cultural icon again. But Hollywood is doing more with this opportunity than merely entertaining us. Some of the recent films carry philosophical messages that can illumine our lives. In particular, the X-Men films address the philosophy of human nature in a way that we can appropriate using the work of the great scholar of mythology, Joseph Campbell, along with some contemporary theories about ethical decision-making.

The Demand for Diversity

In the midst of all the new focus on superheroes, American film audiences are calling for a more diverse range of heroes, including an increase in female heroes. Most well known comic-book superheroes are male, like Superman, Batman, Spider-Man, Green Lantern, Flash, Thor, and Daredevil, and most superhero films of the past have focused almost entirely on these male heroes. However, Hollywood is now attempting to satisfy the shifting need in younger audiences by including gendered heroes for all the many faces of the twenty-first-century viewing public. This new trend of inclusion is helping films like *X-Men* and *X2: X-Men United* to become part of a new superhero mythology. First created on the printed page in Marvel comic books during the early 1960s, and now becoming legendary in a new way, the X-Men and women are being raised to a new height of mythological status on larger-than-life movie screens.

The basic origin story here is simple. In various parts of the world, children have been born with genetic mutations that give them various powers beyond the reach of normal humans. These mutants can do great good for their fellow human beings, or can inflict terrible harm. The normal population fears them, and some even hate them. Two leaders have arisen within the mutant population, the heroic Charles Xavier, and the villainous Magneto. Xavier wants to organize and train mutants to serve the greater good of humanity, and hopes as a result to convince both communities that they can live together in harmony. To this end, he brings together a team known as the X-Men. Magneto takes a very different path. He believes that humans have waged war against the mutant population and that mutants must respond in kind. His actions are all undertaken in the name of mutant freedom, although in the first *X-Men* film[1], he shows that he is willing to murder a fellow mutant to accomplish his goals.

In his evil, Magneto stands opposed to Xavier to represent an important part of the duality apparent in all myth—Good and evil, woman and man, life and death. Recognizing this duality is in classic mythology the first step in moving out into the wider world.[2] And that is how *X2* begins. But that's not how it ends. From his work on world mythology and historic images of the heroic, Joseph Campbell suggests that behind every duality, there is a singularity at play. The main premise of the second X-Men film is that there should always be transcendence through duality to a particular singularity, or unity. The film's title and subtitle, *X2: X-Men United,* are well chosen.

Campbell's definitive work on the mythologies of all cultures is crucial for understanding the parallels between traditional

---

[1] *X-Men,* directed by Bryan Singer (Twentieth Century Fox, 2000)

[2] Joseph Campbell, *The Power of Myth*, edited by Betty Sue Flowers (New York: Anchor, 1991).

mythology and Hollywood superhero myths. It can also be used to construct important elements of a philosophy of human nature, focused especially on the question of what is involved in heroic excellence. According to Campbell, all heroes go on a cyclical journey that involves three main phases: a departure, an initiation, and a return. Launching into the departure phase, the hero leaves the isolation of home after receiving "the call." This enables the hero to cross a threshold into the wider world where he or she can then begin the initiation phase, experiencing a number of different trials. Once the individual has proved worthy of heroic status, the return phase can begin. In this final phase, our hero has somehow transcended duality to an underlying singularity. There is an integration of the familiar and the foreign as he or she becomes a "Master of Two Worlds." This involves a necessary transformation of consciousness and completes the journey. This same three-fold cycle is used in many ways by popular films, and is certainly an underlying part of the hero plots in both *X-Men* and *X2: X-Men United*.

There are times when Hollywood chooses well its mythmaking subjects. In the face of feminist progression, the major motion picture studios have generally had to show more women in leading, heroic roles. And there is perhaps no better comic resource than *The Uncanny X-Men* to meet these needs in creating a new, broader superhero myth. When Marvel comic mogul Stan Lee launched the comic in 1963, he intended a less gender-specific title for the series, "The Mutants." An editor disagreed with him, and renamed the comic "X-Men."[3] Despite the name, this series has always given a significant spotlight to strong women. Of course, most of the great superhero teams of the past have had women members, with, for example, Wonder Woman in the JLA, and the very blonde and beautiful Black Canary joining her in the JSA, Sue Storm in the Fantastic Four, and the Wasp in the Avengers. But the X-Men have more strong female role models than is typical in classic superhero stories. We'll look at three of them to see what philosophical light their mythic journey might shed on the human condition.

---

[3] Stan Lee, in "Special Features" of the *X2* DVD.

The Perfect Storm

The diverse population represented in *X-Men* includes the African American character of Storm. The daughter of an African princess and American photojournalist, Ororo Munroe, code-named "Storm," first appeared in the Marvel comic, *Giant-Size X-Men #1,* in 1975. She was orphaned as a child in Cairo, Egypt, by the collapse of a building that killed both of her parents.[4] As with many heroic journeys, hers began in tragedy. When we meet her, she is intelligent, loyal, and very powerful—her mutant abilities include flight and weather control, hence her name. Storm functions as a teacher in *X2*, as well as a powerful warrior for the good of humanity, despite humanity's insistence on fearing and hating all mutants. She fits perfectly within Campbell's classic definition of the hero, hearing a call to new adventure, leaving the known for the unknown, encountering trials, growing from them, and returning home, at least metaphorically, with new riches of wisdom. Storm leaves the isolation and safety of her surroundings in Kenya, where she is worshipped as a goddess for her incredible powers, to join Professor Xavier in America, crossing that threshold, and facing serious trials, all in the name of justice and good.[5] Campbell describes a hero as "the one who comes to participate in life courageously and decently, in the way of nature, not in the way of personal rancor, disappointment, or revenge."[6] Storm is the image of Campbell's conception, while also broadening our sense of the gender possibilities for a hero.

She is also beautiful. Played in both films by Halle Berry, she has a perfect face and body. Of course, there is a rich tradition in superhero comics of women apparently introduced just because of their exaggerated physical beauty, but Storm isn't on the scene for her physique or face. And she is not the center of a traditional, patriarchal heterosexual matrix—the classic male-female relationship. She is her own person, and brings considerable substance to the X-Men.

In *X2*, Storm shows a keen intellectual interest in a male mutant named "Kurt Wagner," who is also known as

---

[4] *Ultimate Marvel Encyclopedia*, "Storm," edited by Beazley and Youngquist (New York; Marvel Comics, 2003) Volume 1; p.157.

[5] *Ultimate Marvel Encyclopedia*, p. 157.

[6] *The Power of Myth*, p. 82.

"Nightcrawler." He is a demonic-looking character, with fang-like teeth, pointed ears, yellow eyes, three-fingered hands, two-toed feet, and a prehensile tail. He is also covered with evidence of self-mutilation in the form of angelic symbols etched into his skin by his own hand on both his face and body. Nightcrawler explains to Storm that these scars are representations of symbols given to humanity by the archangel Gabriel, and that they match in number his sins. Interestingly, Gabriel[7] is the archangel traditionally known for mercy, truth, hope, resurrection, and humanity. Kurt comes to represent each of these things for his fellow X-Men.

Nightcrawler is very different in appearance from both Storm and the other X-Men. He is such an alien-looking life form and has such odd powers, and yet it is precisely this extreme "otherness" that draws Storm to him in curiosity and questioning. The strangeness that strikes fear into the hearts of most people when confronted with mutants is here presented as the bridge it is capable of being in an individual's trajectory of learning and personal growth. Storm's interest in Nightcrawler shows her seemingly aloof character opening to more possibilities than merely those encompassed in the range of experiences and concepts that have already formed her life. The next step, according to Campbell, is transcendence through duality to singularity, which is of course the natural progression in any ideal relationship—to become of one mind or one spirit, two halves of a whole, as the great philosopher Aristotle and many others have understood.

Storm's contact with this otherness pays off in an unexpected way. She and Nightcrawler at one point briefly discuss faith. She voices a complaint about humans, and in response, Kurt tells her to have compassion for the ignorant, as a spiritual teacher would instruct. In more than one scene, the quiet Kurt prays and puts his faith to work, even to the point of holding and using Rosary beads as he faces difficulties. Storm's own experience of faith grows in *X2* largely through her association with him. At a

---

[7] Gabriel is from the Hebrew "Gavriel", literally meaning "God's man"; the hard 'v' sound was replaced by the soft 'b' as the second and third letters in the Hebrew *Alef-Bet* are 'bet' and 'vet'. Both letters are the same, except for a dot in the 'bet', indicating the soft 'b' sound. Variances in pronunciation occur based on different translations of the Hebrew text.

critical moment in the film, both of them must perform a dangerous task. Nightcrawler expresses doubt, as Storm had earlier in the film, and it is then she who restores him by saying, "I have faith in you," transcending through their duality to a needed singularity—physically as well as spiritually, as the two hold tightly to each other in order to move through a solid steel door, both thereby completing a transformation of consciousness necessary for all heroes.

Psychologist Lawrence Kohlberg famously identified three basic levels of moral development.[8] The "pre-conventional level" is one of obedience to authority. Young children do what's right because they're told to do so by an authority and want to avoid punishment for not obeying. The "conventional level" represents more complex moral reasoning. At this stage of development, people strive to fit in, and act conventionally with respect to others, satisfying more general social expectations and upholding the social order. The "post-conventional level" of moral development displays ethical reasoning of the highest sort. On this level, people act in accordance with higher moral principles focused on justice, allowing them to support or critique their own groups and societies as they seek to do what is right.

Storm characteristically exhibits the post-conventional level of the "ethics of justice" through her work of protecting humans in a rational and objective way. This form of action typically is associated with a rule-based approach to ethical decision-making and often has been known as "masculine ethics." Storm follows her own sense of the demands of justice, based on a strong belief in individual rights, equality, and the common good, despite the nearly constant and active human prejudice against all mutants that she experiences. However, she also has the ability to shift from action in accordance with the masculine ethics of Kohlberg to the alternative "feminine" conception of "care ethics" identified by Kohlberg's most prominent critic and former assistant at Harvard, Carol Gilligan.[9]

---

[8] See Lawrence Kohlberg, *The Philosophy of Moral Development* (New York: Harper Collins, 1981),

[9] Carol Gilligan, *In a Different Voice: Psychological Theory and Women's Development* (Cambridge: Harvard University Press, 1982)

We see Storm at one point in *X2* operating clearly from a center of caring—rather than from just a cold, rational sense of justice and duty—when she saves eight mutant children from their imprisonment in a secret government lab. Gilligan's conception of care ethics puts relationships as the highest priority, and Storm exhibits an almost maternal reaction when she dashes off to save the children she has just seen on a surveillance monitor. She has moral complexity and she masters ethical duality. She is not bound to one conception of ethics over another. She seems clearly to understand that different situations require different ways of thinking. Ethical action may be based on an abstract sense of justice and corresponding duty, or it can arise out of proper emotion. In her understanding of this, she functions outside typical gender expectations, both in terms of mythology and moral psychology. Storm is perhaps the perfect hero. She has mental and physical toughness, beauty, and a nurturing feminine side, as well as a focused rational side. And she succeeds in completing all of Campbell's heroic phases.

One of Joseph Campbell's other insights into myth is that it can aid us in understanding that each person is only a small piece of the total image of humanity. Individuals are limited by such constraints as gender, age, profession, religion, orientation, ethnicity, and education. The "fullness" of humanity lies not in single individuals, but with "the body of society as a whole."[10] Such diverse philosophers as Plato, the apostle Paul, the Stoics, and Pascal, to mention just a few, have stressed throughout history the importance of this vision of unity. These philosophers speak congruently, yet in their own ways, concerning the importance of human solidarity through diversity for maximal human fulfillment. Female heroes are just as necessary as male heroes—in fact, according to Campbell's conception of heroism, it lies within every one of us to be a hero. The character of Storm gives us a fine example of it.

The Shape-Shifting Mystique

The mutant character Mystique is played by Rebecca Romijn Stamos in *X2*. She provides us with some new twists within the

---

[10] Joseph Campbell, *The Hero with a Thousand Faces* (Princeton: Princeton University Press, 1973).

world of the super-powered. She is capable of projecting any form of beauty imaginable, she is very powerful, and she is extremely skilled, both intellectually and physically. She is also evil.

Mystique, also known as Raven Darkholme, first appeared in the Marvel comic *Ms. Marvel #16* in 1978.[11] The comic-book history tells of Mystique's failing, frustrating battles to unite mutants and humans, ultimately forging from her disappointment the cold, manipulative warrior who joins Magneto and the Brotherhood of Evil Mutants. Mystique is the birth mother of Kurt Wagner, our Nightcrawler. We are told in the original comics that she abandoned her demon-like newborn for her own safety. Her chief mutant power is shape-shifting. She is, in her "normal" form, a woman, but she can easily manipulate her physical appearance to become a man.

In *X2*, Mystique appears with indigo skin clumped with patches of scales. She is endowed with yellow snake-like eyes and red hair, and has a definite serpentine look to her agile body. The snake is a primary and ancient mythological symbol associated with the feminine, rebirth, and mystery.[12] Mystique's physical appearance in the film alludes to all of this. Even her name has ancient intonations, as the root for the word *mystique* is the Latin *mystes*, meaning a priest of the mysteries, or one who has been initiated—both definitions fitting her full and complex character.

Her very nature is an unstable, changing duality. She is not just female but may also be male. Stuck in this odd, transmuting physical duality, she may never transcend to the singularity necessary to complete the hero cycle. But that's not her only obstacle to the heroic. She is also a sociopath, seemingly bent on killing all humans. She will do whatever is necessary to reach her goals, which are all ultimately derived from her primal need for self-preservation. She will use her shape-shifting abilities to seduce a man with whatever appearance he most desires whenever it suits her purposes. But when Nightcrawler asks her why she doesn't just permanently shift her appearance to look like everyone else, she replies bitterly that she shouldn't have to. What are the ethics of such a creature?

---

[11] *Ultimate Marvel Encyclopedia*, p.170.
[12] Joseph Campbell, *The Masks of God: Occidental Mythology* (New York: Penguin, 1991).

Certainly, one cannot assign anything remotely like care ethics to Mystique. A mother who abandoned her newborn child to save herself is not a care-giver. In the first *X-Men* movie, she puts Professor Xavier into a dangerous coma. She also helps to kidnap a senator, impersonates him to pursue her own ends, and then participates in what amounts to a terrorist attack on world leaders.

In *X2*, she partners up with the X-Men temporarily to pursue and defeat a mutual foe, a powerful military man who is intent on eliminating all mutants, only to abandon her colleagues to a presumptive death when she gets what she wants. She refuses to acknowledge any thing or person that would distract her from her own goals. From her perverse perspective, her actions may sometimes result in losses, but they ultimately will create what she considers a better world. Her views and actions pervert Kohlberg's ethics of justice by taking his notions of rational, rule-governed action to evil extremes. Her distorted sense of justice demands actions that are contrary to any sensible conception of a just world. Her deeds are rule-governed, but the rules are clearly her own. Her behavior is principled, but the principles are wicked. Her ruthless ethics are even, in the end, ironic—in her blanket hatred of everything human, she unintentionally shows her own underlying, repressed humanity through her insecurity, fear, and hatred. If Storm is the perfect hero, Mystique is perhaps her counterpart as an anti-hero.

Phoenix Rising: Jean Grey

Jean Grey first appeared in the Marvel comic *X-Men #1* in 1963.[13] She is an original X-Man, and was introduced as Professor Xavier's first student. Her character is quite different from Storm or Mystique, who were both created in the 1970s, over a decade after Jean. Both of them represent the shifting attitudes toward women in American society. As we have seen, Storm and Mystique are smart, self-confident, and highly skilled. They both operate completely without any need for a romantic love interest. By contrast, Jean is portrayed as trustworthy, loyal, and intelligent, yet lacking in self-confidence, and dependent on the men around her. She is also physically attractive and is part

---

[13] *Ultimate Marvel Encyclopedia,* p.139.

of a classic love-triangle with her fellow X-Men Scott and Logan—Cyclops and Wolverine. She functions as the focus of a continuing heterosexual matrix, promoting the traditional male-female relationship to the audience.

In the first *X-Men* film, Jean helps save Wolverine's life. Wolverine, a tough and aggressive male mutant, expresses his feelings of attraction, and even adoration for Jean through longing, lustful looks and witty one-liners. In *X2*, the flirtation continues, and so does the resultant animosity between Cyclops and Wolverine over Jean's attentions.

X2 shows Jean early in the film with a group of students from Professor Xavier's School for the Gifted on a field trip in the Museum of Natural History. The director shows us some of humanity's evolution via the museum displays, and continues subtle allusions to the idea of evolution by briefly showing museum banners with the word, "evolution," often outlined in bright colors. Jean's character is suffering from headaches, and because of her powerful telekinetic abilities, they disrupt everything electronic in the museum. The audience sees Jean struggle with her pain, while the camera focuses on her *bling*, a silver-tone necklace of a bird—but not just any bird, a *phoenix*. Fans of the *X-Men* comics will immediately recognize the reference.

Jean has both telepathy and telekinesis as her mutant powers. But her character is shown as a mere shadow of the great Professor Xavier in the first *X-Men* film. In one scene, she makes a presentation at a congressional hearing, and does poorly. Later, she apologizes to Xavier for her performance. With her particular powers, she could easily communicate in a very persuasive way with anyone, but she quickly lost her audience at the hearing because she lacked confidence in herself. After Xavier slips into a coma from a mishap with Cerebro, Jean, who earlier was reluctant to use the machine, bravely decides to give it a try—but can muster the courage only while her male mentor is comatose. In *X2*, she is still accepting guidance from the men around her, including Cyclops as well as Xavier. However, there are subtle signs that she will not be just taking orders for long—she is evolving.

This character is destined for a giant leap in further evolution. For long time comic-book readers, Jean Grey is synonymous with the Phoenix, a cosmic being who takes on Jean's identity after she is exposed to high levels of solar radiation during a rescue mission.[14] Jean's character gradually evolves throughout *X2*, showing personal, social, and philosophical growth, as well as an increase in her powers. And while the ending of *X2* does not give any definitive answers on her future, there is a definite allusion to a great leap forward in evolution beyond physical death as the Phoenix.

Throughout the period of her life depicted in the films, Jean exhibits all three of the main levels of Kohlberg's ethics of justice. She first fits the pre-conventional level, being guided by those around her with authority. She seems almost mousy with her soft tone of voice, explaining her failure to Xavier, or offering excuses as to why she can't perform certain tasks because she's just not powerful enough. She also exhibits on many occasions the second, conventional level of moral development, when she acts primarily to please others in accordance with the expectations she perceives from them.

Ultimately, when, near the end of the second film, Jean sacrifices her life to save her colleagues, it could be argued that she reaches the final, post-conventional level of Kohlberg's ethics. In this act, she rejects the wishes and pleas of others and acts on her own to preserve the common good, regardless of her emotional ties and relationships. She can be viewed in her ultimate act of self-sacrifice as the quintessential utilitarian, calculating what is in the best interest of the most people involved (what will increase the total utility, or the total net sum of pleasure over pain) and, as an act of cool rationality, choosing that action, even though it means her death. But is this the Jean Grey we have come to know? Is she the sort of person who would merely calculate what will yield the greatest good for the greatest number and then mechanically do it? Or could she instead be acting out of the deepest possible form of caring?

When Jean sacrifices herself to save everyone else, she departs from one common understanding of Gilligan's care ethics that insists that women regard themselves as being equally deserving with those around them. Many feminist interpreters have suggested that care ethics, properly understood, preclude any sort of unbalanced self-sacrifice for the sake of others. They recommend instead the balancing of a healthy

---

[14] *Ultimate Marvel Encyclopedia*, p. 139.

concern for the self along with a proper concern for the welfare of other people. However, there actually may be greater resources within a broad understanding of care ethics than within classic justice-centered ethics, such as Kohlberg's, to motivate and explain the ultimate sacrifice that Jean is prepared to make for her friends.

Justice ethics are centered on rules and rights. Care ethics focus on relationships and providing for people. When Jean is faced with a situation where the lives of all her closest friends can be saved only by the sacrifice of her own life, she is not confronted by people who have the sort of right to life that demands her ultimate act as a corresponding moral duty, in service to justice. It is precisely because she goes beyond the call of duty that her act is heroic. She acts not out of duty, but out of love, care and concern, knowing that her death alone can save the rest of the X-Men. In doing this, she becomes something like a female Christ figure, and her death correspondingly seems to foreshadow a resurrection.

The Gospel of John (15:13) says "Greater love hath no man than this, that a man lay down his life for his friends." Jean Grey proves that this is not the privilege of a man alone. And in doing so, she just may be overcoming the duality implicit in both justice ethics and the standard feminist interpretation of care ethics. There is no calculation weighing her rights versus the rights of her colleagues, and there is no question of whom to care for, her own self, or them. It could be that she has transcended through duality to a singularity or unity with the others such as to elide the difference between self-sacrifice and self-preservation. She does what has to be done for the preservation of the greater unity.

While the movie audience does not see the ultimate reward for Jean's act of self sacrifice and salvation, the allusion at the end of the film, along with Xavier's remark to a group of children that "everything is going to be just fine," hints obliquely that Jean's willingness to go beyond the demands and duties of normal ethics into the far heroic reaches of what philosophers call "supererogation"—acting beyond the call of duty—may give her a surprising reward through a rebirth as the extraordinarily powerful Phoenix. This could be a modern mythic presentation of the ultimately transformative power of love. The example of the act can be as powerful for us viewers as the act itself was for the X-Men.

Campbell's stages of the heroic correspond with Jean's meta-morphosis in *X2*. She comes out of her shell, performs bravely through many trials, and undergoes the necessary transformation of consciousness. Then, in her final, self-sacrificing heroic moment, she seems to begin another phase of the cycle, as we see the image of a golden bird-like figure gliding below the surface of the lake where she had apparently met her end. Will Jean return as a "Master of the Two Worlds,"[15] as Campbell suggests? Will she come back to the X-Men? We can't help but feel that the results of her ultimate act would not be complete if she didn't return to Xavier, Cyclops, and Wolverine.

Campbell states, "Wherever the hero may wander, whatever he may do, he is ever in the presence of his own essence . . . social participation may lead in the end to a realization of the All in the individual, so that of exile brings the hero to the Self in all."[16] Perhaps that is the fate of Jean Grey. Her decision to sacrifice herself for the common good, an exile of the most extreme sort, leads to social, philosophical and personal growth. She transcends the dualities within herself—powerful yet timid, intelligent but lacking self-confidence, loving the stable and sensitive Cyclops, yet attracted to the wild and unpredictable Wolverine—and ultimately she recognizes herself in the "all."

X2, Superhero Myth, Philosophy, and the World

Storm, Mystique, and Jean Grey are three very different women. The one of them who might initially have seemed least super-heroic is in the end perhaps the one who is the greatest hero of all, and from whom we can learn the most. The recent film depictions of each of them show a growing awareness of the importance of women and their roles in superhero mythology. And that is important. But these films show much more. Mythology is a powerful vehicle for deepening the human experience. *X2: X-Men United* traces out crucial elements of the evolving gender-based human experience through strong male

---

[15] *The Hero with a Thousand Faces*, p. 229. Campbell suggests that all heroes return with the ability to move back and forth between isolation and the wider world without corrupting either.

[16] *The Hero with a Thousand Faces*, p.386.

and female characters in a way that can bring society as a whole closer to the idea of transcending the duality that is in various ways male-female, self-other, and familiar-foreign, to arrive at a new grasp of the singularity of humankind. The surprise is that this philosophical vision captured in modern myth can be as entertaining as it is enlightening.

8

Barbara Gordon and Moral Perfectionism

JAMES B. SOUTH

I will confess to being something of a latecomer to the joys of comic books. I seriously read my first comic book while in my forties. I mention this fact about me because it helps to explain this essay. When I began reading comics, I assumed that "Year One" stories, that is, those mini-series that go into detail about a character's origin, would be the place to start. I quickly realized, however, that such comics are not quite as fully accessible to the comic-book beginner as I had imagined. There's a good reason for this fact in that these comics tend to be written against a richness of background and decades of continuity (or its lack).

"Year One" story-lines have as one of their primary goals the fashioning of a stable and canonical origin for a character based on a past history that is almost always to some extent unstable. In ignoring any destabilizing stories that may be associated with a character, such comics also provide a kind of truth about the character, at least for the foreseeable future. Hence, the challenge of reading those comics for the novice is that one misses out on an appreciation of the choices made by the author. The observant lifelong reader of comics sees these choices, notices what is absent from the new canonical narrative, and decides to accept or reject this stabilized reading of the character. That pleasure available to the long-time reader of comics is exactly what I could not experience in reading my first "Year One" story. Nonetheless, it's precisely this stabilizing feature of "Year One" comics that I intend to exploit in this chapter, since it is the retrospective work they accomplish that makes the theme of my paper possible.

From Librarian to Batgirl to Oracle

Barbara Gordon is a relative newcomer to the Batman universe, making her first appearance in comic books in 1967 as both Batgirl and niece (later to be the adopted daughter) of police lieutenant James Gordon.[1] One of the more interesting features of the character is the fact that she has had two different super-hero identities. Famously, Alan Moore's *The Killing Joke* shows Barbara Gordon being shot by the Joker.[2] The resultant paralysis effectively put an end to her career as Batgirl. Nonetheless, she re-emerges as Oracle, a highly effective information manager who uses her extraordinary computer skills to help fight crime in Gotham City. In Barbara's unusual case, we have two "Year One" stories, a *Batgirl: Year One* nine-issue series,[2] and an *Oracle: Year One* short story, "Born of Hope."[3] Since becoming Oracle, Barbara has also developed her own crime-fighting team consisting of Black Canary and Huntress, collectively known as the Birds of Prey.

The story of Barbara Gordon illustrates key themes in an important philosophical theory known as 'moral perfectionism'.[4] One very interesting feature of moral perfectionism is that it can be found in the thinking of various philosophers, since the issue it foregrounds is one that works as a kind of precondition for any serious ethical reflection. Thus, it is present not only expressly in philosophical texts such as Plato's *Republic*, but also in works of literature, movies, and the like. In short, wherever we find narratives that concern the moral progress of individuals, we are likely to find a story where moral perfectionism is illuminative. I want to show that a comic-book character can provide such a stable narrative.

There is, famously, or notoriously, no accepted definition of moral perfectionism. Instead, the term denotes a cluster of themes that are central to any life that can be seen as moral. The word 'perfectionism' suggests that 'moral' here is being under-

---

[1] There's a very good biography of Barbara Gordon at the Canary Noir Web site: http://www.canarynoir.com.
[2] Alan Moore *et al.*, *Batman: The Killing Joke* (New York: DC Comics, 1988).
[3] Collected in trade paperback format as: Scott Beatty *et al.*, *Batgirl: Year One* (New York: DC Comics, 2003).
[4] John Ostrander *et al.*, *Oracle: Year One.* "Born of Hope." This short story appears in *The Batman Chronicles* 5 (New York: DC Comics, 1996).

stood in a fairly rigorous way, one that designates the "search" feature that will figure prominently in what follows. The central theme of moral perfectionism is that the self can become better, and that a truly moral life is one in which the self is always trying to improve. Other themes involve the role that exemplars or friends play in anyone's quest for making moral progress, and at the same time the ongoing dangers of inappropriate conformity in anyone's moral adventure. In short, what's at stake in moral perfectionism is the development of a distinctive moral self. And that is a core issue in philosophy.

Where I Don't Want to Be

Consider the following scene from *Batgirl: Year One*. We see Barbara Gordon working at her job in the Gotham City Library. She's sitting in front of a bank of computers: books about crime are stacked around her on the shelves beside her desk; an application to the Gotham City Police Department stamped "denied" lies on her desk, as does a newspaper with a headline about "The Batman." The desk sits in front of a large window overlooking from several floors up a central reading room. The elements of Barbara Gordon's identity to this point in her life are splayed around for her (and the reader) to see. Of course, the significance of these elements is still unknown to her, but the comic is all about what Barbara is going to become, not just as Batgirl but also as Oracle. We are given access to her thoughts: "I want to be in on the action. Anything that will get me out of where I am. Where I don't want to be." (*Batgirl: Year One*, p. 13) I want to focus on this moment in Barbara's life by pointing to a famous passage from the philosopher John Stuart Mill's classic essay, *On Liberty*:

> In our times, from the highest class of society down to the lowest, everyone lives as under the eye of a hostile and dreaded censorship. Not only in what concerns others, but in what concerns only themselves, the individual or the family do not ask themselves, what do I prefer? Or, what would suit my character and disposition? Or, what would allow the best and highest in me to have fair play and enable it to grow and thrive? They ask themselves, what is suitable to my position? What is usually done by persons of my station and pecuniary circumstances? Or (worse still) what is usually done by persons of a station and circumstance superior to mine? I do not

mean that they choose what is customary in preference to what suits their own inclination. It does not occur to them to have any inclination except for what is customary. . . . Now is this, or is it not, the desirable condition of human nature?[5]

Mill is directing our attention to two facts concerning the condition of human nature most of us experience. One fact is that the condition we experience is less than a desirable one. The other is that one way out of this unfortunate condition is by paying attention to our own desires. How is it that so many of us fail to take sufficient notice of our desires, and then fail to act on them, and as a result end up so unsatisfied?

Now, it may be the case that Mill is wrong that these pressures to conform affect everyone, though my own suspicion is that he is correct. Even if, though, such pressures were to affect only one person, we can apply his diagnosis of that situation. In the case of Barbara Gordon, she clearly feels the pressure to conform, to what her father wants, and what society in general expects of a young woman her age, and there are signs throughout the book that she finds this condition undesirable. Here the question that naturally arises for Barbara and for any of us is not so much how we know what we want—though that's a difficult question in itself—but how we can get guidance in following our wants once we do know them.

None of us can get much guidance about how we should live our lives in the standard theories of moral philosophy. There is no help in to be found in a theory of the good as developed by classic Utilitarianism, or in the theory of right posed by traditional Kantianism. Both of these philosophical theories are pitched at a level more abstract than the very concrete question of how I should live my life, and both also cut off precisely the question of what I want. For each of them, the question of what

---

[5] The contemporary philosopher Stanley Cavell is most responsible for bringing the themes of moral perfectionism to the attention of the philosophical community. For a compelling account of the main themes of moral perfectionism, see Cavell's *Cities of Words: Pedagogical Letters on a Register of the Moral Life* (Cambridge, Massachusetts: Harvard University Press, 2004). In what follows, I will not cite particular discussions of specific themes as they occur in Cavell. However, all the themes I discuss can be found in *Cities of Words*.

I want is directly irrelevant to the morality of actions. At the same time, it might seem to hardly make sense to say that the issue of what kind of person I should become is tangential to morality as conceived by these two major theories. Isn't any sort of morality all about both what we do and what we become? But actually, on the Utilitarian view, I simply should be the kind of person who maximizes good in each of my actions. From the Kantian perspective, I should be a person who does my duty. The idea of becoming, or what I am becoming, plays no real part in either theory. And these well-known theories claim that our personal wants are to be excluded rather than consulted when we seek to do the right thing. They insist that I increase the good or act from duty regardless of my feelings, wants, desires, or aspirations. And so they don't really address any of these ingredients of human identity.

Accordingly, it might be better to say that what is at stake for Barbara Gordon as she confronts her future, and for any of us as we consider our own, is not primarily the development of any sort of a rule by which we can measure the goodness or rightness of particular actions, but rather the development of an overall sense of morality, simply speaking. Or if that sounds too strong, perhaps another way of saying the same thing is that we need to understand and prepare the conditions out of which our moral selves will develop. And one way we might make sense of that is by worrying about how it is that we make our desires more fully intelligible, or understandable, to ourselves. Indeed, it is precisely the gap between who Barbara Gordon is and who she wants to be that needs to be bridged. It is noteworthy that she does not experience this need as something extraneous to, or additional to, who she is: "I have to find another path. Divine my own future. One uniquely mine. Not a page from someone else's book" (*Batgirl: Year One*, p. 12). She doesn't just own the question and the challenge—it's actually a part of her.

I Can Become Something More

If we can't turn to standard moral theories for guidance in fashioning ourselves, then where can we turn for guidance? As *Batgirl: Year One* progresses, we see Barbara Gordon fall into the role of Batgirl seemingly by accident. She goes to a costume ball with her father, and she is dressed in a "Bat" costume. She does this mostly to tweak her father, whom she sees as wanting to thwart her ambition for a more active and exciting life, and in effect then to render her future mediocre, though he would never put it this way, or even conceive of his desires for her in such terms at all. But her costume choice is also made surely because at some level she is drawn to the particular life of Batman. While they are at the party, a villain appears and tries to kidnap Bruce Wayne, who, taking a break from his secret work as Batman, is attending the event. Barbara springs into action, rescuing Bruce and chasing the villain. At one point, the criminal calls her "Batgirl" and that, as she notes, makes it all somehow "official."

In the course of her fight with the villain, we are granted access to her thoughts: "I can become something more. Something higher. From out of the shell I once was. I'll emerge better. I'll be lifted up with new wings. Like a moth. Or a bat." It's then that Batman appears on the scene, thanks to Barbara's rescue of Bruce. And there's the answer to the question of how she can get guidance in becoming her new self.

Barbara needs, as we all need, an exemplar, or a paradigm, or a mentor who will help us figure out who we are, or, more precisely, what we want. The role of exemplars in the quest for a moral life has a long history dating back at least to Socrates and his followers. These followers were mostly young men who sensed in the life of Socrates an orientation towards the good that they too were drawn towards. But there are dangers lurking about in such a relationship. The point of an exemplar is not that he or she is to be emulated, but that this person, in virtue of being farther along a path you aspire to go down, somehow understands you better than you understand yourself—at least at the beginning. This point is well made by the nineteenth-century philosopher Friedrich Nietzsche in his essay, "Schopenhauer as Educator." The passage is so central to the philosophy of moral perfectionism that I will quote it at some length:

> Anyone who believes in culture is thereby saying: 'I see above me something higher and more human than I am; let everyone help me to attain it, as I will help everyone who knows and suffers as I do: so that at last the man may appear who feels himself perfect and boundless in knowledge and love, perception and power, and

who in his completeness is at one with nature, the judge and eval-
uator of things.' It is hard to create in anyone this condition of
intrepid self-knowledge because it is impossible to teach love; for
it is love alone that can bestow on the soul, not only a clear, dis-
criminating and self-contemptuous view of itself, but also the
desire to look beyond itself and to seek with all its might for a
higher self as yet still concealed from it.[6]

"Seeking a higher self still concealed" is precisely what Barbara
Gordon is doing. But how is Batman going to aid her in seeking this higher self?

The opening word of *Batgirl: Year One* is "masks." Masks
and costumes are, obviously, tricky affairs for superheroes. We
usually think of masks as concealing identities, but in the case
of superheroes it's almost always the case that in some important sense the mask reveals the identity. Yet in Barbara Gordon's
case, the metaphorical mask she wears at the beginning is precisely the one that conceals her higher self. It's what we might
call the "Barbara Gordon" mask, the "shell" around the librarian
and relative of Lieutenant James Gordon. It's only when she puts
on the Batgirl mask that she begins her journey to her higher
self, her future self—the one she doesn't yet know.

At the end of the comic, Barbara is summoned to the
Batcave. This is her second trip there. The first time she was
brought there, she was tested by a kind of obstacle course,
forced to try to stop a series of cardboard villains. She managed
to run the gauntlet, but only by using "lethal force." While no
one was really killed, Batman took this as a sign that she was-
n't cut out to be part of the team. When asked what a contrary
strategy would have proved, Batman replies, "That you could be
one of us." He goes on to question her own self-understanding,
asking her why she wants to be one of them. Barbara is taken
aback, left without an answer. For Batman, the lack of an
answer, the obvious lack of self-knowledge here, is enough to
rule out the possibility of her joining the team. Barbara isn't
quite finished though. It turns out she does have an answer after
all: "Because I can." This ambiguous assertion—is she saying

---

[6] John Stuart Mill, *On Liberty*, Chapter 3, Paragraph 6.
[6] Friedrich Nietzsche, *Untimely Meditations* (Cambridge: Cambridge University
Press, 1997), pp. 162–63.

that she possesses the ability to help or merely that somehow she sees it as a possibility—is enough to convince Batman to give her a chance. He doesn't tell her that, but over the course of the comic, he indirectly, via his sidekick Robin, provides her with resources to continue her journey. Now she has been summoned again. She is given another test and again succeeds, but this time on Batman's terms: no lethal force is used. At the end of the test, she asks Batman, "Do I pass? Will you finally acknowledge that I can do this?"

Consider that question. Barbara is asking for something from Batman, namely, acknowledgement. In other words, she's asking Batman to accept her desire for a specific better self. This better self doesn't yet exist, but she needs her desire recognized, she needs to know that it makes sense to others, as a sort of confirmation that it is truly makes sense for her. Batman does not immediately respond, instead telling her to follow him. Leading her out of the Batcave, they arrive at the graves of Bruce Wayne's parents. He takes off his mask and they stand there. This is Batman acknowledging Barbara by letting her know who he is, letting her in on *his* past and his ongoing desire for a better self.

At the same time, while it is clear now that Batman will be her exemplar, this scene also makes it equally clear that Barbara's individual path cannot be just a copy of Batman's path. His is rooted in his unique experience just as Barbara's must be rooted in her own experience and desire. This moment is significant to the extent that having exemplars for the path to a better self sounds initially like a kind of movement toward conformity. But this would be a misunderstanding. By seeing how Batman's path is unique, we see that the role of an exemplar is in fact one of reflecting back the legitimacy and specificity of Barbara's own desire for a better self. Batman will help her perform in her life the proper analogue of what he has performed, and is performing, in his life, but with all the differences appropriate to who she uniquely is, and which ultimately she alone will be in a position to know.

There Is What Could Be

There is another possible misunderstanding of moral perfectionism that *Batgirl: Year One* might initially be thought to suggest: namely, that there is one right self, one highest or best self that is a final goal for the quest. If that were the case, then in becoming Batgirl, Barbara Gordon presumably would have achieved her self. The life quest would be complete, the game over. But if it were that easy, relatively speaking, to find yourself, then we would naturally doubt the soundness of Mill's insight. Why would so many people be struggling, as he suggests, with inappropriate or inauthentic forms of conformity if genuine individuality were so straightforward and comparatively simple to achieve? Things are more interesting than that. One fact about human life that makes the attainment of a self a continuing project is its fragility. After all, we as readers know that Barbara Gordon will eventually be shot and paralyzed. In fact, the closing lines of *Batgirl: Year One* point to this present fragility and ironically presage the future: "But despite my great and abiding respect for oracles, I've decided to forgo predictions and portents. There is what could be and there is the life I lead right now" (p. 213). Barbara realizes that there is the self she is on the way to becoming, illustrated in the final panel as she fights alongside Batman and Robin. At the same time, she recognizes that the self she hopes to attain, that she's on the way to attaining, is provisional. There is still what yet could be.

In *Oracle: Year One*, "Born of Hope," Barbara is starting the long process of recovery from her injury at the hands of the Joker. Recuperating at home, she finds out her father is working on a case that involves a villain laundering money by the sophisticated use of computers. Barbara decides to put her own computer expertise to work and begins to track the villain. One day when she is out getting some fresh air, this criminal pushes her wheelchair into the street. Narrowly escaping another grave injury, Barbara resolves to learn new self-defense skills. She arranges to meet with Richard Dragon, a martial-arts expert. At their first meeting, she states that she wants her life back. Dragon replies, "That's who you were, not who you are. Who are you?" Barbara's confused response is "I don't know. I don't know if I ever knew" (p. 13). Later in the story, after defeating the villain, she has another conversation with Dragon in which she tells him that she has found a start of the answer to his earlier question. As she leaves the park where they met, she thinks, "I'm me—more me than I have ever been." She has managed to once again find her higher self, though not, obviously, a highest possible self.

It is significant that finding this new provisional, but higher, self means leaving behind her old self, Batgirl, and the friend whose acknowledgment meant so much to her. That particular path to herself—the one in which Batman played the role of exemplar—can no longer be the path that will allow her to achieve her better self. Above, I noted that in accepting Batman's acknowledgement, Barbara managed to avoid turning herself into an image of Batman. However, it's interesting to note that she recognizes the existence of such a danger.

Indeed, an interesting illustration of her resolve not to let that happen to her is available. For a while after becoming Oracle, Barbara continued to see and even date Dick Grayson, Batman's former sidekick, Robin. Dick had eventually left Gotham City and moved to Blüdhaven where he took on the new identity of Nightwing.[7] In a pivotal issue of *Nightwing*, Barbara decides she can no longer see him. She has come to understand that Dick has become just another Batman. When he explains that he's been overextending himself because he alone provides protection for Blüdhaven, Barbara replies: "Congratulations. You've managed to turn into Bruce after all."[8] She has nicely diagnosed the possibility latent in deformed versions of moral perfectionism in which the quest for a higher self turns into becoming nothing more than a simple copy of another person's higher self.

Barbara also notes a different reason for leaving Dick. Earlier in the story arc, he had inadvertently mentioned the Joker. Barbara starts to cry, and Dick leaps to the obvious, but wrong, conclusion. He thinks that she is still disturbed by talk of the Joker. Barbara makes it clear that the problem is a different one: "It's not about Joker. You don't need to walk on eggshells. What's done is done. But that's exactly the problem, Dick. The past. . . . But something happens when you're with me. You get lost in these yesterdays we shared and . . ." She breaks off the

---

[7] There has been, alas, no *Nightwing: Year One* comic (though DC has announced one for 2005), so Nightwing's origin story remains, as of this writing, unstable.

[8] Devin Grayson *et al.*, *Nightwing* 87. "Snowball" (New York: DC Comics, 2004), p. 14.

thought, but comes back to it: "You can't stop reminding me of what I once was."[9] She sees Dick now, in effect, as something like a retrograde exemplar, not a morally proper one, pulling her back into the patterns of the past. Here, Barbara recognizes the way that the past itself can trap us in a sort of conformity, or what John Stuart Mill called a custom, a habitual pattern that perhaps was once right as a prior stage of the ongoing journey but is no longer proper to its present stage. This past is a constant risk for Barbara as it can hold her back from progress along the new path she now faces for becoming her higher self.

Of Like Minds

If her past is behind her, and her future is open, who is going to help Barbara along the journey? Who will be her new exemplar? Here it is important to realize that sometimes it isn't the acknowledgement and guidance of an exemplar that we need, but someone who will just listen to our attempts to understand ourselves, to come to that measure of self-knowledge that any productive and well-directed journey will require. Sometimes what we need is just a friend. At the same time, the friend cannot block the move to a higher self, as Dick Grayson does to Barbara at this stage. Indeed, it might be better to say that the friend at any given time is precisely someone who can accompany you on your journey by listening with fresh ears, hearing you well, calling you out when you slip, and cheering you on and supporting you when that is what you need.

In Barbara Gordon's new life as Oracle, she has developed precisely this sort of friendship with two others, Dinah Lance (Black Canary) and Helena Bertinelli (Huntress). In the series chronicling their work together, we are shown many moments where what is paramount is their friendship, precisely as it provokes them all to become better. So, for example, in one story arc, Barbara questions whether Dinah should remain part of the team. In a previous story, Dinah had come close to being killed, and Barbara has now decided that she could not face such a loss. Yet by the end of the story, Barbara has realized that the purpose of friendship is not to close off possibility. In Dinah's

---

[9] Devin Grayson *et al.*, *Nightwing* 86. "The Calm Before" (New York: DC Comics, 2003), p. 21.

words, Barbara needs "to learn how to let the small stuff go." At the same time, provoked by Barbara's actions, Dinah has taken up a new training regimen so she will never find herself again in the dangerous position of being a hostage. It's the provocation between friends that pushes both Barbara and Dinah in the direction of growth.[10]

Thus, friends come in various forms. The young Barbara Gordon needed the friend who could also be an exemplar. The mature Barbara Gordon, by contrast, does not need an exemplar. Rather she needs friends who are equals, but also friends who are equal to the task of demanding that her journey to a new, better self be one that she can make understandable to them, and thus one that they can in this way be sure is properly understandable to her.

In a more recent *Batman* story-line, Barbara was forced to blow-up her home and headquarters in Gotham City's Clocktower building. She decides to leave Gotham City along with her friends. Everything in and around Gotham makes her sad, she explains, mentioning Batman, Nightwing, and the rubble of the Clocktower. She and her friends then embark on their new mission aboard a new airplane, named *Aerie One* (after the technical term for the home of birds of prey) that will serve as their new home.[11] The repetition of the term 'new' in the previous sentence is designed to emphasize just what Barbara has accomplished. Living in a moving home may be the ultimate in images of possibility. However, it's not just any possibility, but a hard-won next step toward the Barbara yet to be: her unattained but attainable self. [13]

When philosophers look at ethics, we sometimes consider abstract notions like the good and the right. We often ponder theories of duty and prohibition. But it is an important part of philosophical reflection within the general boundaries of moral philosophy to ponder lives and how they improve. The categories of philosophical viewpoints such as moral perfectionism

---

[10] The reaffirmation of Barbara and Dinah's friendship occurs in Gail Simone *et al.*, *Birds of Prey: Of Like Minds* (New York: DC Comics, 2004).

[11] Gail Simone *et al.*, *Birds of Prey* 75. "Breathless" (New York: DC Comics, 2004).

[13] The phrase "unattained but attainable self" is a favorite phrase of Cavell's and is taken from Ralph Waldo Emerson's essay "History."

can help us to read superhero comics, and the stories in these comics, viewed through such a lens, can then help us to calibrate the progress of our own lives, as we seek to discover, and create, our own best selves.[14]

[14] I'd like to thank the editors of the volume for helpful comments on an earlier version of this essay, and Kelly A. Wilson for instigating it.

9

Batman and Friends: Aristotle and the Dark Knight's Inner Circle

MATT MORRIS

Two are better than one;
because they have a good reward for their labor.
For if they fall, one will lift up his fellow:
but woe to him who is alone when he falls;
for he does not have another to help him up.

—Ecclesiastes 4:9–12

Batman is often thought of as the most solitary superhero. On the surface, this can seem a bit odd, since he often keeps company with a sidekick, Robin, and normally works very closely with his trusted butler, Alfred. There are other superheroes who typically do their jobs as crime-fighters, or as world-savers, totally alone. Consider Spider-Man and Daredevil. Neither of them is often seen in the company of a costumed assistant on the scene. Neither has an associate to help with logistics on a regular basis. But then they do have numerous close friendships in their normal, civilian lives as Peter Parker and Matt Murdock. And this is something almost unimaginable in the case of Batman's alter ego, Bruce Wayne. Bruce, or Batman, has an inner solitude that no one else seems to rival.

Superman has a Fortress of Solitude far away from anyone. Batman has his own heart and mind for the same purpose. Since the moment in his youth when he had the dramatic and horrific experience of witnessing the murder of his parents, he has dedicated himself completely to the most severe regimen of self-development and the most completely focused mission of crime-fighting possible. He's the ultimate paradigm of a man on a mission, and nothing can deflect him from it. His preparation for that mission, and his execution of it, has created an independent spirit, a severely austere focus, and a sense of alienated solitude unmatched by any of his fellow costumed crime-fighters. He is dark, forbidding, aloof, and even scary. This is definitely not a guy you'd go bowling with, or meet somewhere for a pizza. Could he even possibly have a friend, or be a friend?

Yet this most solitary of souls is surrounded by an inner circle of associates, colleagues, and perhaps even friends. This shouldn't surprise us so much. The great philosopher Aristotle understood that we human beings are all essentially social creatures. In the *Nicomachean Ethics*, Aristotle makes a statement that has been used by Jeph Loeb in his masterful series on Batman entitled *Hush*: "Without friends no one would choose to live, though he had all other goods . . ." (NE, 1155).[1] Bruce Wayne is a billionaire industrialist whose mansion and life are absolutely full of material goods. But even he needs more.

From Aristotle to the Bat-Cave

Aristotle's analysis of friendship will help us to understand the various close relationships in Batman's life. But one point of clarification will help us up front. The Greek word for friendship, or friend, and the corresponding concept in the ancient world was a bit broader than our contemporary understanding of friendship.

We think of acquaintances as people we've merely met, and who might or might not be involved in our lives to any significant extent. The term 'relationship' often connotes more of an ongoing involvement. And then, of course, among our relationships we have colleagues, associates, neighbors, family members, and what we now call more specifically friends. In contemporary terms, a friendship is a relatively close relationship. We often think of friends as good companions who, even if they live apart, maintain a strong connection and share a commonality of interests, some aspects of emotional intimacy, and perhaps even elements of at least an episodic sense of

---

[1] Aristotle, *Nichomachean Ethics*, available in many translations. Parenthetical references use the standard scholarly section numbering found in almost any modern edition.

partnership. If we keep in mind that the ancient Greek concept is a bit broader than that subcategory of relationships we now think of as friendship, we can understand Aristotle much better.

Aristotle's claim is that there are three distinct kinds of friendship. More than one kind can be found in the same relationship, but it helps us to understand the varying natures of relationships when we make these distinctions. First, the lowest level of friendship is what Aristotle calls a friendship of utility. This is a relationship in which both parties derive a practical benefit from the other and are in the relationship because of that benefit. Think of business associates, members of a band, or the participants in a superhero team like the JLA, the Avengers, or the Squadron Supreme. Each of them benefits in a practical way from the relationship. Their ongoing usefulness to each other is what keeps a friendship of utility going between any two or more people.

A second, and somewhat higher, form of friendship is what Aristotle calls a friendship of pleasure. This is a relationship based not on mutual usefulness in some project or activity, but on mutual enjoyment. Pleasure friends just like hanging out with each other. They relish each other's company. They get a kick out of each other. This sort of friendship lasts as long as the enjoyment does. Certainly, pleasure friends can also derive other mutual benefits from their association, and utility friends may enjoy their interactions with each other. These categories are not meant to be utterly exclusive. Still, we might categorize any dual-level friendship in terms of its most fundamental nature, as in, "Well, they certainly get along well and seem to enjoy being around each other, but they are basically crime-fighting partners." Or, "Sure, they do business together, but when they retire, they'll still be playing music with each other, smoking cigars, and hanging out at each other's houses—they just hit it off like that." In other words, a relationship can contain elements of both utility and pleasure, and nonetheless, one of these categories might be more fundamental than the other in the particular case.

Aristotle held that there is a third and highest form of friendship, a "perfect friendship," or a "complete friendship" or, alternatively, a "friendship of virtue." This is the admirable relationship that can take place only between genuinely virtuous people who are committed to what is good, are committed to each other, and are at least in some sense roughly equals. A measure of equality is important to Aristotle for any kind of friendship, who believed that if any relationship gets too out of balance and one-sided, it will likely end. But it's possible to interpret the Aristotelian categories of friendship as valuing equality even more as we ascend to higher forms of friendship. It's this highest form of the relationship—the complete friendship—that, in the report of ancient historian Diogenes Laertius, Aristotle famously characterized as "one soul in two bodies."

According to Aristotle, a complete friend wishes good to his friend "for his own sake"—that is to say, for the sake of the friend alone, and not with any selfish concern for residual benefits. A perfect friendship is "other-focused" on the part of both parties. Each wants to give to the other and see the friend flourish. Complete friendship involves benefit, pleasure, and goodness, and Aristotle believed it lasts as long as the goodness of the friends lasts, because goodness produces benefit and pleasure. And since Aristotle believed that true goodness is an enduring thing in any human being, he believed that perfect friendships are, in effect, permanent. But, he also recognizes that they are relatively rare, since truly and enduringly good people are far too rare.

With this three-fold analysis of friendship as a tool, let's look at some of Batman's closest relationships. We want to determine what sorts of friendships they might be, and ultimately whether any of them rises as high as this third and perfect form.

Batman and Robin

Batman has had quite a few sidekicks over the years, but we will focus on his first, and arguably most important. The original story of Robin began at the circus. John and Mary Grayson, otherwise known as "The Flying Graysons," were performing a trapeze act when their ropes snapped and they fell to their deaths. Their son, Dick Grayson, thus witnessed the death of his parents as Bruce Wayne had when he was a child. Bruce was in the audience when the accident occurred and immediately felt very sorry for Dick. The young orphan had nowhere else to go, so Bruce magnanimously took him in. Dick soon found out that his parents' deaths were in fact not an accident, but were planned. Bruce felt that Dick's resultant anger, sadness, and confusion over this terrible crime should be focused into a more positive outlook. In order to try and steer this young man's life in the right direction, Bruce revealed his identity as Batman, and offered to train Dick so that he could help in the fight on crime. And so Dick Grayson became Robin.

It's natural for readers to think of the partnership of these two crime-fighters as a friendship. They are often together, they know each other well, and they frequently join forces to accomplish shared goals. They seem to enjoy each other's company. They certainly appear to embody elements of Aristotle's two lower forms of friendship. Their relationship clearly contains discernible measures of both utility and pleasure.

Consider first the benefits that Robin derives from the relationship. Batman takes on the role of a mentor and helps Robin train to be a crime-fighter worthy of his partnership. On close analysis, we can see that Batman provides a number of services for Robin:

1. Food, shelter, clothing, and other essentials, in addition to very cool transportation, amazing gadgets, and an awesome hide-out.
2. Physical and mental training to help Robin develop his physical and mental crime-fighting skills.
3. A sense of mission for his life.
4. Companionship.

But on Aristotle's analysis of friendship, there must be some form of equality or balanced reciprocity in the relationship, if it is to count as a real friendship, and especially if it is to endure. Since Robin is not nearly as advanced in skill as Batman, and cannot provide his mentor with any material goods that he could not already afford, how then is the friendship reciprocated?

First, Robin provides services to Batman, such as very practical help with fighting crime and ongoing assistance in the continuation of his mission. Of course, it's not as if Batman couldn't do it alone—he was doing so quite well before they met—but Robin brings certain efficiencies to the fight, and extends the range of what can be accomplished at any given time. This is certainly of value to such a mission-oriented individual as Batman. But still, it could be argued that, given Dick Grayson's own motivation to fight crime and stop criminals, this friendship with the world's greatest detective and crime-fighter benefits him in this particular area vastly more than it does Batman. There is still a tremendous inequality in the relationship.

Aristotle's solution seems to be that that the lesser of two friends must give back a proportionate and compensating amount of love and honor. And Robin seems to do this. He clearly cares for Batman, honors him, and is very respectful towards him. He seeks to serve his mentor and never to usurp him. And he deeply appreciates the relationship they have.

In addition, Robin provides Batman with a significant degree of social and intellectual pleasure. This includes the pleasure of teaching such an able and talented student, and the satisfaction of forming him into a great man, as well as the simple pleasure of his company. Robin also derives pleasure from being taught by Batman, and from the ongoing companionship they have. But it could well be that, as many wise philosophers have suggested, the pleasure of the benefactor is greater than that of the beneficiary, and so Batman's pleasure in this mentoring relationship is both deeper and greater than Robin's. Nonetheless, the pleasure is no small part of the relationship to Robin.

Aristotle believed that young people often base their friendships on pleasure, and this seems to be true of Robin. He obviously takes pleasure in all of the situations when he is utilizing something he has derived from Batman, such as the skill and even the incredible tools for fighting crime that Bruce has passed on to him. He enjoys the thrill of the hunt in the presence of his reassuringly strong mentor. And he clearly relishes doing good for the community. In short, he takes pleasure in many aspects of his relationship he has with Batman.

Unfortunately, a young person's friendship of pleasure is not often stable. Aristotle explains: "For their lives are guided by their feelings, and they pursue above all what is pleasant for themselves and what is near at hand. But as they grow up, what they find pleasant changes too. Hence they are quick to become friends, and quick to stop" (NE 1156). We see this to some extent with Robin, though his friendship with Batman does not stop as much as it changes. As Robin grows older, he edges increasingly closer to becoming Batman's equal in skill. As a result, he no longer continues to learn as much from his old teacher. Living in Batman's shadow and always having to do what he is told starts to annoy Robin, and increasingly he no longer finds their partnership as pleasant as he once did. As a result, he eventually decides to take on a new identity as Nightwing, and to leave both Batman and Gotham for a crime-fighting career of his own in the neighboring city of Blüdhaven.

For a time after their split, the relationship between Batman and Nightwing was a bit strained. There was some sense of alienation, mixed with disappointment, and perhaps even resentment. The two of them would cross paths only when cases they were working on caused them to visit each other's city. Eventually, the Dark Knight was able to make amends to his younger colleague Nightwing by displaying a real respect for his abilities and showing that he held no ill will towards him because of his departure. Now they seem to have a renewed sort of friendship based primarily on pleasure, more as equals, or near equals, as they enjoy each other's company whenever they are able to fight crime together. The mutual high regard and respect they have for each other enhances the pleasure they take in each other's company, and in each other's achievements. It moves in the direction of a complete friendship, but never seems to arrive at quite that high a plateau.

The Bat, Harvey Dent, and Two-Face

The story of Batman's relationship with Harvey Dent is one of a real friendship gone bad. Harvey was the district attorney for Gotham City, and often worked closely with police lieutenant Jim Gordon. Through Jim, Harvey became acquainted with Batman. From the start, he had more in common with Batman than Jim did. First of all, Batman and Dent were about the same age, and they obviously had a shared interest in upholding justice. But where Gordon only had an interest in taking down criminals by the book—within the letter of the law—Harvey was always envious of Batman's ability to work outside the law, and had himself no qualms about doing whatever was needed to stop a criminal or gain a conviction. Harvey and Batman grew into a friendship of utility much like the one that already existed, in a somewhat tenuous form, between Batman and Gordon, with the important difference that Batman was on the verge of trusting Harvey with his true identity before a tragic event occurred that sent things spiraling in another direction.

While Dent was questioning a suspect at a trial, he was doused with an acid that horribly scarred half his face. This physical disfigurement triggered a deeply rooted split-personality disorder, and he took on the persona of "Two-Face." Two-Face quickly became a criminal and a killer, everything that Batman despised. Could the committed master crime-fighter under any conditions still be a friend to this individual? If the friendship of the two had been one of the highest form, a friendship of virtue, or a "complete friendship," Aristotle clearly would say that its continuation would be impossible. He also cautions, however, that a virtuous man shouldn't cut off such a relationship rashly. A virtue friendship should and must be ended with an "incurably vicious person." But if a person can be rehabilitated and become good again, then even the highest form of friendship can continue. Dent and Batman, unfortunately, never attained a complete friendship, in Aristotelian terms. They operated mostly at the level of a utility friendship, although the possibility of more had occurred to Batman.

On the surface, it might seem that nothing about the character of one of the parties need preclude a utility friendship from continuing, as long as both parties remain useful to each other. Dent, for example, could decide that, despite being a criminal and killer, he will continue to help Batman put away other criminals, and feed him with clues. And, for his part, Batman could conceivably consider this service to be so important that he decides to overlook Dent's unfortunate new tendencies, and continues to help him as well. But even to imagine such a scenario would be to run up against Batman's clearly intransigent sense of right and wrong. He could do no such thing. He would never continue such a relationship of utility under any conditions remotely like these.

This may shed some additional light on Aristotle's analysis of utility friendships. On his account, it seems that such a friendship can continue only as long as the utility continues in a sufficiently reciprocal way. But clearly we have here a case where it could not. A virtuous man cannot use the services of a vicious man in such a way that it constitutes a friendship. Collaboration with corruption corrupts. And Batman would know that. Moreover, he would not tolerate it. So perhaps we should view utility friendships as having this in common with complete friendships: if one party is virtuous, then that constitutes a constraint on what the other party can be. If one of the friends descends into evil, even a utility friendship with a virtuous person must end.

Despite all of Batman's efforts to rehabilitate Harvey, getting him the proper plastic surgery to restructure his face, and all the therapy that might possibly restore his previous personality, nothing was able to re-establish Dent's original self, the one that Batman had found so compatible. Because of this, Batman ultimately had no choice but to bury the friendship that had otherwise meant so much to him.

The Cop and the Vigilante

It has always been clear that Batman is able to go about his mission alone if necessary, but he has always been open to anyone he respects and who can help. During his first year of fighting crime on the streets, he became aware of two important things that would likely give him an advantage in his mission. First was a way to strike fear into his opponents and take them off guard. His costume and lightning-quick tactics took care of that. Second, he needed someone inside the corrupt Gotham City Police Department, someone who held his same values and would be willing to assist him in the fight against crime. The person who fit this description was police lieutenant James Gordon. Towards the end of *Batman: Year One*, we find Bruce musing on this need when he says to himself: "I can't do it alone. I need an ally—an inside man. I need Jim Gordon. On my side."

From the start, it's obvious that Batman is seeking out Jim Gordon because he wants to use him as a means to an end. At first, Gordon is unsure whether he can trust Batman. As a vigilante, this costumed character is willing to take actions the police cannot. And that gives Gordon concern. But Batman proves to be trustworthy, and he and Gordon become close allies and even friends.

This is another classic example of Aristotle's friendship of utility. Batman is able to use the information and investigative services of the police department to help solve crimes and apprehend criminals quickly. Gordon is able to use the Bat-Signal to call in Batman whenever the department needs special assistance. Both Batman and Gordon benefit from their relationship. Each is getting what he needs and wants from association with the other. The relationship is a two-way street and significant benefits accrue for both parties.

One might come to wonder why this relationship remains only one of utility, and does not develop into a friendship of pleasure as well. But a close examination of the interactions of these two men provides the answer. Whenever Batman is around Gordon, he is always guarded. If Gordon were to find out the true identity of his masked friend, then he would be able to arrest him in case he ever believed that he had overstepped his proper bounds. So Batman withholds important truths about himself from his utility friend in blue. For his own part, Gordon has also always had issues of trust with Batman. He knows that if he makes Batman promise to go about a case in a certain way, he will, but that, otherwise, he can be very unpredictable. There have been some times, including the times when Batman brought in young partners—each of the Robins—that Gordon has had to seriously question Batman's judgment. Furthermore, how easy is it to enjoy yourself in the company of a person who wears a mask all the time? If trust were not an issue in all these ways, then both Batman and Gordon would be able to enjoy their mutual company more, and maybe have a relationship that is a little less purely mission-oriented.

Aristotle notes that friendships of utility can easily break apart. If Batman were to ever go too far and kill someone, even if it may have seemed justified, he would no longer be contributing to Gordon's vision of justice, and the friendship would end. Gordon holds a much narrower view of justice than Batman does. He believes that criminals must be pursued as much as possible, and then punished, within the confines of the law. If the police department had orders to arrest Batman, Gordon would comply and do what he could to arrest him. Under these circumstances, this officer of the law would no longer be open to helping Batman with his mission, but actually would be getting in the way, and so they clearly would no longer be able to continue their relationship. Likewise, there are actions Gordon could initiate that would alienate Batman. If he suddenly became even more of a stickler over the letter and spirit of the law, he might cease to serve Batman's purposes. We have no reason to believe that, in either case, a positive relationship between the two sufficient to count as a friendship would continue.

Batman and Gordon never see each other apart from the

call of duty. In one story, Gordon makes a futile attempt at socializing outside of their shared mission, and finds himself thwarted:

> **GORDON**: You could use a break. Um . . . There's a party at Bruce Wayne's. Costume thing. You could come . . . dressed as you are.
>
> *Batman is silent.*
>
> **GORDON:** It's not that I want to go . . . It's Barbara. Once she gets something in her head . . .
>
> **BATMAN:** Barbara . . .
>
> **GORDON:** The wife. Look. Let's forget it.
>
> *Batman leaves without any further word.*
>
> **GORDON:** That's the last time I try something like that . . .

There's not enough between these two men to support a friendship beyond mere utility. They work together when necessary, and when it's beneficial, and they respect each other, but nothing else in their lives cultivates a broader form of friendship. They are colleagues, compatriots in the fight against crime in Gotham, and ultimately no more.

Batman and Catwoman

Batman has a unique relationship with Catwoman. Their first meetings were not friendly ones, as Catwoman was involved in criminal activity. She was a thief, and it's hard to imagine a thief and a dedicated crime-fighter getting along. But Batman and Catwoman have always been attracted to each other, despite working on different sides of the law. How could this attraction possibly occur?

First of all, Batman has very good vision. If you've ever looked at Catwoman closely, the most superficial level of physical attraction is not at all hard to understand. After all, Batman isn't a bat, he's a man. But there's much more to it than just that. Batman admires Catwoman's incredible skills and personal daring. She has developed herself physically to the utmost, a lot like Batman. She is strong, capable, and even a bit like an Olympic gymnast with an astonishing willingness to take extraordinary physical risks. All this attracts Batman. But how can he overcome his visceral distaste for criminal activity in her case?

One fact saves the day.

Deep down, Catwoman is basically a good-hearted person. She is not in any sense evil, and apart from her gamesman-like exploits of high-stakes theft, she has an affinity for good that she can't shake. Like Batman, she does not kill, and she often will ditch her criminal activity if she sees it could possibly harm Batman. She has always gotten her thrills from stealing, but has also been so attracted to Batman that she would seriously consider reforming. And Batman instinctively knew this. He always had hopes that Catwoman would give up her ways and join the side of the good. Recently, she has indeed changed her life for the better, and has become a protector of her neighborhood. Because of this change of heart and activity, her relationship with Batman has flourished, with Batman recently trusting her with his biggest secret, his identity as Bruce Wayne.

Batman's friendship with Catwoman is clearly one of pleasure. When they were on opposite sides of the law, both enjoyed their cat-and-mouse (or, of course, bat-and-cat) encounters with each other. Batman appreciates a good challenge in the same way that Catwoman enjoys a good thrill. Even while she was still a thief, Catwoman would sporadically help Batman with a case. But these incidents were never consistent and she could not be counted on for help. Batman is not her mentor or her colleague, so she is not literally obligated to help him in his mission or to do what he says. This has kept their relationship from being one of utility.

Most of all, Batman and Catwoman have had a romantic relationship. Aristotle believed that romantic relationships are friendships of pleasure, for each of the lovers enjoys each other's company. And to the present, that's as far as it goes.

The Butler and the Man of the Manor

The most unusual friendship that Batman has with another person may be the one he has with his butler, Alfred. Alfred worked for the Wayne family when Bruce was born. He is the closest person to Bruce, and Bruce has known him for his entire life. When Thomas and Martha Wayne were killed, Alfred took it upon himself to raise Bruce in the way his parents would have wanted. While still remaining, in his own mind and in his demeanor, the butler, Alfred took an almost parental role in

Bruce's life, and also helped from the beginning with his mission as Batman. So, as a result of all this, the question arises as to what kind of friendship Bruce and Alfred might have.

Certainly they have elements of a friendship of utility. Alfred is always working. And the purpose of his job is to help Bruce Wayne, even in his life of fighting crime, which he does in every way imaginable. In return, Alfred is given the highest quality of shelter, food, and clothing, and most likely a very sizable income. It's hard to determine whether such benefits flow between Batman and his butler just because these are the requirements of the job for Alfred, and the obligations of the employer for Bruce, or whether Bruce and Alfred are committed to providing for each other in these many ways because they are friends. It is certain that they are as friendly to each other as two workaholics can be, at all times that Alfred is performing his job, which is basically all the time.

Alfred is unique among Batman's friends in that his own sense of mission is equally strong. He is fully committed to the role of the Wayne family butler. While he is always trying to get Bruce to take time off from his role as Batman and relax, this best of all possible butlers doesn't practice what he preaches. He never takes time off from his work. We never see Alfred go on a date, or out with a group of friends to play poker or attend a concert. And, of course, Bruce never encourages this, largely because he does not see it as a necessary part of leading a normal and well-adjusted life. In the vicinity of the Bat-Cave, different standards for proper living apply.

It is perhaps this mutuality of such a strong sense of mission that keeps Bruce and Alfred from being friends of the highest order. Alfred is committed to being the butler, and Bruce will always be his "master." As we have seen, Aristotle considered equality a strong factor in a virtuous friendship, and this cannot be fully attained as long as Bruce is the boss and Alfred is the employee. And it is almost impossible to imagine a circumstance where this is not the case. If Alfred were to quit, or if Bruce were to let him go, such a dramatic turn of events would surely involve a personal alienation of the highest order, and itself prevent the attainment of a complete friendship. Each of them needs the other in order to fulfill his mission, as each in turn conceives it. Any breaking of this relationship would most likely be considered a terrible act of disloyalty. So, despite the fact that Alfred is probably closer to Bruce than anyone else could be, as long as they remain as they are, they can't be complete friends because each has such an over-riding sense of mission, and if they changed in the relevant ways, they still couldn't be complete friends, because of the inevitable fallout from such a change. Thus, again, a relationship between Batman and one of his closest associates seems destined to ascend no higher in the categories of friendship than the status it has already attained.

The Elusiveness of a Complete Friendship

What keeps Batman from having what Aristotle considered a complete friendship? It's not just his high standards. It's not just a failure on the part of other people. A good measure of the responsibility seems to lie on his doorstep. Such a friendship requires a large personal investment. This is almost impossible for Batman after the promise he made to his dead parents. He has given so much of his time and effort to his crime-fighting quest that he doesn't have much left for friends. This is why, as we have seen before, all of Batman's friends must somehow fit into his mission. Those around him all help out as comrades and partners: Jim Gordon, Harvey Dent (before he became Two-Face), Robin (who became Nightwing), Batgirl (who became Oracle), the other three Robins (Jason Todd, Tim Drake, and Carrie Kelly, in *The Dark Knight Returns*), Alfred, and all the rest. Sometimes Batman forgets how close these people are in his life. In the recent story *Hush*, Batman confesses to Catwoman his inability to keep close friends, and she reminds him how many friends he has.

> BATMAN: I . . . I am not very good at this. Having friends. Partners. It all ends in betrayal and death. If I ever could do it, then I lost it the night my parents were murdered.
>
> CATWOMAN: Tell that to Nightwing. Robin. Oracle. Do I need to go on?

It's true that all of those people are Batman's friends and partners. But do any of them satisfy the requirements for the highest form of friendship? Does he?

In his heart, Batman is probably aware that he may never be

able to have a friendship of the highest order. In becoming Batman, Bruce Wayne made certain sacrifices, one of which was the ability to fully give himself to another person. His life has already been taken, by his promise to his parents and by his commitment to justice. After once being seriously tempted to leave the world of Batman behind, Bruce had to come to terms with the price he pays to continue his mission.

> I learned something over this Halloween weekend. I thought that I didn't have a choice about being the Batman. That Gotham City chose me to protect her. That is wrong. Ever since the night my parents were taken from me, I made the choice. It means that some of my heart's desires may go unfulfilled . . . But many more are satisified . . . It is a good choice.

Aristotle says that good men are, in a way, friends to themselves. And perhaps this is true for Bruce Wayne. He is a friend to himself, and to his own alternative persona. Batman uses Bruce Wayne, and Bruce Wayne uses Batman. So this involves a friendship of utility. And each persona may even take some pleasure in the other's escapades. But if there is any sort of perfect friendship available for Bruce, or Batman, perhaps it is here, in the solitude of the relation of himself to himself. Bruce Wayne is committed to the good. And he commits himself to what he considers his greatest good, which means that he commits himself to Batman. In his case we find, not one soul in two bodies, but one soul in two personae, two identities, two presentations to the world. Because of the all-consuming nature of his mission, it seems like this may be all that is possible for him at the level of virtue friendship.

But the same thing, or at least something similar, may be true for many of the superheroes. And they seem to realize the limits they live under, due to their sense of calling, and the responsibility it brings. In *Superman: The Man of Steel*, John Byrne and Dick Giordano portray a first meeting of Batman and Superman. When they part, Batman says to himself, "A remarkable man, all things considered. Who knows? In a different reality, I might have called him, "friend."[2]

When we philosophically address art, whether it's a novel, a

---

[2] John Byrne and Dick Giordano, *Superman: The Man of Steel* #3 (New York: DC Comics), p. 22.

comic, a painting, or a film, a variety of things can happen. Either we can illuminate the work of art, or we can expand our philosophical understanding, or we can as a result throw light on our own lives. Sometimes we can do all three. But the philosophical endeavor has answered its most important call if it has managed to shed light on our experience in the world. A sense of mission is a good and important thing in life, but the story of Batman is a great cautionary tale concerning the price we risk paying if we are unable to keep things in balance. Some people just feel an obligation to live a life of service that is out of balance. They are often our heroes, and our superheroes. The rest of us should be careful, though, to take their lessons to heart, and exercise as much care as we can not to let our work, and our service to the world, take away from us the most basic necessities of a good and happy life, among which Aristotle counts friendship as crucial.

10

The Fantastic Four as a Family: The Strongest Bond of All

CHRIS RYALL and SCOTT TIPTON

When we reflect on the philosophical issues in superhero comics, we often tend to focus on the individual superhero, in the course of his or her adventures. And that's natural. After all, it's each individual who has been granted superpowers, and who has to choose whether to use those powers for good or evil. Elsewhere in this book, for example, there are numerous ruminations on the question of why individual heroes are good, electing to use their powers for the benefit of humanity, and why, by contrast, other powerful individuals might choose instead to be supervillains, acting in their own narrowly perceived self-interest, to society's detriment. But there is of course more to think about in the classic superhero stories than just how and why individuals choose to act as they do. Aristotle (384–322 B.C.) believed that we are essentially social creatures. And that insight can direct us to another level of superhero life worth examining from a philosophical perspective.

In this chapter, we'll focus on a concept that has been relatively neglected by most of the great philosophers over the centuries, but also one that's of real importance for understanding both human nature and the human condition: the idea of the family. In particular, we'll examine how a team of super-powered individuals can be bound together as a sort of family unit. In most comics, families are relegated to the background of the main narrative, in favor of colorful battles between super-powered individuals. A notable exception is Marvel Comics' Fantastic Four, whose family bonds are as much a part of their story as their adventures.

The First Family

Many super-teams lay claim to something like familial bonds. From the Justice League of America to the Teen Titans, the members of these units often proclaim that their teammates are more than just colleagues in fighting crime, that "they're family." This is even a pretty common theme in comics, almost as common as the shake-up of such teams. Whether through membership changes, internal strife, or solo pursuits, the individuals in these teams inevitably drift apart and back together at various times. The commitment that's distinctive of family is spoken of but, normally, seems not to be truly felt. The Fantastic Four, despite many similarities to these other teams, are somehow different. This team has seen its members stick together for over forty years of adventures. Why? How does the existence of true family bonds hold its members together while other teams change with seeming inevitability?

Of course, long-time careful readers know that even the Fantastic Four has disbanded temporarily and seen the occasional additional member come and go, but, overall, they are still in a different category from any of the other superhero teams. They display a commitment and a form of continuity not often seen in the world of superheroes. Indeed, the Fantastic Four, as created by writer Stan Lee and artist Jack Kirby, and perpetuated by many others over the years, are often referred to as "the First Family of Marvel Comics." The fact that two of the four members of the team are really siblings (Johnny Storm and Susan Storm-Richards) provides us with the first clue as to why they behave as more of a family than other teams. Add in a third member, Reed Richards, being married to Sue, and you have a ready-made family core. However, it's the fourth member who truly makes the team unique as a family unit when compared to any other group in comic-book history.

Ben Grimm, who came to be known as the Thing, is this fourth member of the team, and his only initial connection with the core family is through his friendship with Reed Richards. The two were college roommates and then comrades in the Army. Of course, friendships formed in college and the military often extend throughout lifetimes, so this, too, isn't anything extraordinary—until you look closer.

An unfortunate accompaniment of Ben's powers, which are super-strength and a bullet-proof exterior, is that he was terribly disfigured by the dramatic accident that gave the entire team their superpowers. What's more, this accident was largely a result of Reed's personal *hubris*, or overweening pride. This is not exactly a firm foundation for a lasting friendship or familial bonding.

Forming Family Bonds

The comic book super-team of The Fantastic Four was created at the start of the 1960s. The burgeoning youth culture of the day superficially seemed to be more interested in typical adolescent concerns, so a comic book that touched on more grounded issues of betrayal, angst, and family bickering might not initially have appeared poised to reach its target audience as well as comics featuring super-powered teenagers. However, the comic also dealt with themes of individual alienation, the nature of a family, and the importance of friendship more than other comics of its day. And all these issues are almost definitive of the transitional years through which the typical adolescent struggles.

The origin story of the Fantastic Four seems very unlikely as the basis for a lasting partnership of any sort. Plato (*ca.* 428–347 B.C.) has a character in his treatise, *The Republic*, claim that the dominating motivation in human life is a desire for power. It seems to be just this sort of quest for power and supremacy that drives the scientific genius Reed Richards in his first appearance. His actions, and the family's origin as a superhero team, echo the impetus behind the real international space race in the late 1950s and early 1960s. Both came out of a strong desire that Americans had to beat our powerful rivals, the Russians, into outer space. Plato's character who is focused on power, Thrasymachus, announced that, in his view, the just man always strives to get the better of unjust men, which is how Americans of 1960 viewed themselves relative to their Russian counterparts.

Reed designed a space-ship but had not sufficiently tested it or thought through carefully enough the stresses that it might face on its first voyage. But he was so eager to be first into space that he was heedless of these concerns. His friend and pilot, Ben Grimm, expressed his reticence about taking this experimental, unshielded ship into outer space, fearing the unknown effects of cosmic rays. But Reed was more single-minded in his focus. He felt his desires echoed the country's wishes, and they were given voice by his fiancée, Susan Storm, when she said: "Ben, we've *got* to take that chance . . . unless we want the Commies to beat us!" She even went so far as to question Ben's manhood, stating that she never thought *he*, of all people, would be a coward.

Them's fightin' words, it seems, and Ben's immediate decision to set aside his legitimate worries and fly the ship is cued by anger at Sue's challenge, rather than by any reassessment of the wisdom of this plan hatched by his rash friend Reed. Interestingly enough, over the next forty years of the team's adventures, Reed would become ever more analytical and cautious, while Ben would be portrayed as the rash, impulsive one. Possibly, this role-reversal resulted in part from Reed's deep-seated guilt over what had happened next. The team was complete when Sue Storm's teenage brother, Johnny, impulsively decided to go along for the ride. As he put it, "I'm taggin' along with sis—so it's settled." This dose of teenage logic displays the seeds of family commitment that lie at the core of this little group.

Socrates (470–399 B.C.) believed that virtue is its own reward, no matter what the consequences. Of course, Socrates never ended up on the receiving end of comic-book cosmic rays. Sue paid a heavy price for her loyalty to Reed, and Johnny for his decision to stick with her. While the rocket reached escape velocity and did, in fact, succeed in beating the Russians into space, there were dire consequences for the intrepid foursome. Like the mythological Icarus, Reed's spaceship crashed back to the ground, as a result of his prideful, impetuous action.

But it turns out that this was the least of their troubles. Each of the foursome soon found out that they had been endowed with unusual powers that eerily reflected their individual personalities. Susan Storm, then the shrinking violet of the team, could turn invisible; Ben Grimm's brash, rocky interior soon had an outer hide to match; the intellect-stretching Reed Richards found himself able to stretch his body as easily as he could his mind, and the fiery-tempered teenager Johnny Storm was soon ablaze as the Human Torch.

After the team settled down and thought through what had happened to them, they immediately set about forming a mission statement concerning their new power, as expressed succinctly by the gruff Ben Grimm: "We've gotta use that power to help mankind, right?" The other three members were in complete concurrence. A team was born—the Fantastic Four—and their purpose as stated was clear. But was there more to their bond than just this? Would their relationship grow beyond their basic friendship and their mutual desire to serve mankind?

A Partnership for Living Well

So far, the group's origin, while unique in itself, initially resulted in the formation of a team not dissimilar to others of its day—a group of super-powered individuals intent on helping each other fight against evil and using their powers to safeguard humanity. However, in even their first battle against evil, there is evidence of something going on among them that is more than just the shared desire to do good together. In the midst of a battle, Ben makes an insulting comment to Sue about Reed, her fiancé. He is obviously still harboring anger toward Reed and blaming him for the accident that caused his disfigurement. "Oh, Ben," Sue says in reply, "if only you could stop hating Reed for what happened to you."

This brings up an interesting question, and one that will go unspoken for years. Why does Ben continue in most ways to show such loyalty in his actions toward a friend who, in effect, took away the life he once knew? Unlike the other three members of the team, Ben is the only one whose powers are not something he can disguise from the world at large. While the others can pass as ordinary citizens and members of society, and even as especially attractive people, Ben is now forever an outcast, an aberration, and a hideous monster. In other works of literature, monsters seek to destroy their creators. But in this particular case, Ben's transformation somehow seems to strengthen his ties to Reed and the team, despite his occasional outbursts of anger, in essence shoring up what is becoming a strong family unit. The question is: Why?

Ben's character is a good part of the answer. He was a college football player, and a member of the military. He's by nature a joiner, and he's a loyal teammate. As his exterior changed, his inner character and resolve became even stronger. It was important to him to do right by the world, yes, but it was even more vital that he do right by his friends, who had, in their transformations, if not before, become something like his *de facto* family. They were all different from normal human beings, despite the ability of Reed, Sue, and Johnny to hide those differences. Their differences had a common origin. And they had now chosen to give those differences a common purpose. Ben was clearly there because of these commonalities, and because he wanted to continue to support the group, but it also seems he was there to remind Reed of what can happen if his intellect were again to run unchecked, heedless of the consequences to others. Ben serves, in essence, as Reed's conscience.

In his seminal book *The Politics*, Aristotle sought to understand the essence of any group of people living and working together. At one stage, he asked what a city is. His answer is very insightful: "A city is a partnership for living well." We can take that thought and extrapolate it further. By Aristotle's own reasoning, we can see any group of people associating and working together for good in precisely the same way.[1] A neighborhood ideally can be thought of as a partnership for living well. So can a business. And this may be the best way to think of a team of any kind. More to our purpose, perhaps this same analysis can apply to the family unit. Ideally, a family is a particularly intimate partnership for living well. In fact, if the members of a family don't understand this about their relationship, it's likely that things will never be as good in that family as they are capable of being. It can even be argued that the family is the most fundamental human partnership, and the one that provides for all the others. We come into this world because of a partnership of a special kind, and we survive our early years because of the supporting environment provided by others. As we grow, we learn new ways of participating in this earliest and smallest community unit. And what we learn there will send us into the world with certain expectations and tools for living in the broader community of human beings, whether good or bad.

Of course, not all the members of a family have to be related by birth and blood, but to share this most intimate of bonds with a specific group of other people, an individual not so related

---

[1] For more on this, see Tom Morris, *If Aristotle Ran General Motors* (New York: Holt, 1997).

would typically have to be accepted into the unit with a good measure of support and commitment, and then would himself have to come to display a supportive attitude, a commitment to the others, and an inclination to engage in actions that are in line with the good of those others. In another place, his *Ethics*, Aristotle offered an analysis of friendship that we can also use here to shed some light on the family. He distinguished three types of friendship, those based on benefit or utility, those based on pleasure or enjoyment, and those reflecting the mutual commitment and respect that arise out of virtuous goodness.[2] The relationships between family members typically reflect at least one or two of these bases for friendships, if not all three. Now, no one would doubt that family members can be very unhelpful, hard to take, and cantankerous in their interactions. So can friends, at times. But in order to take on and maintain the bond of a family—even that of an extended family—the individuals who are involved have to be in some way able to forgive, or overlook and overcome contrary attitudes and actions that would otherwise break up their unity and alienate them from each other. No friendship is perfect, and no family is either. The members of the Fantastic Four certainly argue and get mad at each other, but their fundamental commitment to each other, and basic enjoyment of each other always brings them back together.

Let's dwell for just a moment on the three bases of friendship identified by Aristotle. First, consider utility. People are friends at this level because of benefits they both get from the relationship. Ben gets a sense of belonging and family when he is with Reed, Sue, and Johnny that he didn't have anywhere else in his life. At various points throughout his crime-fighting career, he does strike out and experience other friendships, other teams, and other environs outside of his Fantastic Four family. But none of these other experiences, from joining another team of super-powered individuals, the Avengers, to engaging in a super-powered wrestling career, could equal the benefits he received from being a member of the Fantastic Four. In Ben's case, the main benefit is familial love, and a true sense of being both wanted and needed. Other teams may enjoy his company and value his ability, but only when serving as Reed's con-

---

[2] See Chapter 9 in this volume for more on Aristotle's analysis of friendship.

science and sounding board does Ben feel truly of use. Reed and the others need him, and he needs them.

Then there are friendships of pleasure, or enjoyment. These are relationships between people who just like being around each other, even if no other benefits accrue. Ben would be hard-pressed to admit this one, of course. It's in his nature to mask his deeper feelings through wisecracks. But his intellectual and emotional capacity are far greater than he lets himself show to the world, feeling that he must portray a persona as gruff and craggy as his exterior. For years, he and Johnny have enjoyed the analogue of a sibling rivalry that has often led to acrimony, and yet the pleasure Ben gets from being on the receiving end of Johnny's childish machinations cannot be completely masked by the arch comment, the flung couch, or even those times when he stomps off in anger, promising to never return. He always does return, of course, because there is a level at which even these friendly battles give him pleasure and a true feeling of family. Families fight and disagree, he knows as well as any of us. And it's often because they care—which allows them to prevail.

Finally, there is what Aristotle calls a friendship of virtue, or a complete friendship. This is the highest relationship between morally good and virtuous people who respect and care about each other. In this sort of friendship, each friend loves the other for his sake alone. In other words, Ben and Reed can be complete friends if Reed cares about Ben's good for Ben's sake, regardless of whether he, Reed, benefits in any way. And, likewise, the same holds true in the other direction. Not only is this the strongest form of friendship, it's also the one that Reed and Ben experience to the strongest degree. And it's also the form of friendship that causes Reed the most guilt.

Reed genuinely cares about his friend Ben as much as he does his core family—the two are interchangeable in his mind—and yet Ben serves as a daily reminder of Reed's extreme failure as a friend. Does a part of their bond of friendship exist because Reed needs to feel that guilt every day? Perhaps. Seeing Ben's appearance and knowing it was Reed's fault may even somehow strengthen their mutual reliance on one another. For all the great deeds Reed performs, and for all the wondrous inventions and machines that he creates, it never leaves his mind that the one miracle he can't perform is restoring his best friend's human form.

As we survey all the interactions of the Fantastic Four, we find that Aristotle's understanding of friendship, along with the idea that a family can be viewed as a partnership for living well, can both help us understand this superhero team as a vibrant family unit made up of friends who really care about each other, despite their differences and disagreements. Family members, in a healthy family, support each other (utility), enjoy each other (pleasure), and care about each other's good (virtue). Any family is strongest if they have a sense of partnership in support of shared values and goals as well. Ben Grimm, a child of a broken home, realizes this and finds a unique sense of place within the nurturing support system of the team, with these good friends who care about him and each other.

The Family During Turmoil

Every family and every team faces turmoil, and the Fantastic Four has seen more than the average share. Yet they always persevere. Sometimes, their troubles come from the villains they have to fight; at other times they arise out of a normal urge to live an "ordinary life." In their forty-five year history, the team has had its share of break-ups, let-downs, and splits. Ben has wandered off in search of himself, only to find that the path he sought led him right back to the team. His sense of self is grounded in a need to be needed, a desire to do good, and a sense of belonging. Johnny, the youngest member of the team and the person most likely to assert his independence by leaving the supposed confines of the family, has discovered that the independence he has often sought isn't as appealing as the family he'd helped build. Reed and Sue, now married and with children as they are, have experienced their share of marital strife—saving the world and finding time for intimacy can be tricky business—but also have hung in there and stayed committed to each other. Often, the threats to the team have made them ponder whether or not fighting super-powered villains created the proper environment in which to raise a family, and this resulted in an attempt to carve out a suburban life away from the team environment. But, inevitably, each effort to live "normal" lives outside the core family of four somehow turned into a worse environment than the previous one.

All of the team's members have sought to extricate themselves from the group at times, and all have ended up back together, wiser and happier than when they split. The potential to live a good, meaningful, and virtuous life apart from one another existed, certainly. So the appeal of the family unit for each of them has had to do with more than just these things, however vitally important they are. It has had to do centrally with a feeling of comfort, and of being truly able to develop their potential better as a part of the unit than separate from it. The four members have all had solo adventures, but each of them has experienced a feeling of completeness as a member of the team that they couldn't find elsewhere. Only together do any of them experience the deepest feelings of trust and trustworthiness, a real fundamental sharing of common goals, and a firm foundation of confidence.

The best families are not judgmental; they allow for each member's potential to be encouraged and realized. In a good family, each family member's goals run parallel with, and not counter to, those of the other members. And a family exists as the most dependable source of support any of us can have. Good family members seek to pick each other up in times of need. We see all this in the Fantastic Four.

And yet, some of what makes the Fantastic Four more like a family than any other super-team has also served as a detriment. Ben's role within the team in its earliest days could very easily be seen as in many ways dysfunctional, as he early on settled into an almost childlike role with Reed and Sue, often "running away from home," with Reed and Sue continually taking up the parental duties of retrieving the wayward child. On this view, Ben's frequent squabbles with Johnny are even further identifiable as sibling rivalry, with the two bickering to gain the attention of their "parents" Reed and Sue.

Conversely, Reed's misplaced paternal feelings toward Ben have extended even further than the team's early adventures. At one point, Reed realized an important fact about Ben's inability to regain normal human form, and rather than acting as a friend and telling him the truth about what he has discovered, Reed takes it upon himself to keep this unsettling fact a secret from Ben, because, much as a father might say about a son, "It was for his own good." Father, in the form of Reed Richards, knows best.

A sense of betrayal actually once forced Ben to leave the Fantastic Four for the longest of the several times he has departed from the team. But like all the other members of the team who have at one point or another elected to leave, he returned, not from any sense of duty, but finding himself drawn to the others, despite himself. As has often been said, you can choose your friends, but you can't choose your family. The choice seems to be made for you. This often seems just as true of "constructed" families as of natural families. We find each other and then feel a bond; we don't deliberate about it and then consciously decide to set up house as a family unit. It's more like a mutual affinity than decision and duty that brings about this bond of family.

Even the temporary "fill-in" members of the Fantastic Four have more often than not come to the team through a familial connection. Several have come to the group, as new extended family members often do, through relationships with the team's "children," as in the case of Johnny's girlfriends Crystal, of the Inhumans, and Lyja, or Ben's romantic connection to "Ms. Marvel," Sharon Ventura. And even the "replacement" member with the longest tenure, Jen "She-Hulk" Walters, quickly found herself adapting to familial roles, both settling into her own sibling-like squabbling with Johnny and entering into a romantic relationship with Wyatt Wingfoot, the Fantastic Four's longtime family friend. We can see that, even for those who intend to serve with the team in only a professional capacity, the group's true nature as a family eventually subsumes them.

The Ethos of Teamwork

A family is a small unit of society that aims at sustaining the life of its members. Aristotle understood that we derive additional advantages from being part of a larger society; otherwise, he contended, we would be content to live in smaller families, or tribes. But family is where it all starts. As we have seen, living well is the ultimate goal for any group like a family, beyond just living and keeping fellow family members alive. The Fantastic Four, bonded through being a family and banded together for the greater good of society, have achieved both these goals.

Normal families often initially form as a way to create a protective unit to safeguard young children. In a greater sense, the

Fantastic Four turns this protective nature outward—the normal citizens of the entire world become like their children and live under their protection. The members of the Fantastic Four also work to enable each other to live well. But with their powers, wealth, and freedom, they always also turn their attention to improving the lives of others. With their special family bond, they have become friends in the highest sense of that word and partners for a greater good.

Such genuine, self-giving friendships are rare, and they exemplify the differences between the Fantastic Four and other super-teams. Aristotle recognized the complete friendship as that which exists between persons who love one another and wish only to benefit the other. The difference between this team of four and, say, the Avengers, might seem to be negligible in many ways. That team, too, is comprised of friends, for the most part, and they unite to fight evil. However, the friendship between the members there, or on other teams, is most often mainly self-oriented, or even a bit selfish—the people they regard as friends are seen as such primarily because they serve their own primary interests. In contrast, the friendship between the members of the Fantastic Four seems to be more like the true and complete friendship that even amounts to love. It's unselfish, benevolent and aims only at serving the good of the other. In the case of the Fantastic Four, it is this love for each other that finally binds the team together into a family.

11
Comic-Book Wisdom

MICHAEL THAU

You can always find plenty of action in superhero comic books. You can find masterful story-telling, mythic characters, incredibly vibrant art, and great splashes of humor. And you can also come across some real wisdom. That can be a bit of a surprise to people who don't know comic books well. At a time when wisdom seems to have vanished from most of the culture, it can sometimes be found embodied, enacted, and depicted—in fascinating ways—in superhero comics.

Since it's a philosopher's official job description to pay attention to wisdom wherever it can be found, I want to take a brief look at wisdom as it appears in some illuminating superhero story arcs. We'll see that the general cultural skepticism about wisdom is reflected in some of its appearances in superhero comics, but we'll also see flashes of real appreciation for what wisdom is.

Where Has All the Wisdom Gone?

The term "philosopher" comes to us from the ancient Greeks, and it means "lover of wisdom." Everyone in our time knows what a lover is, or at least we all think we do. But it's a curious fact that the concept of wisdom has more or less vanished from our everyday lives—but not completely, in the way that, say, the terms, "trap," "hansom," and other such names for horse-drawn carriages have disappeared from normal conversation, so that they're familiar only to readers of Victorian literature. Everybody still has *some* idea of what wisdom is, and that possessing wisdom is supposed to be a good thing. However, the fact that the idea of wisdom doesn't come up very often in our everyday lives can lead us to wonder whether we indeed believe that it really is a good thing.

When was the last time you heard someone described as wise, or you explicitly thought of someone as wise? Ask yourself whether the notion of wisdom ever occurs in your thoughts, dreams, and plans about what you'd like to be. The word "wise" still comes up occasionally in conversation—you might hear someone ask, "Was that really a wise thing to do?"—but it's much more likely to be used in a negative sense, as in, "Don't be such a wise-guy." We all know from the movies that people in certain neighborhoods refer to a mobster as a "wise-guy." But most of us, in our daily conversations, don't ever think about wisdom or talk in a positive way about being wise.

Not only has the concept of wisdom practically vanished from the common culture, it's also almost completely vanished from most philosophy departments in our colleges and universities. While you can find oodles of books and articles by philosophy professors on such topics as belief, knowledge, desire, and other cognitive dispositions and attitudes, I'd be surprised if you could find much more than a handful of academic essays published in the last couple of decades on the topic of wisdom. And I bet most if not all of what you would find would be historical stuff—people working on exhuming the ideas of the great and long dead.

Nor is the idea of wisdom any more alive in the minds of philosophers when they're not writing their professional journal articles, but just living their lives. Although the word "philosopher" still literally means "lover of wisdom," you'll never listen in on a philosophy department administrative meeting in any college or university in the country and hear one philosopher say to another, "I think Smith should get the job, since, after all, he loves wisdom the most," or even "He's really wise"—you'll hear the words "clever," "brilliant," or "quick," as terms of praise quite frequently, or at least as frequently as you'll ever hear one philosophy professor praise another, but it's almost inconceivable that any contemporary academic philosopher would describe another in terms of the presence or absence of wisdom.

Wisdom is such a neglected virtue that even the official university department where a love of wisdom is supposed to reside doesn't typically seem to care about it any more. Isn't this just odd beyond words? How did we come to this state of affairs? Before the idea of wisdom becomes as antiquated as concepts related to Victorian transportation, it is perhaps a good time to ask why wisdom has seemed to vanish from our thought, and too often, from our lives. We can trace some of the timeline of its disappearance by looking briefly at how wisdom has functioned in those cultural barometers we know of as comic books. Once, wisdom had a recognized place in the stories of at least some superheroes. But even within the comic books, things are not what they once were.

The Wisdom of Captain Marvel

If you know anything about comics, you'll know that wisdom wasn't always a neglected virtue in the modern world. Think of the original Captain Marvel: an old wizard grants young Billy Batson the ability to turn into an adult Superman type figure by uttering the wizard's name, "Shazam." It isn't just that the wizard himself is a comic-book picture of wisdom—an old guy with a long beard in white robes—it's also significant that the first among the six virtues and powers which his utterance of "Shazam" grants him (one for each letter in the wizard's name) is the wisdom of Solomon. And Solomon, of course, was a well-known ancient sage, whose words of wisdom traditionally were said to make up the books of Proverbs and Ecclesiastes, as well as the Song of Solomon, in the Bible.

When he was created in 1940, Captain Marvel wasn't based on some unique and weird concept. Back then, when constructing a completely standard super-hero, it was quite natural to put wisdom on the list of superpowers, or enhanced forms of personal excellence, just like super-strength and super-speed. But here's the difference in the contemporary world: I can still imagine a popular comic-book writer today creating a new character and deciding that one of his or her heroic attributes should be wisdom, but when I imagine this, I can't hear the writer say, "Yeah, let's make him wise" without adding a "but"—"Let's make him wise, but . . ."

We can get an idea of the kind of thing that would follow the "but" by looking at how Captain Marvel's wisdom currently figures into his story as told by Geoff Johns in the pages of *JSA*

(Justice Society of America). As we'll see, Johns gives us the "but" without trashing what comes before it. His story is skeptical about wisdom without falling into full-fledged cynicism and, so, it's also useful for helping us to see why exactly wisdom has fallen out of favor. In this current revival of the JSA, Johns isn't just telling new stories, he's retelling some of the old story. In his distinctive contemporary conception of Captain Marvel, Billy Batson's transformation into the Captain is purely physical. When the teenager says "Shazam," though he's physically transformed into a strapping adult superhero, mentally he's still the same young and naïve boy he was before the remarkable change. In particular, Billy doesn't personally take on the wisdom of Solomon, even though he does still acquire the strength of Hercules. His body changes, but his mind doesn't. Rather, he now experiences Solomon's wisdom as an outside voice that advises him on what to do when he needs such advice.

The idea of wisdom personified speaking to a person from outside his own mind isn't new. This device is used by no less a philosopher than Boethius, in his classic text *The Consolations of Philosophy*, written while he was in prison on false charges. He imagines himself visited by wisdom, and he listens carefully to what she has to say.[1] But the voice of wisdom speaking to Marvel comes to replace the idea of his actually having wisdom himself, as one of his new forms of excellence. We are left to wonder initially whether this is because wisdom is no longer viewed as an excellence, or whether Johns has a deeper understanding that personal wisdom is not the sort of thing that can be instantly added to a person, and thus the best the transformation can effect is a new availability of wisdom to the suddenly changed young man. Regardless of why exactly wisdom isn't among the array of his new personal properties, we can glean some insights into the modern uncertainty about it by looking at the narrative that develops.

Over the course of the new storyline constructed by Johns, Billy and a female teen JSA member called Stargirl—real name Courtney Whitmore—develop a romantic attachment. The Flash, an older JSA member, notices that Captain Marvel is spending a

---

[1] Wisdom, "Sophia" in Greek, was traditionally thought of as in some sense feminine, although the advice she gave was as important for masculine success as it was for women in the world.

lot of time with young Stargirl and, since Flash doesn't know that the Captain is really just a teenage boy, he's bothered that his apparently thirty-something colleague is hanging out with an underage girl, and he mentions his worries to Captain Marvel. The Captain goes to Stargirl to discuss the impression of impropriety that their budding relationship is bound to have on the rest of the JSA, and he breaks off the relationship. But, significantly, this decision to break up with Stargirl isn't Billy's own idea; rather, we understand that he's simply following wisdom's advice on the matter. Indeed, Stargirl, who doesn't want to break up, understands that Billy is only following Solomon's advice, and so she begs him to turn back into his original teenage identity, knowing that, in this state, his decisions regarding her won't be influenced by Solomon's wisdom, and most likely, he won't break up with her after all.

Courtney's attraction to Billy and her fear of losing him cause her to want to maintain the relationship in the face of how problematic it's going to be in the eyes of their teammates. The other JSA members don't know Marvel's really only sixteen years old, so all they'll see is a thirty-something guy getting even more inordinately close to a sixteen-year-old girl. The JSA members view Marvel as the paragon he is, so it's not that the Flash talks to him about the situation because he thinks the Captain might be up to something unwholesome. Marvel's known character not only implies that he wouldn't try to hook up with a sixteen-year-old girl, it also implies that he's not the kind of guy who would do anything to even indicate such tendencies. If Billy and Stargirl are to let their relationship take its course, the towering superhero will have to tell the JSA that he—their greatly esteemed colleague, Captain Marvel—is actually just a mid-adolescent boy. And there's the rub: Billy has to choose between breaking up with Courtney or disclosing to the rest of the JSA that Captain Marvel is in fact merely a teenage boy in a superpowered man's body; and it's the latter alternative—revealing Billy's secret to the JSA—that wisdom's advice is designed to avoid.

Looked at from this perspective, the advice to break off with Courtney might at first seem to be tinged more with self-interest than real wisdom. For the cost to Captain Marvel of revealing his true civilian identity—that is, the cost under these circumstances of staying with Courtney—would be that the JSA would most likely take Marvel much less seriously. A wise and experienced person gets a kind of respect and deference that a teenager—no matter how tight he is with a wise advisor—just isn't going to get. That's simply a fact of life. People with dangerous jobs, who work in hazardous situations, naturally prefer to work with people who have just as much experience, or more, than they themselves have accumulated. Actually having the wisdom of Solomon would be one thing—a very good and advantageous thing—but merely having it virtually available, as a sort of mystically close advisor, is quite another. We know how people get practical wisdom, or at least we think we do—by experience and thoughtful reflection on that experience. But we don't have a clue how the wisdom of one person long dead might communicate with someone now living, and so we would not naturally be as inclined to trust someone who nonetheless assured us that they had such access to great wisdom, despite their youthful inexperience. To make it even worse, the other JSA members would know that, no matter what Marvel might hear from his advising voice, it would ultimately be up to him how he interpreted and used what he heard. And if he didn't have sufficient wisdom of his own, his use of any wisdom otherwise available to him could not be counted on as dependable.

So, at first thought, we might be tempted to suspect that wisdom's advice to Billy concerning what he should do here is motivated by selfish considerations on the part of wisdom—if Billy's secret is revealed, the voice of wisdom, no matter how much influence and power it might still have over Billy, won't have the amount of power and influence it otherwise would have on the rest of the team. Indeed, the dilemma that Johns constructs for Billy is, in a way, ingenious, because, of all the virtues that his utterance of "Shazam" gives him, the only one that will become laughable to his teammates, or at least very dubious, should they learn his secret, is his access to wisdom.

If the other JSA members were to learn that Marvel is really just a suped-up sixteen-year-old, no one would think any less of any of the other virtues—either physical or mental—that he's manifested in the past. They'd presumably still be perfectly willing to rely on him for his strength, speed, courage, stamina, and so on. But—even putting aside the fact that this revelation that they'd been duped so long would likely make them resentful toward, and distrustful of, Marvel—there's just no way that, if the truth were known, Billy could have the kind of authority that someone has with those who think him truly wise. Wisdom's advice to break off with Courtney is clearly designed to preserve its own authority. To a reader with a genuine appreciation of the importance of wisdom, this can seem fully appropriate and right. But to many modern readers, this will just cynically show the personification of wisdom to be as calculating and self-interested as anyone else, and not the sort of admirable quality that stands out above it all, with a purity and insight to which we all should listen.

Skepticism and Cynicism about Wisdom

If we want to look at just how far our contemporary skepticism about wisdom can go, we can easily find examples in other superhero comics. For example, in Jim Krueger's and Alex Ross's *Earth X* series, Odin, the wise all-father of Thor and the other Norse Gods, is revealed to be a complete fraud—he turns out to be a frail and insecure human who took advantage of the one weakness of a powerful alien race to convince them that they are Gods and that he is their King. He takes power from them and rules them entirely under false pretenses, and his alleged wisdom is just a mask for naked self-interest. Though I think the Johns portrayal of wisdom may be tinged with a bit of skepticism, I don't think it goes quite as far as the totally deconstructive characterization of Odin in *Earth X*. True, wisdom's advice to Billy is designed to preserve its own authority, but this needn't mean its advice is in any problematic way selfish and, in the full context of the Johns story, it doesn't look as if it is. Billy, as Captain Marvel, has a job to do; and there's no way he can do that job effectively if his teammates find out the whole truth about him.

The wise person in both western and eastern philosophical traditions is supposed to be detached from the objects of sense—from what we see, hear, smell, taste, and feel. Because the senses deliver us information about the external here and now, the person with true wisdom isn't as bounced around by temporary fears and desires rooted in present appearances. He sees things from a greater temporal perspective, and realizes that his current feelings don't matter as much as they naturally seem to matter. Wisdom doesn't tell Billy to preserve its authority merely because it's afraid—there's no indication that Johns means to reveal or even hint that wisdom is actually a fraud, like Odin in *Earth X*. In trying to preserve its own authority, wisdom appears to be genuinely advising Billy to ignore the passion of the here and now in favor of a larger view of who he is and what his obligations are. Though wisdom's advice to Billy is designed to preserve its own authority, through his continued authority in the JSA, it isn't in any sense narrowly selfish advice. Billy needs to have the stature of a genuinely wise man in the JSA if he's to do his job and, hence, wisdom's advice to Billy does have a whiff of genuine wisdom about it.

And yet, while Johns doesn't portray wisdom as fraudulent, his portrait of it isn't as unambiguously admiring as one drawn at the time of Captain Marvel's original creation would have been. We see Courtney's pain when she begs Billy to change back to his fully teenage self, so that he won't listen to wisdom, and when Marvel flies away from her we aren't certain that he's done the right thing. The fact that wisdom isn't offering insincere advice out of narrow self-interest saves wisdom from fraudulence, but you can be wrong without being a fraud and, as Marvel leaves, the reader isn't entirely sure that wisdom's demand for Billy to ignore his current feelings in favor of the larger picture really represents the course he ought to take. In 1940, the question "Why should the larger picture trump Billy's current feelings?" simply wouldn't have occurred to a comic book reader. In these first years of the twenty-first century, we can't help but wonder.

What Wisdom Requires

The stories written by Geoff Johns in *Flash*, *JSA*, and other titles have a perfect retro feel to them. Like a refreshing number of current comic creators, he manages to tell stories that have the innocent fun that was essential to Golden and Silver Age comic heroes while avoiding the dated feel these stories often have to the contemporary reader. And the way in which his story raises questions about the legitimacy of wisdom's demands on behalf of the larger picture, without questioning its legitimacy or sincerity in claiming to speak on behalf of the larger picture, is a good example of his ability to acknowledge and engage contemporary doubt about the values embodied in the superhero concept without giving that doubt full reign. Because the Johns storyline about Captain Marvel takes into account a contemporary skepticism about wisdom without going into a full-fledged cynicism about it, he offers us a good illustration of what it is about the traditional deliverances of wisdom—and what it is about us—that makes us skeptical.

First, as we've seen, wisdom emphasizes the claims of the bigger picture over the claims of the present moment. And because our senses present us with the here and now, wisdom places reason, in its broadest conception, above mere sensory information as a guide to action. We see this placing of reason above the senses in both western and eastern philosophy. We can find it in Plato's picture of the wise person as one who ignores the temporary objects of sense perception in order to contemplate the eternal forms, as well as in the *Bhagavad-Gita*'s injunctions to detach oneself from the objects of sense.

But our senses don't just present us with the here and now, they present the here and now, as it were, in loud CAPITAL LETTERS—our senses have a natural power over our actions, and so we need to be trained to put them into whatever wisdom deems to be their proper perspective. Because of this, though wisdom in some respect can seem to denigrate the senses, there is a way in which it actually exalts the right kinds of experience. Unless we have actually experienced many times how the senses can often mislead us, and take that insight to heart, we are susceptible to being duped again and again by them. And the wisest people have realized further that if we don't experience some basic training in ways of resisting the immediacy of appearance that can tame the natural power of our senses, reason stands little chance of determining our actions. This is why the revelation that Captain Marvel is just sixteen would most likely completely destroy his teammates' confidence in his wisdom—someone sixteen years old simply couldn't yet have had the range of experiences required to be able to force his attention away from the insistent demands of the present deliverances of the senses when this is needed.

Because wisdom places reason above the senses, it's easy to miss the way in which experience is central to the notion of wisdom. But, according to many schools of thought, the path to wisdom requires meditative exercises explicitly designed to weaken the power that the senses have over us. We tend to associate this kind of training with eastern philosophical traditions—and because of this, many comic-book heroes are said to have trained with eastern masters—but this is because our idea of western philosophy is completely tied to our ideas of the western university and, thus, our idea of western philosophical training is inappropriately associated with such trivia as exams and essay papers on highly abstract, theoretical, or just boring topics. But, contrary to our current ideas, western philosophy has a rich tradition of wisdom, and a tradition of meditative practice—in addition to the religious mystics of the west, the Stoics are perhaps the most obvious example—and, as in the case of eastern meditation, the goal is, in part, to train oneself to withstand, and rise above, the natural power of the senses. The more general idea that wisdom can be acquired only through training is central to Plato's *Republic*, a large part of which is concerned with laying out the very long course of training necessary to achieve real wisdom. Plato's wise person has the vividness and power of the temporary world presented to him by his senses, and yet he manages to direct his gaze toward the eternal truths of reason. It's easy for us to forget that he's able to do that only because of a long and systematic course of rigorous training.

In exalting the larger picture over the smaller, wisdom not only requires that we learn to resist the natural pull of the senses, it also requires us to resist the natural pull of the emotions. In a well-known Daredevil story arc, Matt Murdock's mentor, Stick—the mysterious stranger who is training him in exotic fighting skills and practical wisdom—finally parts company with him because of what he sees as Matt's inability to control his emotions. Emotional control has always been important to the classic wisdom traditions.

Our senses focus us on the smaller picture not only because they present us with the here and now, but because they always present the here and now from *our perspective*. For example, the information about the world that we get from vision is organized along the left-right and up-down axes, but left and right and up and down aren't objective properties of the world. Something is to the left or right or above or below something else only from *a certain perspective*. In addition, all of our senses organize the world in terms of how close or distant to us their objects are. Our own perspective is, likewise, essentially involved in our natural emotional reactions to the world. Your sudden anger, for example, at some perceived insult involves more than the objective fact that someone has said something to you, and the fact that you perceive what was said as offensive, it also essentially involves your *feelings* about this fact. In placing the larger picture above the smaller, wisdom denigrates our natural emotional reactions to the world as reliable guides to action. Even a superhero who acts out of anger rather than reason is always an individual setting himself up for trouble.

Meditative techniques designed to inculcate wisdom by lessening our attachments to the objects of sensory experience are, at the same time, supposed to lessen the effects that our emotions have on us. In the recent Captain Marvel story, Courtney's emotional attachment to Billy is what causes her to fear breaking up with him. Billy has the same attachments and, hence, potentially the same emotions, but the guidance of wisdom directs him toward the larger picture and requires him to ignore these emotions. In the early days of superhero comics when the character of Captain Marvel was created, the counsel of wisdom could be regarded without skepticism because we weren't widely suspicious about the claims of the larger picture against the smaller. We can also see this in other forms of popular entertainment, for example, in the closing scene of *Casablanca*, when Humphrey Bogart tells Ingrid Bergman that, "The problems of two people don't amount to a hill of beans in this crazy world." The audience is meant to feel it's something of a tragedy that the Bogart and Bergman characters' love has to take a back seat to the larger picture, but we aren't meant to have any doubt that the claims of the larger picture *should* trump their personal concerns. And, if, as is the case, we have as a culture grown skeptical about the dictates of wisdom, this is because we've grown skeptical about whether the larger picture does indeed trump our personal concerns.

Our Problems with Wisdom

Some people are dismissive about the claims of wisdom concerning the big picture because they simply think there is no larger picture worth considering. Others have just forgotten how to look. As we've seen, in claiming that we always should look to the larger picture in deciding what to do, wisdom must subjugate our sensory and emotional reactions to the world. Our descent into skepticism about wisdom derives from the fact that we have very different attitudes toward sensory information and emotion than our ancestors had.

In our contemporary way of thinking, the pleasure or pain of current sensory experience is what really matters. We never think of it as just distracting us from what really matters. We tend to think that happiness consists of having pleasant sensory experiences and avoiding painful ones. Our ancestors tended to believe that happiness could be achieved only by learning to discount sensory pain and pleasure. Of course, the idea that there's a strong link between pleasure and happiness isn't unique to our age.

The Epicureans, to name one example, shared our idea that pleasure is central to a happy life. However, it's important to realize that for the Epicureans, discerning what's *really* pleasurable requires serious investigation and training. These ancient philosophers weren't like us in thinking that any immediate evaluation of a whether a sensory experience is pleasurable or not is sacrosanct—they didn't assume that the small picture provided by the senses is always, or even usually, a guide to what's really good. The Epicureans believed that accurately discerning what's really most pleasurable requires training ourselves to look past the immediate pull of the most easily available sensory experience. Peter Parker often overcomes the pressures and pulls of immediate sense experience, and readily available enjoyment, to go out on the town as Spider-Man and help others. Then as a result, he experiences deeper pleasures that he never could have known apart from his exercise of self-discipline and action in behalf of the larger picture of things.

Our attitude towards emotions is similarly distinctive. Our ancestors, in both the east and the west, thought of emotions as things that are external to the self which, when allowed to determine our actions, undermine our freedom and autonomy. We think of the emotions as internal to the self, and we correspondingly consider emotional expression to be an expression of the true self. The word "passion" interestingly comes from the same root as the word "passive," because, for our ancestors, it was part and parcel of being under the influence of a passion that our ability to determine our own actions—that is, our ability to act freely—was being seriously undermined. In Benedict

Spinoza's (1632–1677) terms, it has traditionally been believed that we are *in bondage* to our emotions. But in recent times, we think of emotions as internal forces that we somehow own, forces that rightly demand an external expression. Following Sigmund Freud (1856–1939), we've come to think of the mind as a kind of steam engine, so that for any of us to block the expression of emotion is in the long run impossible—if the emotion isn't expressed, the internal pressure builds and, one way or another, it will in the long run have to be released. Thus, the idea of training oneself not to be subject to one's emotions—an idea common to many older conceptions of wisdom—can strike us now as laughably pathetic.

Our own mode of thinking of things has a way of seeming unavoidable. That's why so many major scientific breakthroughs have often at first been ridiculed by prominent and intelligent people, and often by experts in the field. We grow so accustomed to certain ways of thinking that deeply different suggestions can sound ludicrous, even if they're true. For our ancestors who didn't think of the emotions as basic and natural internal things at all, our modern talk of *emotional repression*, along with our ideas concerning its consequences, would seem equally ridiculous.

We tend to divide conceptions of the world along cultural lines, East versus West, so that Plato, Aristotle, and the contemporary American university professor are thought of as part of one conception, and the Upanishads, along with modern ashrams, as part of another. But one thing our look at comic-book wisdom has revealed, is that a more important division is between contemporary western thought and past thinking across all cultures. Wisdom has similar characteristics and gets similar respect throughout variant cultures of the past, and it's only in the contemporary West that we see pervasive doubt about wisdom and its advocacy of the larger picture.

Now that we've seen the change in conception that's behind our skepticism about wisdom, we can see why this should be so. If you're reading this book, you almost certainly have heating in the winter and air-conditioning in the summer—you can control the temperature in your home simply by setting a thermostat to whatever level you prefer. Within twenty minutes you can very likely get to a store that sells an enormous range of foodstuffs unavailable to the most powerful kings of earlier times. For our ancestors, a life devoted to the small picture of current desire and fear was almost guaranteed to be an unhappy life, since the resources to satisfy sensory experience and emotion were almost completely lacking—their current sensory experience at any time may have told them it's too hot or too cold, or they might have had a hunger or thirst for some special food or drink, but if they had allowed these demands of the small picture to determine their happiness, they would have been guaranteed to be miserable. But, in the contemporary west, and in parts of the rest of the world, this is no longer the case. We've constructed a new human world in which the demands of the moment can increasingly and more easily be met, and no doubt this is a large part of why we've become skeptical concerning any claim that the natural pull of sensory experience and emotion should be resisted in favor of the larger picture. This is part of the reason that we've become skeptical of wisdom.

The material facts of prior ages made it almost impossible to think that happiness could consist in fulfilling the demands of the smaller picture, and nearly inevitable that people would think that a happy life rather required training oneself to often ignore the smaller picture in favor of the larger. However, though our skepticism about wisdom becomes possible only when material progress makes it feasible to alleviate the temporary fears and satisfy the temporary desires of the moment, an attitude's becoming possible doesn't make it right. Socrates and other ancient thinkers believed that satisfying all the demands of the smaller picture, in the end, simply leaves one more unsatisfied. And it's a curious fact that, in a time of unprecedented material prosperity, people seem to complain more than ever. Indeed, in the less materially advanced societies of the past, complaining was almost universally regarded as a bad thing. One of the central injunctions of the *Bhagavad-Gita* is that, no matter how bad things are, one should never, ever complain. Despite our unique ability to satisfy the demands of the smaller picture, it's not at all clear that our skepticism about wisdom and its claims on behalf of the larger picture has made us any happier. And, that's probably why the concept of wisdom, though largely absent from our daily lives, still has some meaning for us, once we properly understand it.

Part Three

Superheroes and Moral Duty

12

Why Are Superheroes Good? Comics and the Ring of Gyges

JEFF BRENZEL

In the course of their long conversation, western philosophers have not had much to say about superheroes. Socrates and Plato did reflect on gods and demigods right at the beginning, and in the last hundred years or so, professional philosophers have chattered to one another about such extraordinary things as Nietzsche's superman, Laplace's demon, brains in vats, and infinite possible worlds. Some philosophers are also conducting lively discussions right now about the "trans-human" future: how genetically engineered or bio-mechanically enhanced individuals will relate to those of us who remain "merely human."

Sad to say, contemporary academics have virtually ignored the richly imagined worlds of superhero comics, where characters have evolved among the minds of artists and readers across multiple generations and through hundreds of story cycles. Philosophical neglect probably only reflects the mainstream devaluation of comic books. Pick your favorite reason why cultural critics have disparaged superhero comics: formulaic plots; creation of subversive subcultures; the peculiar conditions of comic-book distribution; disdain for an audience mistakenly thought to be entirely juvenile. Or perhaps it is only that philosophers would think it unseemly if their colleagues knew they used to curl up under the covers reading Wonder Woman or Spider-Man by flashlight.

For my part, I freely acknowledge becoming a Marvel Maniac about the time that Stan Lee launched the Silver Age. I ran to the drugstore each month during the early sixties and grabbed every issue in which the Fantastic Four, Spider-Man, Iron Man and the

X-Men appeared.[1] When this book's editors invited me to reflect philosophically on superheroes, I therefore got the warm rush that lies in wait for former fans provided with a sufficiently high-minded excuse to catch up on their back reading. Surprised to learn that there was a comic book store within four blocks of my office at Yale, I emerged from it after two hours, enriched by a long talk with the knowledgeable proprietor and a box of graphic novels, classic stories, Golden Age reprints, and current titles.

Getting reacquainted with old friends, I saw that over the years my heroes had kept doing good and fighting evil, often at great cost to themselves. Being the sort of philosopher who likes big, juicy questions, I began to wonder whether it is plausible that superheroes would stick with these jobs for so long. Put another way, why would people with these kinds of powers be so good?

Refining the Question

Satisfying answers to big questions are always hard to cook up, and philosophers often spend considerable time trimming off the fat and bones just to get at the meat. In this case, asking why superheroes are good poses a question that could be taken different ways. There is at least one sense in which the question almost seems to answer itself, simply as a matter of defining the concept "superhero." If a costumed character with unusual powers did not do good and fight evil, in some way that is recognizable to the average reader, then he or she would presumably not be appearing as the protagonist of a superhero story, or would perhaps be a supervillain instead.

But is this really so? Some story lines and breakaway projects have put elements of the traditional comic-book superhero's character into question, without making the hero into a villain. The mid-eighties saw an excellent effort at this in DC Comics' justly celebrated *Watchmen* series. Certain characters in that series were clearly meant to raise questions about the superhero

---

[1] Unfortunately for my retirement plans, my mother chucked the entire contents of my comic book boxes when I went off to college. My regret at the financial loss is tempered by my awareness that this collection was in less than mint condition.

values presented in traditional stories. The character Rorschach, for example, stews in problematic motives and methods that are bound up with the kind of vigilante justice practiced by DC's traditional character Batman. The *Watchmen* creators used another character, Dr. Manhattan, to explore how powers of godlike proportions (think Superman on atomic steroids) might ultimately shape an alien consciousness, one quite morally distant from everyday human experience.

Other writers in the last twenty years have also taken up the graphic novel format to bring traditional characters into deeper confrontations with these questions. Take, for example, the portrayals of Batman in the *Dark Knight* stories and Superman in such works as *Kingdom Come*. Of course, even when writers have adopted what literary critics might call oppositional or subversive postures with regard to superheroes, those same writers are still testifying strongly to, and relying heavily upon, the notion that comic-book heroes are *supposed* to be good. In questioning superhero psychology or superhero values, they remind us how central the notion of goodness has been to the superhero. They also provoke us into seeing that a superhero cannot simply be good by definition. To be a plausible character at all, the super-powered individual must *choose* to be good, and must go on being good in some broadly recognizable way.

A Genetic Fallacy and Something Too Simple

These considerations help us dispose of another way to understand our original question about why superheroes are good. While it may be an interesting fact of cultural history, it is not philosophically significant that, early in their history, good superheroes were virtually legislated for the comic-book industry. As comic-book historians have often noted, the horror comics of the early 1950s led to a burst of anti-comics hysteria, such that the pressure of Congressional hearings in 1954 forced major comics publishers to create a code by which they agreed to be bound. A key provision of the original Comics Code stated that "In every instance good shall triumph over evil and the criminal [shall be] punished for his misdeeds."[2] Though the

---

[2] For the full text of the original Code and a treatment of its history, see Les Daniels's *Comix: A History of Comic Books in America* (New York: Outerbridge

Code eventually dwindled in relevance, it was effective for decades in setting basic constraints on story content and tone. Anyone familiar with the Code's history might therefore be tempted to say that traditional superheroes "became good" merely because the protagonists in comics had to be scripted in conformance with the Code.

But this cannot be a thoughtful answer to our philosophical question. Even if the outlook and motivations of traditional superheroes in subsequent years are in some sense a product of the Comics Code, having their *genesis* in its requirements, the Code's provisions do not explain why superhero stories that conformed to it succeeded in attracting interest among a large audience. Bear in mind that it was not a foregone conclusion that replacing horror tales with superhero stories was going to be commercially successful. The Comics Code might simply have killed comic books. So it must be the case that literary creativity combined with a large and receptive readership to keep morally good superhero characters alive and kicking. That is, it turned out that we the audience paid for and accepted good superheroes. It must therefore have struck large numbers of us as both plausible and appealing that an individual who is granted superhuman powers would choose to do good and fight evil. To frame our question a bit differently, when we ask why superheroes are good, we are also asking why this premise has been a successful basis for fifty years of compelling storytelling.

There are some other ways to dodge the question. For one of them, we could consider the thoughts of Stan Lee, the loquacious, colorful, and sometimes revered spirit behind the rise and growth of Marvel Comics. In his commentary for a 1975 volume of reprinted stories, Lee asked: "Did you ever stop to think that almost every story in the world—not just superhero comic book stories—deals with good guys versus bad guys in some form or other? It's the basic formula not only for comics, but for virtually any and every type of adventure tale—and isn't every story an adventure tale when you get to the nub of it?"[3] If we look past

---

and Dienstfrey, 1971). As of this writing, a copy of the original Code could also be found in several locations on the Internet, including www.comics.dm. net/codetext.htm.

[3] Stan Lee, *Son of Origins of Marvel Comics* (New York: Simon and Schuster, 1975), p. 165.

Lee's quick reduction of all literature to adventure stories, he seems to be telling us that conflicts are central to human experience and that superhero stories simply embody these conflicts and write them in large print that everyone can follow—cops and robbers, cowboys and Indians, good guys and bad guys, heroes and villains, us and them.

Later in this same text, however, Lee adds another thought: "Of course, in writing the typical Marvel type of tale, it's almost impossible not to become involved in some extraneous philosophical or moralistic side issue. After all, the battle between a hero and a villain (which is what virtually all our stories get down to) is basically a conflict between a good guy and a bad guy, or between good and evil."[4] On the one hand, Lee keeps in view the "adventure" component by focusing our attention on the "battle between a hero and a villain." If he had stopped there, he might only have been saying: "Boys sure do love a good fight and we aim to please." Many comic-book critics did think this was what comic books were about, and they also believed that this is what Stan Lee thought. However, Lee also recognizes, though perhaps somewhat reluctantly, that things aren't as simple as that. A writer and an artist can certainly make up characters with fantastic powers and script good action scenes for them, thus enabling readers to project onto those characters their personal fantasies of strength and power. It may be quite another thing, however, to work out all those "extraneous" moral issues that start cropping up when you find yourself pitting good against evil.

It turned out that Lee was better than his word, or at least the words I have quoted here. What revitalized comics after 1961 was Lee's happy inspiration to make superheroes more human. Rather than being the mere vessels of their unusual powers—wooden protagonists engaged in repetitive battles against equally wooden opponents—more fully realized characters such as the Fantastic Four and Spider-Man began addressing unpredictable existential consequences. Story-lines ran over multiple issues, and characters changed over time in response to their experiences. The "philosophical and moralistic side issues" began to take more time at center stage, without ever entirely

---

[4] Lee, *Son of Origins*, p. 188.

interrupting or displacing the action. In short, superhero characters began to grow up. Many heroes began to wonder about
what they were doing and why. It's not incidental in this regard
that one of the more recent superhero films to be released,
Spider-Man 2, dwells almost exclusively on Spider-Man's
motives and motivation for being a hero.

So we have considered one more answer that will not really
do the job. Even if all these claims were true, superheroes cannot be good simply because (1) every story is an adventure
story, (2) every adventure story is ultimately about a fight, (3)
every fight boils down to good guys and bad guys, (4) every
good guy fighting evil is in some sense a hero, and if he has
superpowers, he's a good superhero. Once superheroes start to
grow up and think for themselves, as it were, rather than simply jumping around and banging into other people wearing costumes, things get more complicated for them, just as they do for
us.

The Problem with Origins

As our final step toward refining our question, we need to consider one more way of answering it that will not work. You may
have already been thinking about this. Doesn't each superhero
have an "origin story" that explains why he or she lives or acts
in a particular way? Well, yes. There's no question that origin
stories are important for comic-book superheroes, and over
decades of story development, different writers and artists have
created or embellished or adjusted origin stories in significant
ways. Further, origin stories tend to serve throughout all story
arcs as a kind of touchstone for the basic aspects of superhero
personality or mission. Bruce Wayne became the Batman
because he witnessed the death of his own parents by the hand
of a violent criminal. Helpless at that moment to prevent their
destruction, he ultimately devoted his life to preventing violence
to others and to bringing criminals to justice. Superman is the
son of a good and noble scientist on a planet doomed to
destruction, who rockets the future hero to Earth where he is
found and adopted by a kindly couple, Jonathan and Martha
Kent. The Kents instill in the growing child the virtues and values of rural America, as incarnated in a town provided with the
all too literal name of Smallville. The X-Men are teenaged

mutants and therefore repugnant to normal humans, who both fear and loathe them. A wise professor, a mutant himself, gathers them together and trains them to work as a team for the good of humanity, in order that they may rise above their fates as lonely outsiders.

So it goes. Many super-villains also have origin stories that purport to "explain" why they are evil. Perhaps the thinnest of these was the origin story that Jerry Siegel finally created in 1960 for Superman's archenemy, Lex Luthor. In the story, Luthor is a scientific boy genius and friend of Superboy's. While working on an antidote to protect Superboy from his vulnerability to Kryptonite, Luthor accidentally sets a laboratory on fire. He calls to the passing Superboy for help, and his powerful schoolmate responds by blowing out the fire through an open window. However, in doing so Superboy also douses Luthor with chemicals, which immediately causes all of his hair to fall out. Lex then inexplicably accuses his rescuer of destroying the Kryptonite experiment out of jealousy for his scientific genius. Within two or three more panels, Luthor is swearing eternal vengeance against Superboy, on the ridiculous pretext that his longstanding and faithful friend wished him harm, not only by destroying his bid for scientific greatness but also his hair at the same instant.[5]

I cite this ludicrous origin story for more than its entertainment value as a relic of what used to pass for plot development in comic books. As with the narratives we tend to create about our own origins, these kinds of stories function more as *signs* or *interpretations* of character than as *explanations*. The important fact about Lex Luthor throughout most of his comic-book career is that his animosity toward Superman is almost entirely personal.[6] Therefore most of his intricate schemes combine the standard evildoer's insane ambitions to rule the world with an obsessive focus on destroying Superman in particular. Luthor

---

[5] You can read and look at this story online, at least as of the time I am writing this essay, by going to http://superman.ws/tales2/howluthormetsuperboy/. It originally appeared in *Adventure Comics* #271 (April 1960).

[6] The Lex Luthor character and his relationship to Superman was reworked in the 1980s and then reworked again for the television show *Smallville*. The details are important for the Superman storyline and its fans, but not for the point I want to make here.

therefore required an "origin story" that contained within it some notion of being personally attacked by Superman.

Likewise, when we seek to explain good or bad character in ourselves or those around us, we sometimes bring forward a particular factor, whether in our genetic makeup or in our upbringing, sufficiently noteworthy to play the causal role in shaping our "fates." Although we might use such stories either as inspirations or excuses, and though these stories may make good material for confessional talk shows, the problem with them is always the same. No single event or handful of experiences, however profoundly impressed upon us, altogether determines the choices we make or the attitudes we adopt toward those experiences. People are just not that simple. The principal value of Lex Luthor's origin story is that it happens to be so bad we cannot fail to notice its complete lack of explanatory plausibility.

Superheroes and the Ring of Gyges

We wanted to know why superheroes would choose to do good. We have dismissed a few different ways of understanding and responding to the question. We have seen that it is inadequate to say that superheroes are good by definition. Further, they are not mere proxies for adolescent fantasies of tremendous power and acceptable good guy violence, and "origin stories" no more adequately explain why superpowered individuals choose to do good or evil than our own analogous stories might explain the same things about us. Perhaps we can now come to grips with at least one of the real questions about being good that superheroes must attempt to answer.

In a famous passage near the beginning of Plato's *Republic*, Socrates argues that the man who lives a life of virtue and justice, even if unrewarded with honor or wealth, will be happier than one who falls into injustice, even if the unjust man both prospers and manages to avoid paying for any of the consequences of his evil acts. One of Socrates's friends, Glaucon, believes that most people would find this claim terribly implausible. Human nature is such, says Glaucon, that in the eyes of most people, the best thing is being able to "do injustice without paying a penalty," while the worst thing is "to suffer injustice without being able to take revenge." On that view, the common notion of "justice" turns out to be merely a compromise, an agreement among those who are too weak to get away with injustice themselves, but are fearful of suffering it from the strong.

To put the point here crudely, the many who are weak cooperate to pass laws and whip up sufficient social disapproval to keep the few who are strong from completely taking over. It follows that anyone strong enough to climb to the top and dominate others with impunity, but who then chooses not to do so, would be in some sense unnatural. As Glaucon says, "The reason for this is the desire to outdo others and get more and more. This is what anyone's nature naturally pursues as good, but nature is forced by law into the perversion of treating fairness with respect."

Let's call this the harsh view of human nature. To help show that people are essentially self-seeking except when acting under social constraints, Glaucon tells a story about an ancestor of a man who was apparently known to him and Socrates, Gyges the Lydian (pronounced "Guy-jeez"). In the tale, this ancestor of Gyges is a shepherd in service to a king. He finds a magic ring in a cave that makes him invisible. As soon as he discovers the power of the ring, "he at once arranged to become one of the messengers of the king. He then went, committed adultery with the king's wife, attacked the king with her help, killed him and took over the kingdom." The moral of the story quickly follows: "Now if there were two such rings, one worn by the just man, the other by the unjust, no one . . . would be so incorruptible that he would stay on the path of justice or bring himself to keep away from other people's property . . . This, some would say, is a great proof that no one is just willingly but only under compulsion" (*Republic*, 360b–e).[7]

The idea behind the story is that morality and law evolve only as ways to control unrestrained individual ambition, rather

---

[7] Philosophers have always referred to this story, somewhat oddly, as "the Ring of Gyges," perhaps suggesting that this mysteriously powerful artifact, along with its tempting options, had been passed down through the generations and may have been reputed to be, at the time of the story's telling, in the possession of Gyges himself. Or it may be that the philosophers were just not attending closely to Plato's text. I regret to say that this happens a lot with philosophers.

than as a direct expression of what we all aspire to and value. The more complex our societies become, the greater our need for social cohesion and the regulation of individual behavior, and the greater the payoff to everyone from a system of morals and laws. These systems then make possible the further evolution of even more complex societies. This notion that people invent systems of morality in order to restrain and harness an egocentric and selfish human nature is a plausible and powerful idea with a long philosophical lineage, with much elaboration by later philosophers ranging from Hobbes to Nietzsche.

As an aside to those paying close attention, J.R.R. Tolkien was a well-read classicist who certainly knew his Plato backwards and forwards. The interesting thing here, however, is not whether Tolkien took a cue from Plato in creating *The Lord of the Rings*. The interesting thing is that Frodo Baggins as well as our friends the superheroes are all committed to "resisting the power of the ring." Whether in their intrinsic plausibility as characters or in their power to attract and inspire us, they constitute a powerful denial of the view that human nature is universally and always self-seeking. However, they do not tell us in any immediately obvious way why self-seeking would not be *reasonable*, at least in some circumstances. Plato has Glaucon call this point to our attention by contrasting an unjust man who merely appears just, becomes rich, wins social respect and never pays for his crimes with a just man who suffers wrongful imprisonment and dies a miserable death. Glaucon asks Socrates how anyone could believe that the just man in this instance could really be the happier human being, which is what Socrates wishes to claim.

The rest of Plato's masterwork addresses this question at one level or another. No more subtle, fertile, complex and often frustrating discussion of the matter has ever been written. Since we cannot address all the significant details here, I will simply try to characterize Plato's response briefly, apply it to superheroes and leave it for you to ponder.

Plato presents the first part of his response to Glaucon's objection by having Socrates outline what sounds like a primitive psychological theory. Socrates proposes that our souls can be divided into three parts, roughly speaking: our animal appetites, our emotions, and our reason. As justice in a city-state is a matter of each person making a contribution to the common good under the regulation of the laws, so justice in the soul comes about when the emotions are properly trained and support reason in its governance of our desires and appetites. Justice can therefore be thought of as good order or good health in the soul. Since no one would find it reasonable to take all the money in the world in compensation for a corrupted and ruined body, so no one would be reasonable in ruining the health of their souls for the sake of material gain or social status.

Some modern commentators criticize this reasoning as an answer to Glaucon's question about justice, in part because they take Plato to be proposing that we can equate goodness or justice with some kind of psychological harmony. If this were truly what Plato proposed, he would be open to three serious objections. First, bad people often seem quite content and free in spirit, experiencing some form of inner harmony, while good people are often distressed and uneasy in mind. Second, it is not clear why someone could not both have their appetites and emotions under rational control, while still being coldly calculating and pursuing bad objectives. Third, it is still not obvious why anyone who had the right balance in her soul would by virtue of that fact be motivated to help anyone else.

Following other interpreters, I do not think that Plato was proposing a psychology in our sense, whether primitive or otherwise, but was instead using his initial account of the soul to prepare the ground for the central argument in the *Republic*, which involves the ascent of a person from darkness and confusion to enlightenment. Both Plato's "psychology" and his vision of the ideal and eternal Good turn on the proposition that we have within us an extraordinary potential that we do not all achieve, and an end state toward which we can and should aspire. He also thought that the distress arising from our many internal conflicts and our many inadequate efforts to grasp what it means to be good would lead at least some of us to struggle toward improving our understanding and attaining a better, happier, more completely fulfilled life. When considering the question of whether the unjust person enjoying his or her ill-gotten gains is "happier" than the just person who ends up rotting in prison, Plato wants us to see that though neither character when fully developed would freely choose the other's life, the person who has become fully just and good can be quite reasonable in thinking it better to stay in prison than to live in the way that the unjust person has chosen. In addition, Plato claims that *only* the person who seeks to become good and succeeds in doing so can actually know the full appeal of both a just and an unjust life and weigh them properly against each other. With true goodness comes true wisdom about the relative worth of the alternatives.

This is where Plato links up with the plausibility of superhero motivation. He wants to say that there is something about our nature and about reality that points us in the direction of goodness, though we might at first find ourselves both confused in our minds and surrounded with bad things. Plato identified that "something" as an eternal principle, or form, or idea of the Good, a principle that really exists and in which we can participate. When Aristotle took up this line of thought, he denied Plato's notion that "The Good" is some unified, separately existing thing in which every particular good thing participates. On the other hand, Aristotle retained a very robust sense of teleology, or the notion that by nature we aim or point at a completed or fulfilled state, however dimly we may perceive what it is.[7] For Aristotle, in order for a living thing to achieve its full potential or fully flourishing condition, it must realize or actualize its own particular potential for excellence. To be the best specimens of their kind, horses need to be strong and swift and trees need to grow tall and spread their crowns. When characterizing human beings, Aristotle noted that two things mark us off from other animals, our rational abilities and our unique kind of social and political life. Aristotle therefore devoted considerable reflection to thinking through the qualities, habits, or virtues that would lead people to excel at using their intellect in cooperation with other people to achieve a common good.

This type of thinking in moral philosophy currently goes under the name of "virtue ethics." It emphasizes human aspirations and possibilities more than ethical rules and prohibitions, though of course it does not ignore the role of rules. In the case of superheroes, it's important to see that no matter how extensive their powers might be, they do not and cannot escape the very same questions about their potential for excellence that we must ask. That is, they have to ask themselves what sort and manner of person they are, and what is the best kind of life

---

[7] The Greek word for the aim, or the end state, or the completed purpose is "telos'.

available for that sort of person to lead. They also have to learn as they go whether they have what it takes to realize their particular possibilities. More concretely, they have to figure out whether and how they fit in to the rest of the social world, which includes ordinary people as well as other superheroes, and what special parts or roles their powers and abilities make it possible for them to play in that world. They have to find out what they can offer to others and what they can receive from others in return.

If we think back to Stan Lee's remarks noted earlier, we can now see that he actually came very close to articulating what is special about superheroes with respect to the question of goodness. He said that his stories *inevitably* pitted good guys against bad guys, and that it was "almost impossible" to write such stories without considering "philosophical and moralistic side issues." I believe that he was right on both counts, but for reasons that he does not happen to express. Among other things, their possession of unusual powers simply makes it less possible for superheroes to duck the questions we all need to face about our roles and potential and goals in life. Unlike what usually happens for the rest of us, society does not deliver for superheroes any standard, acceptable ways of fitting into the social world. Since their potential exceeds the normal in some highly obvious way, they *must* wrestle with what that potential means for their life projects and their moral outlook. As Spider-Man's Uncle Ben famously put it, "With great power comes great responsibility." Or as the philosophical humorists of the Firesign Theater once noted, "A power so great could only be used for good . . . or evil."[8] It may not be the case that everyone who obtained a magic ring would turn out like that notorious ancestor of Gyges, perhaps because human nature includes the aspect of questing for completion or fulfillment that Plato and Aristotle address. But it is certainly true that the surprised shepherd had to do *something* with his ring. It is not plausible that he would simply leave it sitting on a shelf.

---

[8] Firesign Theater, *The Tale of the Giant Rat of Sumatra* (Columbia Records, 1974). If you are a superhero fan and have never heard of Firesign Theater, this spoof of Sherlock Holmes is a good place to start having fun with their various recordings. There is an entire subculture devoted to the Firesign Theater's intricate, complex satires, and I would not be surprised to find out that it overlapped heavily with the audience for comics.

Great superhero stories are therefore riddled with personal quests to determine how a person can best live with great powers. Look again at Superman's grim and fateful decision to emerge from retirement and isolation in Alex Ross and Mark Waid's terrific Elseworlds epic *Kingdom Come*. Think of the futile effort that Peter Parker makes to turn his back on his superpowers in *Spider-Man 2*. Remember the various dilemmas that the Watchers face over action and inaction in the early Fantastic Four sagas. Examine the way that Kurt Busiek explores these themes with Samaritan and Winged Victory in his justly praised Astro City series. Among the other things they do, all the great superheroes raise for us the important questions we must ask about our own powers and potential for doing good, and they hint perhaps at some of the ways that our lives cannot help but be explorations of the possible answers.

13

Why Should Superheroes Be Good? Spider-Man, the X-Men, and Kierkegaard's Double Danger

C. STEPHEN EVANS

The idea of a superhero with special powers is not an invention of the modern comic book. Plato's *Republic* (lines 359c–360d) gives a brief description of an "ancestor of Gyges of Lydia" who found a magic ring that made him invisible when he turned it inward on his finger.[1] Using the ring, the man got into the king's palace, seduced the king's wife, and with the aid of the wife, murdered the king and took his place as ruler.

Plato and the Question of Why We Should Be Good

In the *Republic* this story of magical power is told to pose the question as to whether people love justice, or goodness, for its own sake or merely because they realize that if they are unjust, or immoral, they will suffer negative consequences. The story about Gyges's ancestor is narrated by Glaucon, who represents what we might call the immoralist's viewpoint, although he claims it is not his personal view. Glaucon argues that if a just person had such a magic ring, he would behave exactly the way an unjust person would behave. No one, says Glaucon, if he had such a ring, "would refrain his hands from the possessions of others and not touch them," since in such a case the person could "with impunity take what he wishes from the market

---

[1] My quotation from Plato are taken from *The Collected Dialogues of Plato*, edited by Edith Hamilton and Huntington Cairns (Princeton: Princeton University Press, 1963). The Ring of Gyges is also discussed in Chapter 12 of this volume.

place, and enter into houses and lie with whom he pleased, and slay and loose from bonds whomsoever he would, and in all other things conduct himself among mankind as the equal of a god."

If Glaucon is right, then the inhabitants of most comic-book worlds are fortunate that in those worlds the possessors of superpowers have generally been committed to what is right and what is good, using their extraordinary gifts for the benefit of others. It seems all too likely that Glaucon is at least partly right about real-life human beings. In the actual world, many people would surely use any superpowers they possessed for selfish and perhaps even evil purposes.

Glaucon's realistic and sober portrayal of human nature extends even further than this. The problem is not simply that few if any people would be just and good if they possessed powers that gave them the ability to do what is wrong without fear of punishment. He also claims that if there were any persons with special powers who were so committed to the good that they would still seek to be just, then the rest of us would despise them and regard them with contempt, though we might have good reasons for keeping our honest opinion to ourselves: "For if anyone who got such a license within his grasp should refuse to do any wrong or lay his hands on others' possessions, he would be regarded as most pitiable and a great fool by all who took note of it, though they would praise him before one another's faces, deceiving one another because of their fear of suffering injustice."

In the *Republic,* Glaucon goes on, with the help of his brother Adimantus, to pose a challenge to Socrates. Socrates wants to give a convincing argument that people should seek to be good and not merely appear to be good. Glaucon says that if Socrates really wants to give a convincing argument for this claim, then he must show that the life of a person who is truly just but thought by others to be unjust is superior to the life of a person who is really unjust but has a reputation for justice. To discover whether we really love justice for its own sake, we must perform a thought-experiment in which we compare a person who is perfectly just but has a reputation for injustice, along with the consequences of such a reputation, with a second person who is so clever in his injustice that he manages to gain and keep a reputation for justice. In this thought-experiment, the individual who really is just rather than merely seeming to be just must be "stripped of the seeming." Glaucon says that any such person "will have to endure the lash, the rack, chains, the branding iron in his eyes, and finally, after every extremity of suffering, he will be crucified, and so will learn his lesson that not to be but to seem just is what we ought to desire."

Plato presents these ideas to challenge us to think about why we should care about being good. Perhaps it may be helpful to pose the same question for a comic book superhero. Why should someone with superpowers care about being good? Reflection on this case may shed some light on the question Plato wishes to pose about ourselves.

Kierkegaard and the Concept of the "Double Danger"

Plato presents his picture of the good person who is thought to be unjust and suffers accordingly as a hypothetical thought-experiment. Nevertheless there is reason to think that Plato did not suppose the situation to be an impossible one. His teacher Socrates, whom he revered as the best and wisest of men, had been executed by the Athenians on the trumped-up charge that he was a corrupter of youth.

Many centuries after Plato, another great admirer of Socrates, the Danish philosopher and "father of existentialism" Søren Kierkegaard (1813–1855), posed Plato's challenge in a new form. In his insightful book, *Works of Love,* Kierkegaard describes the life we humans are called upon to live as a life of universal love.[2] He claims that we are called by God to love our neighbors as ourselves, and we are not allowed to say that any-one falls outside the category of "neighbor."

Obviously it is not easy to live such a life of love. To become loving in this way we must overcome the natural selfishness and simple inertia that push us towards the satisfaction of our own desires when those desires conflict with the good of others. We might call the problems that these difficulties create for us the

---

[2] Søren Kierkegaard, *Works of Love,* translated and edited by Howard V. Hong and Edna H. Hong (Princeton: Princeton University Press, 1995), p. 192. All quotations from this work will be given in parentheses with the abbreviation "WL".

"first danger" that threatens us as moral beings. It is an inner obstacle to goodness, justice, and love.

Kierkegaard says, however, that if we surmount this first danger and begin to make headway towards the love that the highest morality demands, we will face a second difficulty—an external one—and thus we are confronted with a "double danger" in our challenge to be good and loving. Identifying the struggle to become a truly loving person with the struggle to become a true Christian, Kierkegaard says that "the truly Christian struggle always involves a double danger because there is a struggle in two places: first in the person's inner being, where he must struggle with himself, and then, when he makes progress in this struggle, outside the person with the world."[2] Kierkegaard believes that the thought-experiment described in the *Republic* is not a hypothetical, contrary-to-fact situation, but that it captures the reality of life for a person genuinely committed to the good.

We all understand that a moral person must engage in a certain measure of self-denial, as he or she overcomes the firm pull of selfish desire and breaks free to act in the interests of others. Kierkegaard contrasts two understandings of self-denial. What he calls the "merely human" view of self-denial is that you should "give up your self-loving desires, cravings, and plans—then you will be esteemed and honored and loved as righteous and wise." The genuine self-denial of the Christian (meaning the person who really loves his or her neighbor) is different. Kierkegaard says: "give up your self-loving desires and cravings, give up your self-seeking plans and purposes so that you truly work unselfishly for the good—and then, for that very reason, put up with being abominated almost as a criminal, insulted and ridiculed" (WL, p. 194).

Why should this be so? For Kierkegaard, as for Glaucon, it is a simple consequence of the fact that the ordinary level of moral virtue is not very high. We may admire saints at a safe distance, but an actual encounter with heroic selflessness is likely to disturb us. This is one of the themes insightfully explored by Kurt Busiek and Alex Ross in their masterpiece graphic novel, *Marvels*. In the New Testament, Jesus says that his contemporaries build monuments to the prophets who suffered persecution and death in their lifetimes. At this stage in history, the birthday of Martin Luther King Jr. is a national holiday, and every major city has a street named for the martyred civil rights leader. However, during his lifetime King was a controversial figure who incurred much criticism and, of course, finally suffered the fate of Socrates, Jesus, and Gandhi. The life of such a person is a standing rebuke to us, and it is thus not surprising that we do not respond with universal acclaim.

Some comic-book superheroes who work unselfishly for the good do not seem to face either of these dangers. Superman is an excellent example. For the most part, the Man of Steel does not seem to agonize about whether he should use his superpowers for anything remotely like selfish purposes. The typical Superman episode does not revolve around a painful inner conflict in which he must conquer the temptation to amass riches, or to assume political power, in order to be able to continue to work for the good. Certainly, at times, Superman is pained by the necessity to put aside what might be personally satisfying, such as courting and marrying Lois Lane, to continue his important work for the greater good. But his character seems to be so committed to "truth and justice" (not to mention "the American way") that the outcome of any such inner struggle is not really in doubt. Nor does Superman appear to face the second danger that Kierkegaard mentions. He seems rather to enjoy nearly universal acclaim and good will from those he helps, as well as from the broader general public in his fictional setting.

Spider-Man's Struggles

Not all superheroes possess Superman's relative serenity. Spider-Man, for example, seems to face both kinds of temptations mentioned by Kierkegaard. Perhaps that is why the Spider-Man comics and movies have been so extraordinarily successful. Spider-Man offers us a superhero we can identify with—Peter Parker is a young man who struggles with ordinary human temptations as well as the many travails of the teen years.

The first kind of difficulty Kierkegaard mentions is quite evident in Spider-Man's life. He is deeply in love with Mary Jane Watson, or "M.J." His personal happiness, however, comes into conflict with his vocation as a superhero, in both small and large ways. In *Spider-Man 2,* he agrees to come to see M.J. perform in a theater, and promises not to disappoint her. However, on the way there, he comes across some evil-doers and goes to the rescue of an innocent person, causing him to be late, and giving M.J. the impression that he is unreliable and uncaring. At a more profound level, Peter has come to realize how a personal relationship with him can be dangerous for those he cares about. Both his Aunt May and M.J. are threatened by villains who want to get at Spider-Man. He thus decides he must put aside his feelings for M.J. for her sake.

The decision is not an easy one, however. We see Peter's agony every time he encounters Mary Jane. In *Spider-Man 2,* he actually chooses to give up his vocation as Spider-Man, throwing away his costume and attempting to live a normal life. His personal happiness at that point seems more important to him than his superhero work, and it appears to him that he can have only one or the other. We sense his personal anguish and almost applaud his decision to give up being Spider-Man. The cost of his devotion to the good of others is too high.

Notice that even in this case we do not see Spider-Man being tempted to use his powers for evil, despite a brief flirtation with exercising them for simple financial gain, when he first discovers he has them. The choice is ultimately between using these powers for good or withdrawing to a normal, private kind of life. There is never any worry that Peter will become an arch-villain. What is in doubt is whether he can achieve the kind of selflessness that a real love of neighbor demands. When it seems to him that what must be sacrificed for this is his personal happiness, Peter is tempted to be ordinary, not evil. To this extent, he still does not confirm Glaucon's prediction that a godlike person with superpowers would surely seek to do evil with impunity. Nevertheless, Spider-Man does experience the inner struggle that Kierkegaard calls the "first danger." Here, too, he is like the rest of us. Most of us are not tempted to become Hitlers or Green Goblins. We only want to be free to tend our own gardens, to attain our individual happiness, regardless of the needs of others.

To some degree, Spider-Man also experiences Kierkegaard's second danger. To be sure, most of the people he helps seem properly grateful for his good works. However, J. Jonah Jameson, the editor of the newspaper where Peter Parker works as a photographer, consistently portrays Spider-Man as a menace to society. His good deeds are all reinterpreted and "spun" so as to make them appear to be the opposite of what they are.

The real truth is that Jameson may be as uncomfortable in the presence of super-powered goodness as Kierkegaard predicted most people would be. Whether Jameson really believes Spider-Man is a danger is unclear. The editor is simply a paradigm of the "practical" man. His only interest is in making money by selling newspapers, and if portraying Spidey as nefarious helps him toward that goal, he will continue to do it with enthusiasm.

Curiously, despite this consistently negative press, ordinary people do not seem to hate Spider-Man or fear him. However, if the world of Spider-Man is anything like the actual world, then a consistent portrayal in the media as a villain is bound to have an effect in the long run. We can predict that, besides his personal struggles with his vocation, Spider-Man will increasingly face the painful situation Kierkegaard describes, in which "the world" does not applaud his heroic virtue. Either people will cynically refuse to believe in his goodness, or else, if they do acknowledge it, they may follow Glaucon's prediction and ridicule him as a major chump, at least behind his back.

The X-Men and the Double Danger

The case of Spider-Man shows that Superman's relative freedom from struggle is not the condition enjoyed by all superheroes. However, the X-Men provide an even better example of Kierkegaard's "double danger." Both in the comic books and in the movies, their stories are set in the near future, at a time when children with striking mutations are being born all over the world.

The X-Men are a group of mutants with special powers of various kinds. Some have telepathic or telekinetic abilities—for example, Professor Charles Xavier possesses both, and Dr. Jean Grey has the latter. Others have more bizarre qualities, such as Storm, who can control weather, or Cyclops, whose gaze has a destructive, laser-like power. The differences between mutants and "normal" people have led many ordinary citizens to fear and even hate the mutants, who are therefore often forced to remain "in the closet." Powerful politicians, such as Senator Robert Kelly, exploit these fears and prejudices and call for special laws that require mutants to be registered, laws that disturbingly recall the initial measures put into effect against Jews by Nazi Germany.

How should the mutants respond to this situation? Interestingly, there is disagreement, symbolized by the confrontation of two old friends, Professor Xavier and Erik Lensherr, who is known as "Magneto" because of his special power to control electro-magnetic fields. Magneto in effect calls for a war on ordinary humans, and gathers a group of mutants to assist him, while Xavier believes that it is possible to work peacefully for a tolerant world where those who are different are accepted. To this end Xavier has started a boarding school for mutant children and, from the mansion that serves as its campus, directs a group of mutants known as the X-Men (though the group includes many women) who try to thwart the plans of Magneto, while working to help and protect ordinary humans, and hoping for a broader acceptance and understanding of who they are.

The X-Men associated with Xavier in many ways grow to embody the neighbor-love that Kierkegaard sees as the fundamental human duty. They work for the good of others by fighting for a world where everyone is accepted, not just those who are alike, who are part of a network of family and friends, or who are likely to repay any beneficence in some way. The X-Men work for the good of all, including even those who are trying to persecute and harm them. At their very best, their love and concern for others seems unconditional in quality and ideally universal in scope.

Yet it is clear that they face struggles of various kinds, and not just the struggle of protecting themselves against Magneto and the political authorities who seek to harm them. The mere fact that the mutant community contains both the followers of Xavier, who seek to pursue the goal of an inclusive peace, as well as the followers of Magneto, who seek their more exclusionary ends through violence, shows that the choice of the good is not easy or automatic for mutants.

The story of the mutants embodies both of the two dangers that Kierkegaard describes, and these difficulties are most memorably dramatized in the character of Logan, or Wolverine. Wolverine, who has suffered a great deal as a victim of a disturbing medical experiment that has wiped out most of his memory, initially seems uninterested in helping Xavier and his group. His own personal agenda is all that counts. Early in the first X-Men film, he seems motivated more by inner rage than by any desire to do or be good. However, as he becomes part of Xavier's community, he increasingly seems to care about them and their cause. Though some of this may be due to a romantic interest in Dr. Grey, there does seem to be some awakening of moral concern in Wolverine as he begins to make personal connections. This moral growth is certainly not easy for a person possessed by the inner demons that appear to drive him, and thus well illustrates the first difficulty Kierkegaard discusses.

The X-Men as a whole seem to illustrate the second difficulty Kierkegaard describes. Although they are committed to the good, and they put that commitment into practice in serious and costly ways, they are rewarded for their concern over others' wellbeing with fear, persecution, and hatred. Of course, their illustration of Kierkegaard's second danger is not as perfect as we might like—the mutants are hated not simply because of their goodness, but rather because of their difference. But it's uncontroversial that their good deeds don't result in their being generally liked, respected, or appreciated. And, as a matter of fact, when you add their goodness to the greatness of their powers, you get the grounds for a distinctive sort of resentment on the part of many regular people. Indeed, it's possible to see the basic mutant differences themselves as a kind of dramatic, metaphysical symbol of the ways in which a community of those who truly cared about the good would likely be viewed by their broader society. And, in any case, it's interesting to note that the love or caring concern displayed by the X-Men towards others seems in no way to even decrease the general persecution they suffer. Perhaps, when people who are despised show themselves to be good, it is natural for their adversaries, and even many onlookers, to resent and despise them even more. After all, they have by their behavior demonstrated how irrational and perverse it is to despise them in the first place, and no one likes to realize or admit that his own attitudes are irrational or unjustified. We unfortunately, but naturally, often lash out against those who bring us such unpleasant self-knowledge.

Why Are the X-Men Good?

Why are the X-Men good? Why should they care about others, particularly when those others do not care about them? An answer to this question might suggest an answer to Plato's question about why we ordinary humans should be good. However, determining what motivation the X-Men might have to be good and just is not easy. Let's consider some of the possibilities that naturally suggest themselves.

One possibility is that they are motivated to be good by a conviction that this kind of life is the most effective way of securing tolerance and acceptance from others. On this interpretation, their commitment to the good is the result of a strategic calculation as to what policy will most effectively help them secure their own ends. However, this appears to be most implausible. As we have seen, ordinary people seem to fear and revile all mutants, including the X-Men. The fact that the X-Men face the second aspect of the "double danger"—a hostility of the outer world toward them and their efforts for good—seems to undercut the idea that their motivation for being good could be purely self-interested.

It does not seem generally true that human beings react positively to genuine saintly behavior, especially if it's uncomfortably close by—as shown by the fate of most great prophets—and the reaction of other people to the X-Men does not seem to be an exception to this rule. In any case, though the X-Men certainly wish and hope to be accepted by others, at least in the long run, their commitment to the good does not seem to be based on an expectation that this will occur. In fact, the argument of Magneto, that they should abandon any commitment to love and care for normal humans, is based on the actual lack of acceptance the X-Men experience. If the X-Men had a commitment to the good that was rooted in self-interested calculation alone, then the argument of Magneto would have some genuine force.

A second possibility is that the X-Men simply have no choice but to follow the good. Perhaps they are psychologically so constituted that they just naturally care strongly about others. Perhaps the genetic variation that has given them superpowers has also given them an unswerving desire for the good. The motivation for ethical action in this case could simply be the inner satisfaction that they derive from doing the good.

This suggestion suffers from several defects. First of all, it would fail to explain why some mutants, such as Magneto, have made the opposite choice. Secondly, it would seem to make the X-Men so different from ordinary people that they would be scarcely human at all. They would be more like Superman, an alien from Krypton, than real humans who happen to have a genetic difference that gives them superpowers. And this just seems false. The X-Men appear to have the full range of normal human desires and emotions. The romantic conflict between Cyclops and Wolverine over Jean Grey shows that they struggle with ordinary human desires and exhibit normal human behavior, including the most petty and self-interested behavior. They don't appear in any way to be the kind of angelic beings who simply can do no wrong. So this second possibility seems no more plausible than the first.

A number of other possibilities can be quickly dismissed. The X-Men do not appear to worry about legal sanctions or punishment; they are not doing what is right because, if they don't, they might run afoul of the police. And any suggestion that they do what they do out of a sort of pity for others that, as the German philosopher Nietzsche (1844–1900) surmised, was a sign of decadence (the invention of a "herd morality" that fears and hates those who are strong) is similarly implausible. The X-Men appear quite strong and self-confident, and their attitudes do not seem to stem at all from the sort of base resentment that Nietzsche believed was the inner motivation for altruistic morality. The X-Men are for the most part very positive people, not driven by any envy or resentment of those who are "strong and healthy." If anything, they appear to be the strong and healthy ones themselves.

So far our search for the motivation of the X-Men has been fruitless. Perhaps we should turn the question around and ask what motivates ordinary humans to be good. If we can come up with a plausible answer, we can then see if it fits the specific case of the X-Men. We might begin by asking what is known about bringing up children to be good. No one seems to have a formula that is guaranteed to work. Even the best of parents sometimes face heartache when their children pursue self-defeating patterns of behavior. However, in general, it seems to be true that children who are brought up in loving, accepting homes by parents who are concerned about the good are themselves more likely in turn to also become people who care about the good.

Why should this be so? I think the most likely answer is that when children are really loved by their parents, they naturally want to identify with their parents and be like them. They feel gratitude and admiration for their parents and any others who show goodness to them, and this gratitude and admiration produce within those children a personal love for the good as well. It's worth pointing out that this is not like the imagined possibility I considered and dismissed above, in which an individual might be so constituted that there is no choice about loving the good. Perhaps this is why even very good parents are not always successful in passing on their ethics. However, the child who has internalized the values of a good parent, or a good set of parents, at least has, as a result, an additional inner motivation to do what is right and good, some internal, emotional or psychological push that might provide a reason to resist the universal temptation to be purely self-interested.

The example of child rearing can be generalized, since I don't mean to suggest that someone who has had poor parenting is condemned to be a moral monster. It may be more difficult for a child who has had poor parenting to develop good character, but there are lots of children who as adults have risen above the examples of their parents. Surely, however, in most cases these people have somewhere along the way encountered a positive role model, someone who exhibited goodness and also was good to them, and thus could stimulate gratitude and admiration. In general, perhaps the best advice that can be given on how to produce moral growth in yourself is that you should hang around people who are already better than you are.

I believe that this answer is on the right track for the X-Men as well. We can certainly imagine that Xavier reflects an upbringing that nurtured a love in him for the good. We actually don't know a great deal about his upbringing. His father died when he was quite young, but he seems to have had a devoted and caring mother, and perhaps it is her loving care that has nourished a love for goodness in him. An important aspect of Xavier's school for mutants is that it is a place where the students can be accepted and loved, and thus naturally come to desire to be like those who are dedicated to helping them. Wolverine, who seems at the beginning not to have much concern for others, has suffered great evil. He too begins to change as a result of his being incorporated into a truly moral community. On the other side of the ledger, Magneto has suffered the destruction of his family at the hands of the Nazis and clearly reflects the emotional scars of horrible abuse. It is not too surprising that he finds Xavier's love to be naïve and even ridiculous. So perhaps the best account we can give of the motivation of the X-Men to the good is that they have learned to love the good as a result of a relation to those who are good.

This explanation also sheds light on Peter Parker. Although most readers naturally trace the motivation for his career as a superhero to the tragedy of his beloved Uncle Ben's murder, it's clear that this event was able to spur Peter on to good deeds and the protection of his community rather than just to mean-spirited vengefulness because of the positive moral upbringing he had enjoyed with Uncle Ben and Aunt May. They were clearly loving and caring people, and their treatment of young Peter was naturally formative for his own sensibilities and values, despite a very temporary departure from the moral high road that he took right after he acquired his powers, a serious lapse that indirectly resulted in his uncle's death.

Finding a Strong Basis for the Good

Psychologically, I believe the answer I have arrived at so far makes sense. It fits what we know about child development and moral growth. However, I am not convinced philosophically that this is all that is needed as an explanation for why we are good, or as anything like what can count as a reason to be good, either for us normal humans or for such superheroes as Spider-Man and the X-Men. A variety of problems arises out of supposing otherwise. One is that children do not only want to be like their parents; they also want to distance themselves from their parents and form their own views, and hence may have a reason to reject their parents' ideas about the good. They may grow up to read Nietzsche and decide that their parents' views are just the invention of weak people afraid of claiming their true destiny. Furthermore, no one has perfect parents; and many do not even have very good ones. There are other possible role models for the good, but not everyone is fortunate enough to have sufficient contact with such people. Even those who do have access to good role models always also have other, negative examples around that they may learn from. It's natural then to seek for a firmer, deeper reason why anyone decides to be good, and to look for a reason that could apply to anyone, not just those who have had the right kind of upbringing.

The reply that Plato has Socrates give to Glaucon in the *Republic* turns from such psychological factors to ask deep philosophical questions about the character of the human self and the kind of universe we find ourselves in. Plato wants to argue that our nature is such that in the long run, despite our current desires, we will be happier, both in this life and after death, if we live in accordance with justice by turning our attention to the good. In effect, Plato tells us that despite what may appear to be the case, morality reflects the true, deep character of the universe. Those who are committed to the good are committed to what is profoundly and eternally true. It is no accident that Plato's worldview has often been seen as religious in character. Christian writers, for example, from St. Augustine to C.S. Lewis, have often viewed his metaphysical vision of the world as fully congruent with their own faith.

Kierkegaard also believes that a religious vision is needed to give us a reason to be good. His account, like Plato's, attempts to show how such a vision fits with our psychology. As Kierkegaard sees it, moral duties in general are grounded in relationships between persons. To be a parent, or a son or daughter, or to be a citizen of a state, or to be a husband or a wife, is to be implicated in a web of mutual responsibilities. Certain obligations simply are constitutive of these kinds of relationships. So far this fits what I have said already about our reason to be good being bound up with our relationships to others. But it also goes beyond this by noting that sometimes those relations do not merely ground a love for the good, but motivate that stricter part of morality we call duty.

There are lots of actions that are good but that we do not think of as duties or consider strictly obligatory. Driving at a moderate speed is in itself a good thing to do, for example, but if there is a legal speed limit, this creates a further legal obligation to drive at a slower speed. It may be good for a man and a woman to love each other, but when they exchange marriage vows, they create further specific obligations to love each other faithfully. Kierkegaard believes not merely that it is a good thing to love our neighbors as ourselves, but that we have a duty to do so.

How could we come to have such a duty? On Kierkegaard's view, this obligation is generated the same way other types of obligations are produced: through a relationship. Only the relationship in this case is first with God, who calls us to love our neighbors as ourselves. Why should we heed the call of God? What authority does it have? For Kierkegaard, we should heed the call of God, not because God is powerful and we fear punishment, but because God is the one who loves us and has created us for eternal life with him. Just as two lovers become obligated to each other by the history of their acts together, the promises made, and the goods bestowed and gratefully received, so our own hearts are "bound infinitely" to God by our relationship to our Creator. Kierkegaard says: "But that eternal love-history has begun much earlier; it began with your beginning, when you came into existence out of nothing, and, just as surely as you do not become nothing, it does not end at a grave" (WL, p. 150).

God has created us out of nothing and bestowed upon us every good that we have. Furthermore, God has destined us for the greatest good of all, eternal life with himself, a life we cannot enjoy if we do not love the good, because God is pure goodness. If a relationship with a good person who is good to us can move us toward the good, then surely a relation to the one who is himself pure goodness and who is the source of all goods can do so. Such a relation gives all persons, not just those fortunate enough to be around other good humans, a cause and reason to be good, and, for those who understand what has been given, this relation should motivate the kind of gratitude and emulation that underlies genuine moral goodness.

As a Christian, Kierkegaard also points to Jesus as the ultimate expression of God's love. Christ is God's way of showing humans that they are accepted as they are. Even if Glaucon is right, and the truly good person will be crucified, there is hope, because the person who suffers for the good suffers as Christ did. And it is Christ who suffers with and for that person as well. For those who love Christ, even persecution may be something to rejoice over, and this gives powerful motivation for facing the double danger.

If Kierkegaard is right, then we humans do have an excellent reason for caring about the good. Our own deepest and ultimate happiness is found by following the path of neighbor love. But what light does this shed on the goodness of the X-Men? Perhaps not nearly as much as we would like. But it does point to a puzzling gap in their world. Ordinary human beings can be described as *Homo religious*, or naturally inclined toward a religious sensibility. No human culture has been found in which our deepest hopes and fears are not bound up with religious convictions and attitudes. Yet in the world of the X-Men, as well as in the world of most superheroes generally, religion is quite conspicuous by its absence. To be sure, there are some notable exceptions. But by and large religious concerns do not seem central in the worlds of the superheroes.

Do the X-Men wonder about their own deepest nature? Do they ask themselves what kind of universe it is that they inhabit? Do they consider whether they are merely meaningless collections of atoms, with no final purpose, and with no hope beyond the grave? Their deepest intuitions, elicited by the impetus of community, may be what have pointed them in the right direction, whether they have ever reflected on this issue philosophically at all. But if they begin to ask these philosophical and spiritual questions, deep in their hearts, and with all their minds, they may find answers that truly give them a reason to care about loving their neighbors, even when those neighbors do not love them in return. For they may discover that it is in loving the neighbor that they best connect with the love of the One who perfectly loves them and called them into existence for a life together with himself. In doing so, they would perhaps also be discovering their deepest destiny, the thing they most have in common with those from whom they might otherwise seem so different.[3]

---

[3] My thanks to Charles Evans, Jr., for reading this essay and making several good suggestions dealing with the superheroes.

14

With Great Power Comes Great Responsibility: On the Moral Duties of the Super-Powerful and Super-Heroic

CHRISTOPHER ROBICHAUD

Halfway through *Spider-Man 2*, Peter Parker does the unthinkable: he quits being Spider-Man. He throws in the towel, er, costume, in the hopes of salvaging what's left of his personal life, a life reduced to shambles by his exploits as a crime fighter. Peter finds that walking away from wall-crawling improves his social and academic pursuits, but not without a cost.

In the absence of Spider-Man, the crime rate in New York City rises a whopping seventy-five percent. Indeed, Peter can't even stroll down the street without encountering someone who could use Spidey's help. Pleased that his life is taking a turn for the better but troubled by the thought that he's shirking his responsibilities, a frustrated Peter Parker looks out the window of his tiny studio apartment and asks both himself and the city he once swore to protect, "What am I supposed to do?"

With Great Power Comes—*What?*

This is a good question. What should Peter Parker do? Uncle Ben famously tells his nephew that with great power comes great responsibility. But what does this mean? Does Peter have a responsibility to use his amazing powers to fight crime and offer help to those in need? Is he obligated to take up the role of Spider-Man? And what are the duties that come with this role? Must Peter always put his personal interests in thrall to it? Is it right for him to deceive his friends and family about his web-slinging escapades? How should he interact with a public that distrusts him and a city that often seeks to arrest him? And what responsibilities does he have regarding the colorful cavalcade of villains that he battles on a regular basis?

One of the things that make *Spider-Man* such compelling fiction is that it isn't afraid to show us a superhero grappling with these issues. Needless to say, though, Peter Parker isn't the only kid on the block with superpowers. Comic books have given rise to a universe chock-full of people with amazing abilities, and all of them face the same fundamental moral concerns. What should they do? Is it their duty to don a cape, or cowl, or a primary-colored spandex jumpsuit and take up the role of hero? And then, duty or not, for those who do embrace this role, what obligations do they thereby gain?

Notice that these questions aren't asking how super-powerful and super-heroic persons *do* in fact live their lives. To answer that, we don't need to look any further than the chronicles of their adventures. Rather, these questions are asking how they *ought* to live their lives. This makes them what philosophers call normative questions. And normative ethics is the branch of moral philosophy that provides us with the resources needed for answers. We'll begin our investigation, then, by examining what one of the more prominent theories within normative ethics— utilitarianism—has to say about the duties of super-powerful individuals. But first, we need to tackle two hobgoblins.

Any philosophical investigation into moral duties inevitably brings with it considerations of what is good or bad, and what is right or wrong.[1] Two extreme philosophical views would make any such investigation a waste of time. Ethical nihilism claims that moral properties just don't exist. Nothing is really good or bad, and nothing is morally right or wrong. Ethical relativists make the different claim that moral properties are always relative to a point of view, and a set of standards. On this perspective, there are no universal and objective answers to the questions we want to ask.

---

[1] Here and throughout, the normative properties I have in mind—properties having to do with value—are moral ones, to be distinguished from, say, aesthetic ones. For example, helping the poor is good and my mother's cooking is good, but only the former is good in the moral sense (saint-like though my mother is, her home cooked food does not fall into the category of things that are morally good).

Fortunately, we can reasonably dismiss these views. Philosophers who have tried to defend them have run into some notorious difficulties. And, on examination, neither of them reflects our ordinary beliefs about these matters. Most of us don't think that actions are never good or bad, nor do we think that actions are good or bad only relative to a limited perspective. On the contrary, most of us believe, for example, that Mother's Teresa's assistance to the poor was objectively good and that Hitler's policies of genocide were actually and absolutely bad. For these reasons, we won't let ethical nihilism and ethical relativism hold us back, and our discussion will just take it as given that both these views are false. Morality is real, and it's not just all relative.

Start Stitchin' That Costume, Bub. Duty Calls

Now, let's dive right in to what is perhaps one of the most famous philosophical views in history, utilitarianism. Utilitarianism is an ethical theory that comes in several shapes and sizes. Jeremy Bentham (1748–1832) and John Stuart Mill (1806–1873), its two most famous proponents, offered different versions of its specifics,[2] and contemporary utilitarians have made many further refinements. We're going to bypass a lot of these nuances, though, and focus primarily on Mill's version, or at least an interpretation of it, in what follows.

Utilitarianism builds its account of what makes an act right on its view of what makes an act good. The big picture looks like this. The rightness or wrongness of an act is determined entirely by its consequences; specifically, it's determined by the amount of goodness the act produces. Goodness, for its part, is essentially tied up with happiness, and happiness is taken as consisting both in the presence of pleasure and in the absence of pain. So the rightness or wrongness of any action is a result of the pleasure and pain it produces.

It's the *overall* happiness resulting from an action that determines its rightness or wrongness, not just the happiness produced in the person performing it. This means that the pleasures

---

[2] See Bentham's *An Introduction to the Principles of Morals and Legislation* (1789) and Mill's *Utilitarianism* (1861). Sadly, first editions of these philosophical classics are probably worth less than a mint copy of *Detective Comics* #27.

and pains brought about in all beings capable of having such experiences are taken into account when morally evaluating an action. In addition to physical pleasures, there are intellectual pleasures, emotional pleasures, artistic pleasures, and so forth— and likewise for pains. Needless to say, beings who are capable of experiencing pleasures and pains do not always have the same spectrum of experiences available to them. A cat, for example, is capable of enjoying the pleasure that results from eating fine tuna, but is incapable of enjoying the pleasure that results from reading *Watchmen*.

According to utilitarianism, then, a person does the right thing when, of all those actions available to her at the time, she chooses the one that produces the most good, which is determined by the amount of happiness that results from the action. And this is to be judged by the extent to which that action maximizes overall pleasure and minimizes overall pain.

There are several reasons to find this view appealing. Perhaps the most obvious one is that it captures what appears to be a core insight into morality, namely, that the right action in any situation—the action that ought to be taken—is the one that results in the greatest overall good. That certainly sounds correct. If given the choice between two actions that will produce different amounts of goodness, it doesn't seem as if it would ever be right to choose the one that will bring about the lesser amount. Another mark in favor of utilitarianism is that it links goodness with happiness, and happiness with the maximization of pleasure and the minimization of pain. It's quite plausible to think that good things are good to the extent that they are pleasurable and not painful. And a further appealing reason to endorse this view is that it provides a clear rule to guide our behavior: we should always act to bring about the most overall good.

Let's look at how utilitarianism works. Suppose Clark Kent faces the choice either of representing the *Daily Planet* at a press conference or of rescuing a plane that's experiencing engine failure. If he doesn't attend the conference, he'll lose his job. If the plane crashes, hundreds of people will die. What should he do? Utilitarians answer that he's obligated to perform the action that brings about the greatest overall good. Presumably, then, he ought to rescue the plane, even though that will cost him his job.

What this illustrates is that if utilitarianism is correct, we must be prepared to make difficult personal sacrifices in order to fulfill our moral duties. Of course, a run-of-the-mill reporter wouldn't have been obligated to forgo attending the conference in order to rescue a plane, as rescuing a plane wouldn't even have been an option for him. Utilitarians don't claim that we have a duty to do things we *can't* do. But they still make significant demands on us. When we face the choice of spending a hundred dollars of discretionary income on a pair of designer jeans or of donating that money to charity, these philosophers typically tell us that we're obligated to give the money away.

The theory of utilitarianism lends itself to evaluating broader courses of action. Should you be a teacher? A parent? A rocket-scientist? More relevant to our concerns here, is there a duty for anyone with the proper abilities to become a superhero? Unsurprisingly, utilitarians claim that the answers to such questions are determined by the consequences that would be brought about in virtue of adopting these various roles. On the supposition that taking up such a role is a genuine option (after all, you need a keen mind to be a rocket scientist, and super-powers—or at least very highly developed normal powers—to be a superhero), you are obligated to adopt a particular role in life if and only if doing so will bring about the greatest overall good. Needless to say, this suggests that folks with superpowers have a duty to become superheroes, since it's the very business of superheroes to promote the good of all. So now we have an answer to Peter Parker's query from *Spider-Man 2*. According to utilitarianism, he's obligated to remain our friendly neighborhood superhero. Doing so may cause him great personal pain, but this pain is outweighed by the overall good that his super-heroic activities bring to the world.

Aw, C'mon! Do I Have to Save the Day?

But there's more to the story. Utilitarianism isn't the only philosophical theory on the market, and it faces some serious objections. Can it really be true that Peter *must* be Spider-Man? Is it his duty to be a superhero even if his personal life continues to spiral downward? In general, are people with superpowers always obligated to act in a way that promotes the overall good, even if doing so comes at great personal cost? Before we accept the conclusions that utilitarianism draws, we need to look at some of its problems.

Any moral theory worth its salt is sometimes going to require us to make personal sacrifices. Utilitarianism, however, demands too much. Suppose Juggernaut is on the rampage again, and Jean Grey has been using her telekinetic powers to slow him down. Juggernaut being who he is, this has not been an easy task. Jean finds herself severely weakened. Juggernaut, in turn, seizes upon an opportunity to get her off his back by knocking a bus packed with people over the side of a bridge. Jean's abilities can bring the passengers to safety, but in her current state, she knows that rescuing them is going to cause her to undergo massive brain trauma and death. Jean no doubt will choose to save the passengers anyway. Let's grant, too, that doing so brings about the most overall good. Surely we'd all admire Jean's selfless action. The problem, however, is that utilitarians claim that Jean would've been wrong not to have sacrificed her life. And that, as philosophers say, is unintuitive. It goes against our pre-theoretical moral beliefs.

Do we really think that Jean would have deserved any serious moral blame if she had made the anguished choice to remain alive rather than to kill herself by expending the last of her mental powers? Surely not. Utilitarianism obliterates the possibility for actions to be *supererogatory*, which means above and beyond the call of duty. Supererogatory acts are acts that are good to do but not bad not to do.

A utilitarian might respond to this worry by suggesting that we shouldn't have assumed that Jean's saving of the passengers would in fact bring about the most good. After all, if Jean were to die saving them, she'd never again be able to save any other lives. And certainly there will be countless people who need to be saved in the future. So if it's the production of the most overall good that we're after, we ought to conclude that Jean shouldn't sacrifice herself for the sake of the passengers. This response, however, poses just as serious a problem for the utilitarian as the one she is trying to address, for now she's committed to claiming that Jean is obligated not to save the passengers. But just as it seems inappropriate to find Jean blameworthy for saving her own life in the situation, so it would seem at least as inappropriate to find her blameworthy for sacrificing her life. Imagine criticizing such selflessness! The bottom line here is that our intuitions tell us that the choice of sacrificing herself to save the lives of the passengers, and the alternative of sparing her own life by regretfully letting the passengers die are both permissible actions available to Jean, and utilitarianism simply lacks the resources needed to capture such intuitions about supererogatory acts.

A related problem is that utilitarianism forces us to choose actions that oppose the very core of our character.[3] Consider the following situation. Wonder Woman once more finds herself battling Ares, and the god of war has really outdone himself this time. He confronts her with a little girl and tells her that if she doesn't kill this child, he'll set in motion a global biological war sure to doom millions. Let's grant that Ares is telling the truth and that Wonder Woman cannot, despite her best efforts, stop him any other way. Needless to say, killing little girls runs contrary to everything Wonder Woman stands for. But utilitarianism would demand that she take the girl's life, for clearly that's the act that will bring about the greatest overall good. Wonder Woman, according to this view, would be doing the wrong thing if she spared the child's life. But our intuitions suggest just the opposite: She would be doing something terribly wrong if she killed this innocent child. Again, utilitarianism delivers a judgment that we intuitively reject.

Another problem with a utilitarian philosophy is its handling of justice. In *The Joker: Devil's Advocate*, Joker finds himself on death row.[4] But, wouldn't you know it, he's been found guilty of a crime this time that he didn't commit. We can all agree that letting Joker nonetheless die would bring about a greater overall good than rescuing him from this odd situation. Innumerable future killing sprees on his part would thereby be avoided. But Batman knows that Joker didn't commit this crime, and he has the evidence to prove it. Should he let Joker die for a crime he didn't commit? Utilitarians will say he should. But doing so would clearly be unjust, and no one ought to do what's unjust. Batman knows this, and refuses to let his wicked nemesis be executed on false grounds.

---

[3] This criticism is due to Bernard Williams. See J.J.C. Smart and Bernard Williams, ed., *Utilitarianism: For and Against* (Cambridge: Cambridge University Press, 1973), pp. 93–100.

[4] *The Joker: Devil's Advocate*, by Chuck Dixon and Graham Nolan (New York: DC Comics, 1996).

A remaining issue to raise against utilitarianism concerns its complete emphasis on the consequences of actions. Once more, this leads to unintuitive results. Suppose the Green Goblin decides to grab Spider-Man's attention by terrorizing pedestrians. Speeding along on his bat glider, he spots an appropriate target walking down Fifth Avenue. Lassoing this man with a cable, Green Goblin pulls him along behind the glider as he streaks up and down the street, cackling maniacally all the time. As it turns out, the man is a disgruntled dishwasher who was on his way to the restaurant that employs him, where he planned to unload his handgun on an unsuspecting group of diners. Not only does the Goblin's action interrupt this nefarious plot from unfolding, but the experience so traumatizes the deranged man that, after Spider-Man comes on the scene and frees him, he abandons his murderous plan, destroys his gun, and signs up for an anger-management course. As it stands, then, Green Goblin did something that brought about a greater overall good than if he had just left this man alone. His action prevented twenty or more lives from being taken. So did he do the right thing? Utilitarians are forced by their view to answer in the affirmative. But surely that's not correct. Dragging this man around Fifth Avenue with the intention of traumatizing him and baiting Spider-Man is wrong, even if doing so unintentionally produces great good.

I'm a Lover, Not a Fighter!

These considerations show that utilitarianism faces some formidable obstacles in its attempt to provide us with a viable ethical theory. Of course, many gifted philosophers inclined towards utilitarianism continue to develop arguments in response to the sorts of objections we've raised. But the problems we've highlighted certainly justify us in looking for a different moral framework with which to analyze our question of what superpowerful persons ought to do. So let's explore instead the main alternative available to us in moral theory, a broadly nonconsequentialist ethical stance.

Nonconsequentialist theories, true to their name, deny that the moral worth of actions is determined entirely by their consequences. Kantianism is the most famous of these, and it goes so far as to claim that the consequences of actions don't matter at all in determining their moral worth. The great philosopher Immanuel Kant (1724–1804) maintained that our fundamental duty is to act in a way that satisfies what he called "the categorical imperative," one formulation of which states that we are always to treat persons as ends in themselves and not merely as means.[5] This comes down to something like always respecting people as having intrinsic value, and never just using them for our own purposes, as if they had just instrumental value. But Kant also emphasized that performing an action in accordance with the categorical imperative is not enough to make it good. Crucially, the action must also be done for the right reasons; that is, you must do it precisely because it's your duty to do it. On this view, then, our intentions are crucially relevant to the moral worth of what we do. So if an action treats individuals as ends in themselves and not merely as means to attaining further ends, and if a person performs that action because she intends to follow her duty by acting in a way that treats people appropriately, then her action is good, regardless of its consequences.

Most contemporary nonconsequentialists aren't strict Kantians, but all take their lead from Kant's system, and we'll follow suit. Our immediate concern is to determine what a nonconsequentialist perspective has to say about the obligations of folks with superpowers. Does it require them to be superheroes, as utilitarianism does?

Let's begin to answer this question by attending to an important distinction that some nonconsequentialists make between positive and negative duties. Positive duties are obligations to do things that aid people, like tending to the ill or feeding the poor. Negative duties, in contrast, are obligations to refrain from doing things that harm people, like maliciously lying to, or assaulting, an innocent person. They are constraints on our actions. Fulfillment of our positive and negative duties is one way to flesh out the Kantian idea of treating people as ends in themselves and not merely as means. In particular, by fulfilling our positive duties, we treat people as ends in themselves (we show them respect), and by fulfilling our negative duties, we avoid treating them merely as means (we refrain from simply

---

[5] See Kant's *Groundwork on the Metaphysics of Morals* (1785), translated by Mary Gregor (Cambridge: Cambridge University Press, 1997).

using them). And just as Kant put more of an emphasis on the importance of not treating individuals merely as means than he did on the importance of treating them as ends in themselves, so nonconsequentialists who subscribe to the distinction between negative and positive duties put more of an emphasis on negative duties than on positive ones.

To see what this amounts to, suppose that Doctor Doom has left two badly wounded people in the wake of his most recent attack against The Fantastic Four. Reed Richards, a.k.a., Mr. Fantastic, can save their lives with one of the many wonderful devices he's built, but these poor people are in such bad shape that he needs certain vital internal organs in order to do so. Is he permitted to kill a nearby pedestrian and use her organs to heal Doom's victims? If a utilitarian were to answer this question, she would say that not only is Mr. Fantastic permitted to kill the pedestrian, he's obligated to do so since, all else being equal, saving the two lives in this case promotes more good than not taking the one life. But our intuitions tell us that Reed Richards most assuredly is not permitted to do this. And the nonconsequentialist agrees. Since negative duties are stronger than positive duties, we are prohibited from fulfilling our positive duties by violating our negative duties. So Mr. Fantastic isn't permitted to violate his negative duty not to kill an innocent person in order to fulfill a positive duty to heal the wounded.

One important upshot of this is that nonconsequentialists often don't come down on one action over another if it turns out that it's not possible to perform both of them, but doing either would satisfy some positive duties while not violating any negative ones. In such a situation, either action is permissible. With that in mind, let's return to the case that began our discussion. On the plausible assumption that no negative duties are violated either by Peter Parker's choosing to be Spider-Man or by his choosing not to be Spider-Man, and assuming that either choice will allow him to satisfy some positive duties (helping people, for example, by doing the things that superheroes do, or alternately by investing his energies in medically beneficial scientific research), nonconsequentialists will conclude that both options are allowable.

Peter, of course, opts to be Spider-Man. Presuming that he does so with proper intentions, nonconsequentialists will go on to claim that his choice is not only permissible, but is good. Had he chosen not to be Spider-Man, though, he wouldn't have done anything wrong. Indeed, presuming that he made this contrary choice with the right intentions, a decision not to be Spider-Man could also have been good.

According to this perspective, opting to be a superhero is a supererogatory act, one that goes beyond the call of duty. Nonconsequentialists, therefore, don't think that folks with superpowers are obligated to serve the world as superheroes. This means that if Peter wants to hang up his costume to pursue science and the love of his life, Mary Jane, he's permitted to do so. And if Clark Kent wants to give up his powers to be with Lois Lane—a choice he faces in *Superman II*—then that, too, is permissible.

This is as it should be. After all, we think that part of what makes the superheroes heroic is that they don't have to do what they do. It's permissible for them to live ordinary lives. Their choosing to do otherwise is what makes their actions that much more praiseworthy. The great responsibility that comes with their great power isn't a duty to use that power as a superhero, it's at most an obligation not to harm others by misusing it.

An interesting question, though, still remains. For those who do choose to take up the role of a superhero, how should they conduct themselves? We already know that it's the business of superheroes to fight crime, to help the helpless, and to protect people from the twisted machinations of supervillains. Superheroes aggressively pursue these noble tasks, even at great risk to themselves. But they also often behave in ways that might not be morally appropriate. And this is a matter we need to explore further.

I Fought the Law and the Law Won

One issue worth investigating is how superheroes, in their pursuit of criminals, ought to interact with law enforcement agencies. Needless to say, there is at best a relationship of convenience between most costumed crusaders and the police officers who protect the same neighborhoods that they watch over. Batman, for example, though mistrusted by many on the Gotham police force, has an ally in Lieutenant (later Commissioner) Gordon. As a result, he is able to work with the authorities to apprehend criminals. But his methods still raise questions.

Gotham's police officers are legally bound by certain rules. They are prohibited from searching people's homes without legal warrants, from using physical intimidation tactics to gain information, and from arresting people without having evidence against them or without reading them their rights. But Batman isn't a police officer. He doesn't get warrants before crashing into criminals' lairs, he uses physical intimidation tactics all the time to gather information, he often apprehends criminals without having legally sufficient evidence against them, and he surely doesn't read them their rights. Should Batman be doing these things?

It could be argued that Batman's procedures result in a lot of good. And there's no doubt about that. But as we've learned from our examination of utilitarianism, a course of action that produces the most overall good still might be the wrong thing to do. Indeed, building on our discussion of nonconsequentialism, it seems reasonable that police officers are bound to act under certain constraints because the law in this case reflects our negative duties. We all have a negative duty not to barge into people's homes without good reason, not to intimidate them physically, and not to apprehend them without appropriate cause. Acting otherwise would not just be illegal, it would also be immoral. In the absence, then, of circumstances that might override these duties (and most nonconsequentialists maintain that negative duties can be overridden under some conditions), Batman ought to amend his crime-fighting tactics. And so it goes for all superheroes.

But this might come as just too much of a shock. We could easily be tempted to argue that just as super-powerful people can reasonably be thought to take on special obligations when they opt to be superheroes, they also gain special privileges. After all, people who adopt other exalted roles in society sometimes gain privileges by doing so. In Washington D.C., for example, members of Congress are exempt from receiving traffic tickets if they break traffic laws while on official government business. Foreign ambassadors likewise have important forms of diplomatic immunity to arrest and prosecution. So perhaps superheroes, given their extraordinary talents and their willingness to take on perilous risks in their pursuit of criminals, ought to be exempt from some of the laws that bind ordinary officers of the law.

This way of thinking is flawed for two reasons. First, police officers also take on perilous risks in their efforts to fight crime and help people. Superheroes shouldn't gain special exemptions for that reason, then, unless we think that police officers should as well. But, of course, we don't think that. We would therefore need to justify exempting superheroes but not police officers from normal constraints by appealing to the fact that superheroes have greater powers than police officers do. But power alone doesn't justify special legal treatment, for laws are meant to bind both the weak and the mighty. Second, and even more important, the privileges being considered aren't just exemptions from legal duties, they're exemptions from moral ones. And that's a crucial difference.

Let's acknowledge that what's moral and what's legal don't always coincide. Jaywalking is illegal, but not immoral, and lying to a friend is immoral, but not illegal. Often, however, what's moral and what's legal do coincide. Murdering someone is both immoral and illegal. Keeping this in mind, exemptions from some laws might be permissible if those laws don't express our negative duties, which, recall, are the most important moral duties we have. The immunity to traffic tickets granted to members of Congress under certain circumstances is one such example, since exempting persons from traffic laws is not exempting them from their negative duties. But an exemption is not permissible if the law in question does in fact convey relevant negative duties. That's because it's the essence of negative duties that they apply to *all* people, regardless of their roles in society. And as we already agreed, the laws that police officers must obey in pursuing criminals are laws that do reflect their negative duties: it's not just illegal to beat up a person during questioning, it's immoral. So although it might be permissible to exempt Superman from no-fly zone laws, or Batman from traffic laws (the Batmobile goes pretty fast), it is impermissible to exempt them from laws that reflect basic negative duties.

A related topic of interest has to do with the responsibilities superheroes have towards police forces that seek to arrest them. Poor Spidey, misunderstood as he so often is, finds himself pursued time and again by the NYPD. Sometimes this is just for questioning, but other times there's a warrant out for his arrest. Peter chooses to evade the police on such occasions. He figures that either the charges will be dropped once the actual criminals

involved are apprehended—a task he then sets about performing himself—or that the charges are politically motivated and
will be dropped anyway in due course. And let's suppose he's
right. Nonetheless, is evading arrest permissible?

Doing as Peter does seems to display a rather cavalier attitude toward the state and the entire institution of law. Peter, like
the rest of us, is a citizen of his country and therefore subject to
its authority. And as Socrates so eloquently argues in Plato's dialogue, *Crito*, all of us have a *moral* duty as citizens to yield to
this authority.[6] Of course, there are obvious circumstances in
which this duty is overridden, such as when the laws of the state
are immoral or when its authorities are corrupt. But Peter does-
n't evade arrest because he thinks that the police who are pursuing him are corrupt or that the laws he's accused of breaking
are immoral. He knows that he's been wrongly accused, but this
fact alone doesn't warrant him in thumbing his nose at the
authorities. It seems to be his obligation in these situations to
yield to arrest and then to pursue appropriate legal means of
exoneration. And for that, he can turn to a great attorney like
Matt Murdock.

We've ignored, however, an important response available to
superheroes in defense of their evasive tactics. Should they be
captured, the thought goes, they would be forced to compromise their secret identities. And those who opt to be superheroes have good reasons to keep the public ignorant of their
real identities. As they themselves rightly point out, were their
enemies to learn who they really are, these villains would stop
at nothing to terrorize, perhaps even kill, their family and
friends, either for the purposes of simple revenge, or else for
leverage to block their interfering actions as superheroes. So by
acquiescing to the authorities in situations in which they've
been falsely accused, not only do superheroes jeopardize the
lives of their loved ones, they also jeopardize their ability to
continue serving as superheroes. This being the case, the serious consequences that would come about from the world
learning that, say, Peter Parker is Spider-Man do warrant his
evading arrest.

---

[6] Translated by Hugh Tredennick in *The Collected Works of Plato*, edited by
Edith Hamilton and Huntington Cairns (Princeton: Princeton University Press,
1980).

This position is perfectly consistent with nonconsequentialism, or at least its non-Kantian varieties (since Kant himself couldn't abide a lie of any sort). Nonconsequentialists, after all, don't claim that consequences *never* matter in determining the permissibility of actions. They simply claim that consequences aren't the only things that matter.

But It's Just a White Lie!

The topic of secret identities brings us to the last of the issues we'll be examining. We've acknowledged that superheroes have good reasons to keep the public ignorant of their true identities. But does the same hold true concerning their families and friends? Superheroes don't usually deny outright that they've adopted the role they have, if for no other reason than because their families and friends don't typically confront them with such questions. Their loved ones do, however, often ask them where they've been and what they've been doing. And this is when superheroes often choose to lie and engage in other deceptive strategies (withholding the truth, allowing false inferences to be made, and the like). But is it permissible for them to deceive the very people they care about the most?

Kant maintained that our negative duty not to lie is absolute and cannot be violated. Whether he felt the same is true for other cases of deception is less clear. Regardless, most nonconsequentialists take a more flexible approach. We can easily imagine cases where our duty not to deceive is trumped by other considerations. Take the case of good-hearted Aunt May. Peter fears that telling her he's Spider-Man would cause her irreparable harm. She just wouldn't be able to handle the news; indeed, learning of her nephew's exploits might literally kill her with worry. In such a situation, it is surely permissible for him to deceive her. One could look at this as a resolvable conflict between two negative duties. Peter has a duty not to deceive his aunt, but he also has a duty not to cause her serious physical harm. The latter duty is intuitively more important than the former, and so he's permitted to deceive the sweet old lady.

But other cases of deception aren't so clear. Clark Kent loves Lois Lane. Is he permitted to keep her ignorant of his role as Superman? (Let's ignore the fact that in *Superman II,* he does tell her that he's Superman, only to wipe out her memory of his

identity by the end of the film, without even so much as seeking her approval before doing so. Yikes!) Clark might reason
that if he tells Lois the truth, his enemies most likely will somehow learn his secret identity and her life will therefore be put in
danger. Peter Parker reasons in this same way when justifying to
himself why he shouldn't tell Mary Jane that he's Spider-Man. So
Clark has a duty not to deceive the woman he loves, but he also
has a duty not to put her life in danger. The latter duty is more
important than the former, and hence Clark is permitted not to
tell Lois the truth about who he is.

But does telling Lois that he's Superman really put her life in
danger? Admittedly, were the public to learn his secret identity,
Lois's life would clearly be endangered. But how does telling
her the truth result in the same threat? There can seem to be an
implicit and disturbing assumption going on that Lois can't keep
a secret—or, in other words, that telling her is equivalent to
telling the world. Peter seems to make this same assumption
about MJ. But surely the women these men love ought to be
trusted in their discretion more than this.

Perhaps, though, there is another harm that Clark and Peter
can point to in justifying their deception. Clark may know Lois
well enough to realize that, despite her tough façade and professional daring, she would simply worry about him too much
if she knew his true identity. As long as she just thinks of him
as ordinary Clark Kent, she doesn't have to be constantly on the
lookout for Kryptonite when they're together, or always be wondering what new nefarious scheme Lex Luthor has up his sleeve.
Peter also may have wanted to spare MJ the worry that when he
swings out the window, he'll never return. The idea is that
Clark's duty and Peter's duty to avoid inflicting long-term psychological harm on their loved ones outweighs their duty to tell
them the truth about who they are. But as well-meaning as this
thought might be, it just doesn't hold up. It's more than a bit
patronizing of Clark and Peter to assume that the women in
their lives couldn't learn to live with their roles as superheroes.
Not telling them the truth fails to treat them with the proper
respect they are owed as persons. Superheroes, therefore, have
a duty in such cases, just like the rest of us, to tell the people
they love who they really are.

We've seen that individuals with superpowers face many
important ethical questions, and we've done our best to suggest

some answers. Having great power does not obligate a person to become a superhero, but should such an individual choose to adopt this role, there are many responsibilities that come with it. In addition to fighting crime and helping those in need, our super-guardian must also adopt the same standards that the police conform to, and should acquiesce to their authority when it's appropriate. And such a person must also be willing to trust their closest loved ones with the truth. Needless to say, these are but a handful of the ongoing issues that superheroes face. And our discussion, like most philosophical examinations, has reached tentative conclusions at best. But that's the most we should expect. After all, we're not superheroes.

15

Why Be a Superhero?
Why Be Moral?

C. STEPHEN LAYMAN

Would you like to be a superhero? Don't answer too quickly! Of course, there is something very attractive about those special powers. Most of us would love to amaze our friends, bag some bad guys, make the world a bit safer, and become famous in the bargain. But first thoughts are apt to be superficial. I want to explore the question, "Why be a superhero?" using insights from the original film *Spider-Man*. I'll suggest that, as it turns out, the simple question, "Why be a superhero?" is one of the great, classic philosophical questions in disguise.

The Problem for Spider-Man

The film *Spider-Man* depicts a moral world, chock full of good and evil. There are plenty of small-time bad guys as well as a world-class villain, the Green Goblin. And from the very beginning of the film, the characters of Uncle Ben and Aunt May stand out as clear examples of moral virtue—honest people you can trust, people who care about others, people with a strong sense of right and wrong.

When a genetically designed spider bites the young, academically inclined Peter Parker, he acquires astonishing new powers overnight. Using these new powers, Peter easily defeats the school bully—the athletic Flash Thompson—to the amazement of their fellow students. And almost immediately, he is tempted to use his powers for very self-interested purposes. In order to buy a sports car to impress Mary Jane, the girl of his dreams, Peter enters a wrestling contest for a prize of three thousand dollars. He wins the match, but the wrestling promoter pays him only one hundred dollars, claiming unfairly that Peter won too quickly. Peter responds, "But I need that money," to which the promoter retorts, "I missed the part where that's my problem." Peter leaves in frustration, and within moments, an armed bandit robs the promoter and, in making his getaway, runs right past our newly empowered young man. Peter understands what's going on, but does nothing to stop it, and the robber gets away. The promoter is furious: "You could have taken that guy apart! Now he's gonna get away with *my* money." But Peter calmly savors his revenge, responding, "I missed the part where that's my problem."

The entire incident vividly raises the classic philosophical question, "Why be moral?" Why do the right thing, especially in a world where other people so often don't? Why should Peter help the wrestling promoter, who has just cheated him out of two thousand and nine hundred dollars? Why not use his special powers only when doing so serves his own personal advantage? Why be a superhero, making sacrifices and taking risks for others? What's the reason? Where's the payoff?

Of course, Peter's Uncle Ben had already delivered that memorable line, "With great power comes great responsibility." But is it indeed so? After all, with great power comes a great opportunity to satisfy your wants and desires, and this suggests an alternative slogan: "With great power comes great personal satisfaction." Perhaps the idea of being a superhero loses much of its attractiveness if more power carries with it a proportionally greater burden of moral obligation. Why be a superhero, using your powers to help those in need, when you could have a super *life*, using those powers for your own advantage and the benefit of friends and family?

In any case, if we agree that, "With great power comes great responsibility," then, "Why be a superhero?" seems to be a thinly disguised version of one of the all-time classic philosophical questions, "Why be moral?" The traditional superhero is, after all, committed to promoting good and fighting evil. He is dedicated to seeing justice prevail over injustice, and this is the core concern of morality as a whole.

Spider-Man not only raises the question, "Why be moral?", it also suggests some answers—at least two. I want to explore those possibilities and also consider some other answers given by philosophers down through history.

Phony Answers

Are there good reasons to be moral? Do the strongest reasons that we have to act in one way rather than another always favor doing our moral duty? Most good people normally assume a "yes" answer to this question. If we find someone's behavior odd, but then become convinced she was doing her duty, we are usually satisfied that her behavior was fully rational after all. Ethical theorists also normally assume that the strongest reasons always favor doing our duty. After all, the institution of morality lacks the authority of rationality if the strongest reasons *do not* always favor doing our duty. We humans generally seem to have a tendency to believe that the strongest or overriding reasons always support doing what's morally required.

Because of this tendency, some philosophers have defined "moral reasons" simply as "strongest or overriding reasons." But this is certainly not a definition that appears in any dictionary, and the connection between "moral reason" and "strongest reason" does not seem to be necessary, for we can imagine situations in which moral reasons do not appear to be the strongest. Here's an admittedly far-fetched situation, just to establish the principle: What if we somehow *knew* that there is an all-powerful but malevolent Deity who delights in making morally virtuous people eternally miserable after death, while perversely rewarding the morally wicked with endless happiness? In such a literally *demoralizing* situation, it seems clear that moral reasons would not be the strongest. Under these conditions, simple self-interest would counsel avoiding the everlasting punishment of this evil Deity, and this would presumably trump any conflicting reason you might have to be moral.

Of course, we want to know what the situation is in the actual world, the world in which we live. In particular, we want to know whether the strongest reasons for acting in one way rather than another always support doing those things that have traditionally been understood to be morally right or good. For example, do the strongest reasons always favor refraining from murder, theft, adultery, and punishing the innocent? Do the strongest reasons always support keeping our promises, telling the truth, acting fairly, and helping those in dire need (when morality tells us we are required to do these things)? If the answer were, "No," then it would sometimes be irrational or unreasonable to do our moral duty—in the sense that doing our duty would then involve acting on the weaker reasons in a situation involving alternative possibilities. And if the strongest reasons sometimes backed immoral actions, then the system of traditional morality, taken as a whole, would be called into question. Why indeed would we then want to be moral?

Reasons to Be Moral

The *Spider-Man* narrative presents us with reasons to be moral. The first reason has to do with the consequences of not being moral. Go back to the scene involving the robber who has just stolen a bag of cash from the wrestling promoter. Peter could easily block the robber's escape and apprehend him, and surely this would be the right thing to do. But he doesn't do it. He is understandably angry at the promoter, who has cheated him, and he lets his desire for revenge get the best of him, and fails in his moral duty. The robber escapes and hijacks a car, fatally shooting the driver. The driver of that car turns out to be Peter's beloved Uncle Ben. Now, this narrative-sequence suggests a reason to be moral—call it "Reason One":

> **REASON ONE:** If you fail to do your moral duty, there will be negative consequences that affect you, directly or indirectly.

The phrase "negative consequences" is admittedly vague, so let me sharpen it up a bit. If the negative consequences are minor (such as a literal or figurative slap on the wrist), they won't provide a good enough reason to be moral. So, the negative consequences must be *countervailing*, that is, they must be more than enough to offset whatever you would gain by not doing your duty. Also, the negative consequences here are not supposed to be negative merely from the *moral* point of view, such as a loss of moral integrity. Rather, they must involve types of suffering or loss we would wish to avoid even if we were otherwise unconcerned about morality. In short, Reason One tells us that we will never advance our self-interest, overall, by doing something morally wrong.

Unfortunately, Reason One is questionable, for at least two reasons. First, there at least seem to be cases in which, if you fail to do your moral duty, no countervailing negative consequences occur. Consider the following case:

The Case of Ms. Poore, who lives just a few miles from Peter and his aunt May. Ms. Poore has lived many years in grinding poverty. She is not starving or homeless, but has only the bare necessities. She has tried repeatedly to get ahead by hard work, but to no avail. An opportunity to steal a large sum of money arises. If Ms. Poore takes the money and invests it wisely, she can obtain many desirable things her poverty has denied her: for example, a college education that would enable her to get a job that is personally rewarding and pays well. The stolen money can solve other problems too, such as outstanding debts, substandard housing, inadequate heat in winter, unreliable transportation, lack of funds for vacations and amusements, and so on. In addition, if she steals the money, her chances of being caught are extremely low and she knows this. She is also aware that the person who owns the money is well off and will not be greatly harmed by the theft. Let's add that, at this point, Ms. Poore reasonably believes that if she leaves this money alone, she will likely live in burdensome poverty for the remainder of her life. In short, she thinks she faces the choice of stealing the money or staying in a terrible situation for the rest of her life. Ms. Poore has a moral duty *not* to steal the money, and yet if she does steal it, there will apparently be no countervailing negative consequences.[1]

A second problem with Reason One is also illustrated by this story: There seem to be cases in which, if you *do* your moral duty, the consequences for you will be more negative than positive, all things considered. After all, if Ms. Poore takes the moral high ground and doesn't steal the money, she will in all likeli-

---

[1] This case is borrowed in its essentials from an article of mine, "God and the Moral Order," *Faith and Philosophy* 19:3 (July 2002), pp. 304–316. Throughout this chapter I am making use of key ideas initially developed in that article. Incidentally, the case here does not presuppose that stealing is *always* wrong. Most moralists will grant that stealing is morally permissible in extreme cases— for example, suppose that (a) I have a child who will die unless she receives expensive medical treatment and that (b) stealing is the *only* way for me to obtain the funds needed to pay for the treatment. However, our case here does not contain such extreme elements.

hood live a life of desperate poverty, and what in the consequences of being moral would offset that? There is, apparently, nothing.

The Case of Ms. Poore suggests a general principle: *If prudence (self-interest) and moral duty conflict, and if the results of behaving immorally are relatively minor while the results of behaving imprudently are momentous, then the moral reasons do not override the prudential reasons.* And, given this principle, Reason One does not seem to be an adequate answer to the question, "Why be moral?" Even if being moral is often or usually in our self-interest, the case we've looked at suggests that being moral might not always be in a person's self-interest.

So, Reason One is not fully convincing. But *Spider-Man* suggests at least one other reason to be moral. In the midst of a fierce struggle with the Green Goblin, Spider-Man is temporarily paralyzed with a chemical spray. Thus rendered helpless, he is interrogated by the Green Goblin, who scornfully demands to know the reasons behind his super-heroism: "In spite of everything you've done for them, eventually they will hate you. Why bother?" Spider-Man, though desperate and in agony, answers:

REASON TWO: Because it is right.

As applied to the broader question, "Why be moral?" this would amount to the answer, "Because being moral is right." Now, this may seem too simple, but some great philosophers, such as Immanuel Kant (1724–1804) and F.H. Bradley (1846–1924), have taken it very seriously. The basic idea is this: We cannot get people to do their moral duty by appealing to their self-interest, since if they do the right thing for merely self-interested reasons, they are not really acting morally at all. We must do the right thing because it's right, and not for some sort of self-interested reward.

This seems to capture the apparent motivation of most superheroes. Spider-Man isn't out there protecting people from self-interested motives. Neither, for that matter, is Daredevil, or Wonder Woman, or Flash, or Green Lantern. The classic superheroes are on the job because they think it's a good thing to do, and not because they think it's going to bring them self-interested benefits.

Nevertheless, it is pretty clear that Reason Two does not provide an ultimately satisfying answer to the question, "Why be moral?" No doubt, we should do the right thing because it's right and not just in order to obtain a narrowly self-interested reward. But what if, in a given case, we have stronger reasons to do the wrong thing? Then doing the right thing would be irrational. And it would be demoralizing to live in a universe in which we could be fully moral only by being irrational. So, while we should do what's right because it's right, we need to be assured that in doing so, we are not being irrational.

Now, let's try to get our bearings. We can do this by contrasting Reasons One and Two with some different reasons offered by prominent figures in the history of philosophy: specifically, Plato and Aristotle. To our question "Why be moral?" Plato gave the following answer:

> **REASON THREE:** Doing your duty is the only way you can have harmony in your soul (roughly, peace of mind).

According to Plato, a person's soul consists of reason, the appetites, and what he called "the spirited element." Reason includes the conscience, that faculty or inner ability through which, in most situations, we know what's right and wrong. The appetites are bodily desires for such things as food, drink, and sex. Through the spirited element, we are competitive or willing to strive and struggle. For Plato, reason (hence, conscience) must govern the soul, otherwise the soul will be disordered and lacking in harmony. So, harmony of soul (or peace of mind) is possible only if we are moral.[2]

Plato's answer may work for some morally upright people. Because such people have a well-formed conscience, they feel very guilty whenever they violate what their conscience has told them, perhaps flagellating themselves endlessly for even relatively minor moral infractions. After his uncle's death, Peter Parker seems to have a new sensitivity to what his conscience tells him. Like many other superheroes, whenever he's attracted to the idea of abandoning his responsibilities, the inner turmoil of a guilty conscience eventually gets him back on track. He

---

[2] *Plato's Republic*, translated by G.M.A. Grube (Indianapolis: Hackett, 1974), pp. 98–104.

can't feel right in his own soul unless he's out doing good in the world.

But to test Plato's answer, we have to consider two kinds of cases. First, we have to consider people who do not have a strong moral formation, happy-go-lucky types who seem not to approach life from a dominantly moral perspective. Think of Peter Parker's classmate, Flash Thompson, or so many of his fellow students, immersed as they are in superficial amusements. It's not clear that these folks can have peace of mind only by doing their duty at all times. For them, peace of mind can apparently be achieved by assigning conscience a relatively minor role. Second, we have to consider the types of cases that test even morally upright people. Don't all morally upright people give in to temptation at some point in their lives? Perhaps they are selfish with their money on occasion, or they fail to stand up for what's right when doing so would be dangerous or unpopular. Now, many of us have done such things, and we aren't proud of it, but we may see no point in berating ourselves forever. We forgive ourselves and get on with life, and in this way achieve substantial peace of mind. Thus, it's far from clear that Plato's answer really works.[3]

Some moral theorists such as Aristotle emphasize character traits, virtues and vices, rather than duties in their account of morality. The virtues include such traits as being wise, just, moderate, and courageous. The vices include such traits as being foolish, unjust, immoderate, and cowardly. From Aristotle's point of view, the good life for a human being is a life lived in accordance with virtue.[4] This approach to ethics suggests the following reason for being moral:

> **REASON FOUR:** Virtue is its own reward; that is, having a good moral character (having the virtues) is necessarily a greater benefit to you

---

[3] My comments on Plato's reason for being moral owe a debt to Peter Singer, *Practical Ethics* (London: Cambridge University Press, 1979), pp. 201–220.

[4] *The Ethics of Aristotle: The Nichomachean Ethics*, translated by J.A.K. Thomson (London: Penguin, 1953). For an insightful collection of essays on virtue ethics, see Roger Crisp and Michael Slote, eds., *Virtue Ethics* (Oxford: Oxford University Press, 1997). In the introductory essay, the editors note that Aristotle "can be understood to be saying that there is *nothing* worth having in life except the exercise of the virtues" (p. 2).

than any benefit you might obtain at the expense of your good moral character.

Now, I do not doubt that moral virtue is a benefit to those who possess it. But the suggestion that *perfect* virtue is *necessarily* a great enough benefit to its possessor to compensate fully for any loss it might entail strikes me as implausible. Consider the following brief thought experiment:

> The Strange Case of Norm Osborne and Arachnid-Girl. Imagine that Norm Osborne is a morally dubious individual who happens to be widely regarded as a paragon of virtue. He is admired by most people, is very prosperous, is loved by family and friends, and enjoys life a great deal. Arachnid-Girl, by contrast, is a copy-cat, or copy-bug, who has sought to emulate Spider-Man in every respect. Imagine that she is genuinely virtuous—honest, just, and pure in heart. Unfortunately, because of some clever enemies, Arachnid-Girl is widely regarded as extremely wicked, diabolically clever, and very dangerous. She is in prison for life on false charges. Even her family and friends, convinced that she is guilty, have turned against her. Her life in prison is lonely, dreary, and unrewarding.[5]

Which of these two people is better off? Which is more fulfilled? To all appearances, it is Norm Osborne, not the virtuous Arachnid-Girl. And note that even if virtue is of value for its own sake, it isn't the *only* thing of value. In particular, freedom is valuable too. Suppose the corrupt warden agrees to release Arachnid-Girl if (but only if) she commits one morally wrong act. Perhaps she can help the warden cover up an injustice that he has committed—not an injustice that caused a great deal of harm, but one that would cost him his job if it were known. (Maybe the warden has engaged in inappropriate favoritism toward prisoners he likes.) Now, it certainly appears that it is in Arachnid-Girl's long-term best interest to act immorally in this sort of case. The choice, as in the Ms. Poore Case, is roughly between a moral stance that perpetuates life-long misery and a

---

[5] This thought experiment is borrowed in its essentials from Richard Taylor, "Value and the Origin of Right and Wrong," in Louis Pojman, ed., *Ethical Theory: Classical and Contemporary Readings* (Belmont: Wadsworth, 1989), pp. 115–121.

single action that is immoral but does not produce major harm, and that has the unusual side-effect of resulting in great good for the person doing it. So, it does not seem *necessarily* true that the rewards of perfect virtue compensate for the rewards of wrongdoing; nor does it seem necessaril*y* true that being perfectly virtuous is in everyone's long-term best interest. And thus, "Virtue is its own reward" is not by itself a convincing answer to the question, "Why be moral?"

In It for the Long Run

So far our discussion has avoided some of the deeper questions that philosophers sometimes explore concerning the big picture for life in this world. In particular, we haven't yet raised an issue that many philosophers of the past have thought of as crucially relevant to the question we are seeking to answer. What I have in mind is the possibility of life after death, a topic often broached in comic-book superhero stories. From various religious and philosophical perspectives, this idea has played a key role in answering the question, "Why be moral?" We can give a generic version of the answer as follows:

> REASON FIVE: Being moral always pays in the long run, where "the long run" includes life after death.

Traditional theists—believers in a perfect God—generally accept Reason Five. A perfectly good God clearly would not set up a moral order that ultimately penalizes virtue and moral action. And an all-powerful Deity is able to raise people from the dead, recreating us and providing us with a life after death. So, even if being virtuous does not always pay in this Earthly life for Peter Parker, or you, or anyone else, if such a God exists, then this very God can ensure that no one is ever penalized for being virtuous in the long run, where "the long run" includes life after death. In addition, from the theistic perspective, to act immorally is to sin; to sin is to alienate oneself from God; and it is never in one's long term best interests to alienate oneself from the Creator of all. In short, if a perfectly good and all-powerful God exists, it is never in anyone's long-term best interests to be immoral.

The Eastern doctrines of reincarnation and karma also amount to an endorsement of Reason Five. If reincarnation occurs, then after one dies, one's soul enters another body, and so one lives another life—a life after death, not in heaven, but on Earth. According to the doctrine of karma, one's degree of moral virtue determines one's circumstances in the next life: *The more virtuous one is in this life, the better one's circumstances will be in the next life*. Being moral always pays in the long run, from this perspective, and being immoral never pays in the long run.

Notice that Reason Five is in fact rather similar to Reason One, which is suggested by the narrative in *Spider-Man*. Both tell us that being moral pays off in the long run, although of course Reason One, as stated, makes no mention of a life after death. Also notice that the Ms. Poore and Arachnid-Girl cases do not give us a reason to reject the claim of Reason Five. At worst, these sorts of cases show only that immoral actions can sometimes pay off in this Earthly life—in the relatively "short run."

Now of course, we are not forced to accept Reason Five. We have two other options, at this point. (1) We could just accept that the strongest reasons for action do not always support doing one's moral duty. This option is profoundly disturbing to the morally serious person and it is apt to lead to "hedging our bets" whenever morality requires major sacrifices. (2) We could simply revise the moral code so that it is less demanding, so that it never requires that we do anything that does not promote our self-interest *in this life* (prior to death). Again, this option is profoundly disturbing to the morally serious person and it is apt to lead to very substantial departures from traditional morality. In addition, it's clear that Peter Parker, Uncle Ben, and Aunt May would never go for this. And neither, I think, should we. So, if we take the moral life seriously, we probably believe that the strongest reasons always favor doing our moral duty, where "moral duty" is understood in a fairly traditional way. Let us proceed tentatively, then, on the assumption that the strongest reasons *do* always favor being moral in a traditional sense, and notice where it leads us.

Superheroes, Duty, and the Biggest of Big Pictures

As we've seen, Reason Five for being moral, the claim that moral behavior always pays in the long run, where that includes life after death, seems to be the only claim we've examined that underwrites our belief in the full rationality of morality (that the strongest reasons always favor doing our moral duty). Reason Five, however, seems to call for some pretty strong metaphysical positions, views about the ultimate nature of reality—namely, either theism or reincarnation-plus-karma. Theism and reincarnation can be combined, and indeed they are combined in some forms of Hinduism. But theism and the doctrine of reincarnation are also sometimes regarded as rival hypotheses, and some Eastern religions, like certain forms of Buddhism, endorse reincarnation but not theism. In closing, I wish to offer an argument to the effect that any forms of reincarnation that reject theism undermine themselves.

If it were given that reincarnation and karma are true *in the absence of any Deity*, then it would follow that the universe is governed not only by physical laws (such as the law of gravity) but by *impersonal* moral laws as well. These moral laws would have to be very complicated, for they would have to regulate the connection between each soul's moral record in one life and that soul's total circumstances in its next life, including what sort of a body it has and the degree of happiness (or misery) it experiences. Accordingly, these laws would have to somehow take into account every act, every intention, and every choice of every moral agent and ensure that each agent receives nothing less than his or her just desserts in the next life. Now, the degree of complexity and co-ordination involved here is not only extraordinarily high, it is also complexity *that serves a moral end*: namely, justice. Such complexity could hardly be accepted as a brute fact. Highly complex order *serving a moral end* is a phenomenon that calls for explanation in terms of an intelligent cause. And if the order is on a scale far surpassing what can reasonably be attributed to human intelligence, an appeal to a divine intelligence seems entirely justified. Thus, the moral order postulated by non-theistic reincarnation would paradoxically provide evidence that there is a God.[6]

Every superhero has an interesting origin story. We want to know where the superpowers came from, and how the mission

---

[6] The main point of this paragraph is borrowed from Robin Collins, "Eastern Religions," in Michael J. Murray, ed., *Reason for the Hope Within* (Grand Rapids: Eerdmans, 1999), p. 206.

got started. What I'm suggesting is that if a physical universe like ours does have a highly complex moral order, then that would be evidence that it too would have to have a pretty interesting origin story involving great intelligence, power, and moral concern. In other words, it's plausible to suppose that this story would start with something like a God.

Swinging from One Idea to Another

The film *Spider-Man* is both extraordinarily entertaining and interestingly philosophical. It asks the question, "Why be a superhero?" But if we agree that, "With great power comes great responsibility," then, "Why be a superhero?" is a thinly disguised version of one of the classic philosophical questions, "Why be moral?" *Spider-man* not only raises this question, but it offers some fascinating and fairly plausible answers. In the end, I've suggested that those answers alone are not fully adequate, and that, in order to get an adequate answer, we seem to be pushed in the direction of large-scale metaphysical claims. This is part of the enduring fascination of philosophy—stumbling across connections between ideas that initially may have seemed hundreds of miles apart. Like Spider-Man swinging from building to building, when we move logically from one idea to another, we can find ourselves eventually coming across something surprising that is very important indeed.

Would you like to be a superhero? Given Uncle Ben's insight about power and responsibility, this is a loaded question indeed. To be a super*hero*, you would have to be super-responsible, that is, you would have to take on responsibilities in proportion to your enhanced powers. And would it be rational to take on such responsibilities? Isn't it interesting that, in order to answer that question, you come up against some of the biggest cosmic questions of all—"Does reality ultimately favor good over evil?" "Is there life after death?" and "Does God exist?" How you answer these questions may be more important than you might have realized concerning how you live your life, whether you're a superhero or not.

16

Superman and *Kingdom Come*: The Surprise of Philosophical Theology

FELIX TALLON and JERRY WALLS

We're going to do something a bit different, a little off the beaten path. We propose to talk about philosophical theology through interaction with a particularly famous superhero comic book. To some, perhaps, any sort of theological reflection might seem completely unnecessary for any discussion of super-heroes—an unwelcome intrusion, like when the police show up at a roaring party, or when a humorless English major corrects your grammar while you're telling a joke. But the philosophical theologian and the comic-book writer aren't necessarily working at cross-purposes.

For one thing, both camps are obviously interested in *ethical* issues. Matters of life and death concern the philosopher, the preacher, and the caped crusader alike. Second, Christian theology in particular and comic books as a whole occasionally share some of the same characters in their respective role-calls. The devil, for instance, shows up in the Bible, the Marvel Universe, and Todd McFarlane's *Spawn* series, among many other places. Demons pop up in both contexts, and even angels sometimes make a fleeting but important appearance in both worlds.

As a third and interesting specific point of contact, and one especially relevant for our purposes, the classic superhero Superman in particular bears many similarities to the central Christian figure, Jesus Christ. Of course, the original creators of the Superman story, Jerry Siegel and Joe Shuster, were both Jewish, and parallels have long been pointed out between Moses and Superman. But since Christians see Moses as a fore-shadowing image for Christ, it should be no surprise to discover further Christian parallels. Superman and Jesus both have strange circumstances surrounding their arrival on Earth. Kal-El was sent by his father from the exploding planet Krypton to the Midwest—to Smallville, Kansas, as it turns out—by a rocket. Christ, on the other hand, was sent by his Father from heaven to the Mideast—to Bethlehem, in particular—by a virgin birth through the Holy Spirit. Hence, both share amazing entrance stories and a parallel stranger-citizen dynamic. Superman is both an alien from another planet and an all-American farm boy, turned big-city journalist. According to traditional theological claims, Jesus is both a savior from another realm and a small-town Jewish boy, turned prominent itinerant preacher, who is both fully human and fully divine. Perhaps most significantly, both are uniquely able (in their own ways) to help out the average Joe.

One could go on like this all day, but it is enough to say that philosophical theology shares sufficient common ground with the world of superheroes to make for an interesting conversation—as we hope to show. Specifically, we mean to discuss "eschatology" (pronounced "es-ka-tó-la-jee"), the branch of theology that deals with final things or ultimate outcomes. In other words, eschatology considers huge issues that any thoughtful person will naturally care about—and care about deeply. Where are things finally headed and what is it all about at the end of the day? What is the eventual fate of humanity, and indeed of the cosmos as a whole? Is there life after death and ultimate justice, or is the hope for justice nothing more than an empty utopian dream?

Questions of this nature are raised in a fascinating way by one of the best-known comic books ever written, the DC graphic novel *Kingdom Come*. This novel will be the focus for our conversation between philosophical theology and the world of superheroes.

The Background of *Kingdom Come*

The phrase "kingdom come" is taken from the Lord's Prayer: the prayer that Jesus taught his disciples. The Lord's Prayer says, among other things, "Thy kingdom come, thy will be done, on Earth as it is in Heaven." The word "Thy" refers to God the Father, and the phrase "kingdom come" is often understood in two complementary ways. In the first way, the "kingdom" is seen as the present reality of God's reign in the world, as we see it in the person and ministry of Jesus. In the second way, it is seen as a future reality, when God's reign will encompass the entire Earth after the second coming of Christ.

The DC comic *Kingdom Come* takes its cue from the second emphasis on the phrase. The graphic novel deals with dark days in the Earth's future—and is peppered with allusions to the book of *Revelation*, the last book in the Bible. *Revelation* also describes dark days but ends with a hopeful vision of the second coming of Christ and his everlasting kingdom. In *Kingdom Come*, however, we read about the return, not of Christ, but of Superman.

The story, superbly told through the words of Mark Waid and the paintings of Alex Ross, begins some decades in the future. Superman, Wonder Woman, Aquaman, the Green Lantern, and Hawkman have all retreated from fighting crime into lives of relative isolation. The old Justice League has disbanded and a new breed of vicious superheroes has taken their place. What's worse, these new superheroes seem little concerned about protecting innocent life and supporting freedom. The graphic novel's narrator, an aged minister, describes these new superheroes as being inspired by the *legends* of the old Justice League, "if not the *morals*." According to the narrator, the new heroes "no longer fight for the right. They fight simply to fight." The solid and sturdy morality of yesteryear has been replaced with a postmodern drama of superhero power plays. Even Batman's war on injustice has become tyrannical, as he rules Gotham City by fear. In other words, the world is in sad need of heroes who are good as well as powerful.

The prevailing mood of the older, retired heroes is that their mission has failed. Superman, Aquaman and others feel that the world has become so much more brutal, and therefore that the old ways of fighting crime no longer apply. At the beginning of the book, we find Superman hiding out in his Fortress of Solitude. There he has recreated his old life on the farm in an effort to forget about the real world. Wonder Woman comes to talk him out of his funk, but he refuses to be encouraged. His faith in the crusade for justice has been crushed.

Superman's dilemma is obviously nothing new. Many people share the feeling of disillusionment and despair in the face of large-scale and pervasive injustice. Elliot S. Maggin, the writer of the novelization of *Kingdom Come*, picks up on this shared situation and common plight. In this day and age, Maggin says, "The superhero is Everyman." The implication of what he is saying here is that Superman's dilemma is our own. Any of us, when faced with injustice and suffering, can become utterly discouraged and totally apathetic. Therefore, we should look closely at Superman's situation, and in examining it ask questions about the human obligation to combat injustice, as well as our prospects for succeeding.

Hope, Obligation, and the Big Picture

At the outset of the story, Superman is profoundly discouraged about the likelihood of success, isolating himself in the Fortress of Solitude, and wondering why he should bother trying to save a world that cares so little about real justice. What could stir Superman to action? When Wonder Woman confronts him, she tries to coax him out of his inertia by saying that he "must face this." But her use of the word "must" raises a very big question. Is Superman actually *obliged* to rejoin the fight? Is there any real sense in which he indeed *must* respond to Wonder Woman's arguments?

How you answer this question depends on what you believe about the universe, including what your eschatology is. In deciding on matters of right and wrong, and in making decisions about obligation, we have to consider *deeper* issues that involve what we believe about the big picture for life. In this regard, there are at least two obvious and opposing worldviews we should consider. We could ponder even more, but these two represent the main lines of available worldviews, and should suffice for our purposes here.

One is the view we have mentioned briefly already, the framework of ideas that has been dominant in the West for most of the past two millennia—the worldview of Christian theism. Christian theism states simply that there is a God who created the universe for a purpose, who then entered this creation in the person of Christ, and who will direct the future of it all to a proper moral and spiritual culmination. The second worldview is the major *opposing* philosophy, one that can be found in ancient times but that has become much more prevalent in the past two centuries—the view of naturalism. Naturalism roughly states that there are no supernatural forces operating in the universe, only natural ones. So there is no God, or anything like God, that can create or interfere with the material world. Matter in motion, governed by natural laws, is all that exists.

Interestingly, naturalism has its own eschatology, an account of the final outcome of things very different from the one to be found in Christian theism. To see this, we can reflect for a moment on this famous statement of naturalism by the distinguished twentieth-century British philosopher, Bertrand Russell:

> That man is the product of causes which had no prevision of the end they were achieving; that his origin, his growth, his hopes and fears, his loves and his beliefs, are but the outcome of accidental collocations of atoms; that no fire, no heroism, no intensity of thought and feeling, can preserve an individual life beyond the grave; that all the labors of the ages, all the devotion, all the inspiration, all the noonday brightness of human genius, are destined to extinction in the vast death of the solar system, and that the whole temple of man's achievement must inevitably be buried beneath the debris of a universe in ruins—all these things, if not quite beyond dispute, are yet so nearly certain that no philosophy which rejects them can hope to stand. Only within the scaffolding of these truths, only on the firm foundation of unyielding despair, can the soul's habitation henceforth be safely built.[1]

The eschatology here is obviously bleak—everything we value is ultimately to be "buried beneath the debris of a universe in ruins," including, notably, heroism. Destination ruination for everything we love, including the marvelous world of DC Comics! What could be more hopeless? What a philosopher like Russell stated so eloquently decades ago is a view that many contemporary cosmologists affirm—the grim, ultimate fate of the entire cosmos is dissolution and destruction. The world system in which we all live is destined to continue expanding forever, breaking up and further disintegrating as it goes until all its suns burn out and all its life forms have died.

---

[1] Bertrand Russell, "A Free Man's Worship," in *Why I Am Not a Christian* (London: Allen and Unwin, 1957), p. 107.

Gloom, Doom, and Morality

The naturalist worldview, with its gloomy eschatology, is rife with moral implications. First of all, note that, on it, we are all the product of causes that had no awareness of what they were producing. In other words, there is ultimately no rational intention behind our existence, no overarching reason for us to be here, no purpose at all for our presence in the universe. In the deepest sense, our existence is accidental. Consequently, there is nothing remotely like a blueprint for how we ought to live or what we should be doing with our lives. And the fact that it will all come to a bad end anyway, no matter how we live, does not exactly provide any degree of moral inspiration. We have only Russell's foundation of "unyielding despair" to build upon, and it is pointless to pretend otherwise. This is a cosmic despair that goes beyond the understandable despondency that Superman felt at the persistent injustice in this life. Despite this, however, Russell believed he saw something beautiful about recognizing the ultimate tragedy of life, and he thought that sensitive people could find in the beauty of this tragedy sufficient motivation to pursue certain moral values in their lives.

Of course, this is not the only account of moral motivation available to naturalists. Another interesting option that appeals to many contemporary naturalists draws from the field of sociobiology. Two well-known proponents of this view are the noted Harvard biologist E.O. Wilson and the philosopher Michael Ruse. Wilson and Ruse acknowledge that naturalism does not support traditional accounts of moral obligation. However, they affirm that evolution has programmed us to *feel* that we have an obligation to do what is right. In reality, however, we are under no such objective obligation. Indeed, Wilson and Ruse have written as follows:

> In an important sense, ethics as we understand it is an illusion fobbed off on us by our genes to get us to co-operate. It is without external grounding. Ethics is produced by evolution but not justified by it, because, like Macbeth's dagger, it serves a powerful purpose without existing in substance.[2]

---

[2] Michael Ruse and Edward O. Wilson, "The Evolution of Ethics," in James E. Huchingson, ed., *Religion and the Natural Sciences: The Range of Engagement* (Fort Worth: Harcourt, Brace, 1993), p. 310.

According to the naturalist scheme of things, this illusion is a *helpful* one, since it motivates individuals to self-sacrifice in service to the larger community. But there is obviously a large potential problem here. If what motivates moral or sacrificial action is in fact illusory, is there any good reason to follow our conscience once we see through the illusion? Is an illusory dagger effective in any way once we discover that it is illusory?

According to Wilson, what naturalism has discovered is that there is no God or any other supernatural source or ground of morality. He never says how that discovery has been made, and gives no compelling argument that we should think so—but we can still trace out what he thinks follows from this. If there's no God, there's no guarantee that evil ultimately will be punished and that good will triumph. If the naturalist is right, then there is no kingdom coming in which all will be set right by God, there is no heaven or hell, and there is nothing after death but the extinction of consciousness and an eventual, universal silence.

Ideas like heaven and hell may seem like old-fashioned Sunday School scare tactics, but in reality the notion of an afterlife has played a crucial role in grounding morality in the West until quite recently. This is true not only of Western theology, but mainstream philosophy as well. One of the most notable examples is in the work of Immanuel Kant, whose moral philosophy has been deeply influential in Western thought. Kant argued that morality does not make rational sense unless we assume the existence of God and immortality, endless life after death. For if a perfectly good and powerful God exists, we can be confident that virtue will be rewarded in the end and that evil will be punished. Only if we have such "moral faith" in the ultimate outcome of things can we avoid the despair that arises out of fearing that moral effort may not be worth the trouble it takes, and may in fact be utterly futile in the end.

Naturalism simply has no *equivalent* grounds for morality. True, the naturalist may know that evolution has trained him to react morally, and still may often act on those feelings. He might do so because it feels right, or to avoid social disapproval. But if those feelings and reactions are produced by blind forces working on our minds, and are associated with beliefs that we consider to be false, is this enough?

Obviously Superman (and, hopefully, each of us) grew up in the sort of home where he was trained to desire to do the right thing. And in most average, everyday situations it behooves all of us to be moral. Doing the right thing can help us to become well liked, it can assist us in achieving important goals, and it can fill us with a great sense of personal satisfaction. But in the face of a very difficult moral demand, or a particularly onerous duty, I think almost anyone takes stock of whether he or she is really *obligated* to do it. If one is facing great danger (as in war or an emergency), much more is at stake than simply being well liked or filled with satisfaction. When we stand to lose our lives, the ultimate basis of morality becomes crucial—and it seems that naturalism has no deep basis for morality.

Worldviews, Values, and Superheroes

In a naturalist universe, where would any sort of objective morality come from? What would be the source for a real moral structure in the world? Subatomic particles, force fields, and multi-dimensional strings of energy don't generate obligations or duties by any remotely plausible natural law. In a naturalist universe, there would not be any metaphysical foundation for moral principles, no grounding for any objective and real distinction between good and evil, and thus no possible justification for any plausible discrimination between what we call justice and what we see as injustice. These are sobering implications of the naturalist worldview, and they certainly raise the bar for what would count as sufficient reason to believe it to be true. If there were some proof available for the truth of naturalism, or if indeed someone had somehow "discovered" naturalism to be true, we would just have to accept these shocking consequences of its claims, and learn to live with the revolution in our normal judgments and beliefs it would require. But without a good and compelling reason to think it's true, we can take the strength of our normal moral intuitions and judgments as evidence that it is an inadequate view of reality.

So if naturalism were true, there would be no real obligation for anyone like Superman to fight evil and injustice, partly because there would actually be no such thing as moral evil or injustice at all, and partly because there would be no obligations concerning anything. But it is possible that somebody in Superman's boots could say "Who cares if I really *must* fight evil or not, I want to and I'm going to!" To such a person, the major-

ity of us would offer kudos. Yet, such a resolution, as praiseworthy as it might be, seems deliberately to ignore basic facts
about the universe. It places the moral sentiment of sympathy at
a high value, to be sure, and it delights in a desire to be helpful,
but at the same time it downplays the importance of truth. If
there is no ultimate grounding for moral distinctions, then there
is really no truth to calling one thing good and another evil. An
announced desire to "fight evil" would then have no grounding
in the truth about values. And this is quite problematic, because
most people want to affirm both morality *and* truth with equal
vigor. Returning to the initial confrontation between Wonder
Woman and Superman for a moment, it's striking that in urging
Superman to confront evil, she says, "Here are two words. See if
they sound familiar. Truth and justice." Truth and justice! Are
there any words more closely associated with The Man of Steel?
Is anything closer to his heart than truth and justice?

But here we must confront some fundamental questions.
What is the relationship between truth and justice? Is there in
truth a real distinction between good and evil, or between justice and injustice? Is it the *truth* that justice will ultimately prevail, or is the sad truth that it will not? To put it another way, are
truth and justice in league with each other in such a way that
both will finally reign supreme? Or do they finally part ways, so
that when we reach the ultimate truth about things, we will see
that the idea of ultimate justice is just another illusion?

These questions are variations on one of the great issues in
the history of philosophy: what is the relationship between
truth, beauty, and goodness? Most classic philosophers believed
that these three are in a league together, that they are closely
related and that they are all mutually supportive. Indeed, some,
such as Socrates, have even argued that they are one and the
same thing. By contrast, one of the hallmarks of postmodern
philosophy is skepticism about all of this. Indeed, this was a
central theme in the thought of Friedrich Nietzsche, the godfather of postmodernism. Consider his following comment: "For a
philosopher to say, 'the good and the beautiful are one,' is
infamy; if he goes on to add, 'also the true', one ought to thrash
him. Truth is ugly."[3]

---

[3] See Damon Linker, "Nietzsche's Truth," *First Things* 125 (August–September
2002), p. 52.

The notion that truth is at odds with goodness and beauty creates serious dilemmas if we are forced to choose between them. Similarly with truth and justice. If they were at odds, what would we choose—to believe in justice, even if it isn't true that it is really possible or that it will in the end succeed, or to accept the truth that there is no ultimate justice and give up on the moral enterprise? Naturalism, it seems, faces us with this rather disheartening dilemma.

The practical upshot of naturalism is that we may be able to find little compelling reason to fight what strikes us as injustice, especially when facing the apparent evil that may place our own lives in danger. The truth of the matter is that the belief that there is no ultimate justice stands in sharp opposition to any strong motivation toward serious self-sacrifice in the face of apparent evil. Given a naturalist view of things, there will be moments when what strikes us as truth and what we take to be justice stand in conflict in the choices we face. If resisting evil might shorten one's life and therefore cut down on one's total enjoyment of whatever pleasures are available in this world, then why bother? If one knows there will be no ultimate punishment, or any other sort of sanction, for committing undetected wrongs, then why worry? If the universe is ultimately unjust, or if there is just ultimately no such thing as justice or injustice, good or evil, in the fundamental nature of things, then why make any real sacrifices at all? Such is the dilemma naturalism creates in regard to morality.

A Theological Basis for Super-Heroics

Here is where the theologian would like to suggest a resolution to the dilemma. Since it seems that naturalism drives a wedge between truth and justice, or in other words, between our *feeling* of moral obligation and our *explanation* for it, let us propose a system that explains moral feeling, *and* gives solid grounds for real moral obligation. Simply put, a metaphysical view of reality that allows a real place for moral principles and for objective distinctions between good and evil, along with an eschatology that allows for an appropriate system of reward and punishment, can resolve the tension.

The view of Christian theism obviously affirms this with its idea of a morally concerned, personal Creator, and its doctrines of heaven and hell, as well as with its anticipation of the return of Christ. To some, this sort of worldview may seem tantamount to believing in Zeus, Santa's elves, and the Tooth Fairy, but the majority of great philosophers in the West (including Augustine, Aquinas, Anselm, and even through Descartes and Kierkegaard, among many others) would have seen this as an entirely plausible worldview with a very serious eschatology. Even still, perhaps we can reframe these ideas in a simpler way. What the doctrines of heaven, hell, and the return of Christ basically affirm is that the fundamental structure of reality is such that there is a difference between good and evil, and therefore between justice and injustice, that moral decisions have ultimate long-term consequences, and that justice will prevail in the end. These doctrines give real grounding to difficult moral decisions. Our moral feelings aren't all illusions. Moral impulses aren't all irrational. On a Christian worldview, one is able to understand from where moral laws or decrees come (the perfectly moral nature of God), and one is also able to see why we should obey them (aligning ourselves with the plan of a loving God). So long as the Christian is being fully rational, or intellectually virtuous (not believing in this worldview or in any particular deliverance of conscience against his better judgment), then he can place a high premium on both truth and justice.

There still may be another intellectual problem lurking in the neighborhood. Besides asking about the truth of Christianity (a good question, but not our focus here), one may inquire whether a belief in ultimate justice may not actually *discourage* one from bothering to fight evil. Elliot Maggin, in the introduction to *Kingdom Come*, seems to suggest something like this. He writes:

> In the story you hold in your hands, Mark Waid and Alex Ross tell us that our proper response to the inexorable march of progress that has brought us to this place and time in the history of civilization is to find a way to confront it responsibly. Not modestly. Not unself-consciously. *Not with faith in a power greater than ours to descend from the sky and set things right . . .*

Maggin's interpretation of the story is interesting. He seems to say that faith in a greater power leads either to irresponsible action or else inaction in the face of evil. But is this so?

Returning to Superman's situation, let us ask, "What if Superman believed in a power greater than himself who would set things right in the end? Would this prevent or even inhibit the Man of Steel from bothering to fight evil?" Now, it is possible to imagine certain situations where knowing that a "power greater than ours" will make things right might be de-motivating. Placing exclusive faith in the police or government to clean up problems and right wrongs might let us off the hook and deflect us from even thinking about the things we ought to be doing in our own neighborhoods, and with our own resources of time and energy. But when it comes to a supreme being, the situation is quite different. Christian theology, and the classic Jewish theology that lies behind it, has usually maintained that humans do play a crucial role in preventing and resisting present evils, and indeed, that humans have a responsibility to do so which is both serious and binding. God works not only directly to accomplish his will, but in the unfolding course of history, he typically works through human agents who seek to promote whatever is true and just. The idea is that God has created us to be co-creators of good with him. We are in a partnership to work in our realm to realize the justice that is within our reach. What is outside our reach will be taken care of by that power that is greater than ourselves. Superman's power is tremendous, but not even he is omnipotent. He can't do everything, but like all of us, he has a duty to do what he can, while knowing that the ultimate triumph of truth and justice is beyond his range and his responsibility. In other words, we all are deeply beholden to work to promote truth and justice while recognizing that securing them in all things is not finally up to us.

This brings us to an additional benefit provided by any eschatology that promises eventual justice—namely, an objective grounding for hope. In both Superman's situation and Batman's, as depicted in *Kingdom Come,* we see the inherent problems that arise with a loss of hope. In Superman's case, his problem is obvious and understandable—faced with so much injustice and the knowledge that he is just one man, however super, he despairs and falters in his mission. Batman has been affected differently. As the story begins, he has taken to ruling Gotham City with an iron hand. His Bat-Knights patrol the streets, constantly evoking fear in the hearts of both honest citizens and criminals. Quite simply, his quest for justice has become tyrannical. He too knows that he is just one man, and so, because he desires justice, he must seek it through extreme means.

It seems that both cases could be helped by a worldview that made room for a robust sense of real, well-grounded hope. If one believes that justice has an ultimate supernatural source, and that it will prevail in the end, this can not only spur one on to take action, but also to recognize genuine objective moral constraints on the actions that we do initiate. In *Kingdom Come*, Superman and Batman both see the inherent limitations of being just one man, and react in opposite, though equally negative, ways. The hope of ultimate justice can act as corrective to both, encouraging human efforts to bring justice through moral hope, while also providing limits through moral restraint.

Because of this, it is surprising to us that Elliot Maggin, in his introduction to *Kingdom Come*, thinks the story tells us to confront injustice without faith in a power greater than our own. It seems that the essence of the classic superhero story is much the same as the core of the traditional religious story. Both emphasize, each at their own level, the *importance* of a hope in powers greater than ourselves to motivate us to action and sustain us in that action, however futile it might at times look. As all the great philosophers have urged us to realize, things in this world are not often what they seem. A theological worldview like Christian theism offers one way to articulate this that makes sense of our deepest moral sentiments and inclinations.

Hope and the Human Challenge

The benefit of hope in a greater power is seen very clearly seen in *Kingdom Come*. After their confrontation, Wonder Woman leaves Superman with her questions unanswered. The reader has no indication from Superman that he will ever return to crime fighting. A dozen pages later, however, the elderly preacher who acts as the narrator of the book is watching two teams of vicious "superheroes" fighting one another. He realizes the bad state of affairs the world is in, and turns to his supernatural guide, The Spectre, saying, "If any of us are going to survive . . . We need hope!"

Right then, of course, the wind whips up, and we see a blur of red. Someone says, "Look!" and someone else says, "Up in the sky!" Superman has returned—fighting crime, wearing tights, and bringing hope. The story progresses and other superheroes, taking their cue from Superman, also return to the fray. As they band together, the world shakes off its despair. In the words of the narrator, "A world, hungry for hope, gradually surrenders its fears to the skies." Hope in a greater power encourages the average person in the struggle against evil. The theological symbolism of Superman is even driven home by the writer of *Kingdom Come*, as later in the book, Superman is standing on the steps of the UN and one onlooker hails it as "The second coming of Superman."

So, while Superman's dilemma is like our own in one way, because of his great power he also represents something else. The superhero story is not *simply* a magnification of the human dilemma, but can also be an adaptation of the story of divine intervention. In his doubt and questioning as well in his hope-giving power, Superman shows the human need for faith in a greater power. Both sides of this story can also be found in the divine and human person of Jesus Christ.

One of the final scenes of *Kingdom Come* takes place in a church, where the narrator of the story, preacher Norman McCay, is given his final charge. He has witnessed the entire story of *Kingdom Come* through the assistance of the Spectre. As the Spectre departs he says, "Well Norman, you have watched the titans walk the Earth and you have kept stride. Perhaps you are more like them than you realize. You exist to give *hope*." The theistic philosopher heartily agrees. A supernatural eschatology, such as we have outlined, does exactly what the Spectre says of the preacher, or Superman, and more. It provides the truthful possibility of unbounded hope, in contrast to a naturalistic eschatology built on a foundation of unyielding despair. What's more, such an eschatology allows one to hold consistently together hope and truth, as well as individual responsibility and a belief in ultimate justice. This is a great deal for any worldview to accomplish, and it is certainly a worldview that can help us accomplish a great deal.

Part Four

Identity
and Superhero
Metaphysics

17

Questions of Identity: Is the Hulk the Same Person as Bruce Banner?

KEVIN KINGHORN

Imagine you're a judge in San Francisco presiding over a criminal trial. Recently the city jolted to a standstill. An awesome force had rampaged through the downtown area damaging automobiles, cable cars, power lines, and the buildings of several city blocks. The defendant in the trial is Bruce Banner, who has been charged with numerous counts of destruction of property. When asked to enter a plea, Bruce Banner's lawyer offers the following defense: "Your honor, the person who perpetrated these acts was a large, greenish hulk of a person. But my client, as you can see, is a smallish, light-skinned man. In short, my client is clearly not the same person as the individual who perpetrated these acts."

Now, when the lawyer says that the Hulk and Bruce Banner are not the "same person," he is not using the term in the colloquial sense in which we might say, "You know, Bob is just not the same person when he doesn't get his morning coffee." No, the lawyer is making the stronger claim that the Hulk and Bruce Banner literally are *not the same individual*. The lawyer continues, "Your honor, my client is merely another victim in all this. Yes, we acknowledge that Bruce Banner was somehow changed into the person of the Hulk, and then somehow re-emerged as himself once again. But the fact remains that when the acts in question were perpetrated, it was the person of the Hulk and not the person of Bruce Banner who was perpetrating them. So, if the prosecuting attorney wants to put someone on trial, let him capture the Hulk and put him on trial! But it's plain to see that my client is simply not the same person as the Hulk."

As the judge, you must now rule on whether Bruce Banner should stand trial. And this means you must rule on whether Bruce Banner and the Hulk are indeed the same person. What criteria will you use to reach your decision?

The search for such criteria has a long history in philosophical circles. Typically, philosophers frame the issue in terms of the "continuity of personal identity over time." Put another way, the question is: What makes you the same person today that you were yesterday, or were ten years ago, or will be ten years from now? If you could answer that question, then you would have the criteria for determining whether the person before you on trial is the same person who weeks earlier went on a rampage through the city.

The Hulk's Bodily Identity

In our day-to-day lives, we generally never question whether Bob, or Sue, or anyone else we know is literally the "same person" today that he or she was yesterday. This is because we tend to equate *personal* identity with *bodily* identity. That is, we see a physical figure that resembles closely the physical figure we saw and talked with yesterday (or ten years ago), and we assume the two physical figures are the same person. Indeed, even in courts of law, bodily identification is typically all we look for in determining personal identity. This much can be learned by watching any old episode of *Perry Mason* or *Matlock*, where something like the following exchange inevitably takes place.

> **PROSECUTOR**: Do you see the person who committed the crime in the courtroom now?
> **WITNESS** (*pointing*): Yes, he's sitting right over there.
> **PROSECUTOR**: Let the record reflect that the witness has identified the defendant.

If we were to use bodily identification as the way of identifying the person of Bruce Banner, then Bruce Banner would *not* be the same person as the Hulk. After all, the Hulk's body is much larger than Bruce Banner's body. It follows from this that the individual atoms that comprise Bruce Banner's body haven't simply been rearranged to form the body we identify as the

Hulk. Rather, there is a widely different number of total atoms in each body. To grasp how widely different this number is, we need only think back to the 1970s TV series where Dr. Banner (in the TV series, oddly enough, *David* Banner) would transform into the person of the Hulk. He would burst every seam in his clothing except, unrealistically, the seam in the seat of his trousers (the one seam in any tight fitting pair of pants that is always the *first* to go).

Because the atoms that comprise the body of the Hulk number many more than those that make up the body of Bruce Banner, the physical constitution of the Hulk clearly differs from the physical constitution of Bruce Banner. On the assumption that bodily identity is the same as personal identity, this would mean that the Hulk is not the same person as Bruce Banner.

But is bodily identity the correct criterion for determining personal identity? On closer analysis the answer seems to be "no." It's true that the atoms of Bruce Banner's body cannot be the same ones that comprise the Hulk's body. Yet we should remember that the atoms of *all* people's bodies change over time. In the course of a year or two, all the cells in each of our bodies will die and be replaced by new ones. Over the course of a mere week, half our red blood cells will regenerate. Yet we retain our personal identity through this process. The actor who played Don Vito Corleone in the movie *The Godfather* may in his later years have contained in his body nearly as many atoms as the Hulk. But he was nonetheless the same person as the star of *On the Waterfront*, a man who at the time of this earlier film was about the size of Bruce Banner—the trim and muscular Marlon Brando. And so, just because Bruce Banner's body at the time of the trial is very different from the Hulk's body during the time of the earlier rampage through the city, it does not automatically follow that Bruce Banner is not the same person as the Hulk.

At this point perhaps we could reasonably seek to salvage the importance of bodily continuity by suggesting that there need only be *some* degree of bodily continuity in order to establish personal identity. An analogy might help make this suggestion clear. Suppose you bought a sailboat and named her the *Stan Lee Schooner*. As the years go by, your boat will need repairs. At various points you'll need new decking, new rigging, a new mainsail, a new keel, and so forth. Eventually, perhaps, if you own it long enough, you'll end up replacing every single part of the boat with new parts. The question then becomes: Is your current boat still the *Stan Lee Schooner*? Our intuitions are probably pretty clear that the answer is "yes." In the clearest sense, you still own the same boat, however refurbished it might be.

Similarly, it can be argued that, as long as there exists some certain degree of physical continuity between bodies over time, these bodies do belong to the same person. Hence, as long as Bruce Banner and the Hulk meet these minimum physical continuity requirements (whatever the correct minimum requirements are), then it might be argued that Bruce Banner and the Hulk are the same person.

Despite any initial plausibility this line of argument might have, on further analysis it leaves us with some unwelcome outcomes. Suppose I were to die tomorrow after having agreed to become an organ donor. Suppose further that the body parts of mine needed by doctors for medical transplants all go to the same person, whom we'll call "Herb Trimpe." Conceivably (given continued medical advances), over fifty percent of my body might be used as replacements for Herb's internal organs, his limbs, and so forth. In such a case, the majority of Herb's post-operative body would consist of physical parts that now belong to my body—including perhaps such things as my current fingerprints. Herb's post-operative body would therefore have a greater physical continuity with my body today than with Herb's own body today. But certainly we would not want to say the person who emerges from the operating room is Kevin Kinghorn and not Herb Trimpe. Whatever the merits of my donation, surely my generosity hasn't helped me defeat death— it is Herb who as a result avoids that fate.

Thus, whatever it is that provides continuity of personal identity over time, it is not the continuity of physical cells or atoms. It is perhaps an interesting question just how much physical continuity there is between the body of the Hulk and the body of Bruce Banner. But this question does not serve as an adequate criterion for determining whether the Hulk and Bruce Banner are the same person.

The Mental Realm of the Hulk

Aware of some of the problems with trying to reduce personal identity to the physical realm, philosophers have often explored whether the mental realm might be a more promising place to locate personal identity. Following the seventeenth-century philosopher John Locke (1632–1704), much of this exploration has involved the role of memory.

Locke defined a person as a "thinking intelligent being, that has reasons and reflection, and can consider itself as itself, the same thinking thing, in different times and places." For Locke, what is unique to all persons is the ability to be aware through introspection that one is indeed a thinking being. Continuity of personhood over time is secured because you are able—through the use of memory—to reflect on the fact that at earlier times you were aware through introspection that you were a thinking being.

On the surface, this is a very attractive account of personal identity and could help us understand the continuing identities of many famous comic-book characters who undergo radical physical change. A member of the Justice League of America, Jonn J'onnz, a.k.a. the Martian Manhunter, is able to shift shape at will and assume many different bodily appearances. And yet he continues to consider himself, in a mentally self-reflective way, the same being both before and after the shifting. We share that belief. The Fantastic Four would seem to offer us four more examples of this same phenomenon. After their exposure to cosmic rays, Reed Richards, Sue Storm, Johnny Storm, and Ben Grimm take on vastly different physical characteristics, and yet their mental continuity is such that there is no question whether, despite those changes, they are the same people who went up in the experimental spacecraft. In each such case, mental continuity seems sufficient for personal identity.

Applying Locke's criteria, should we then view Bruce Banner as the same person as the Hulk? The answer here may depend on how we conceive of the Hulk character. In the early Marvel comic books, the Hulk kept the same mental states and self-awareness as Bruce Banner. It was as though Banner—or at least his mind—was trapped in the body of the Hulk. On this conception of the Hulk, Bruce Banner's transformation into this monstrous creature in no way violates Locke's criteria for continuous, single personhood.

On the other hand, in later comics, as well as in the 1970s TV series and in the 2003 movie, the mental capacities of the Hulk are much more blurry. The Hulk can still recognize friends like

Betty Ross, and he feels protective of them. Correspondingly, he can identify who the bad guys are, and he's none too happy with them. Still, we often see the Hulk looking with evident confusion at people and at his surroundings, seemingly trying to make full sense of his environment. His contribution to ongoing discussions is most often rather general, like the nonspecific announcement of intention, "Hulk smash!" There appears to be no suggestion in such depictions of the Hulk that his mental states include the memories of Bruce Banner's previous introspective experiences. So, on these later conceptions of the Hulk, Locke's criteria for continuous personhood seem not to be met.

We have looked briefly at whether John Locke's famous mental criteria for continuous personhood can be met in the case of the Hulk and Bruce Banner, and we've arrived at conflicting results. Now we must ask whether these mental criteria are themselves satisfactory. And on closer analysis we'll find that there are severe problems with this alternative and otherwise apparently plausible account of what it is to be the same person.

One problem is that Locke's criteria seem far too restrictive. After all, I cannot now recall what my introspective experiences were at the time of my eighth birthday. But surely it does not follow that my personal identity somehow hasn't remained the same.

Another problem with Locke's criteria was identified by the philosopher Thomas Reid (1710–1796), who wrote on the subject of personal identity a century after Locke did. Reid described a scenario that was meant to illustrate the absurd conclusions to which Locke's criteria lead. He has us imagine a person whose life includes the following three events: (1) as a boy, he is flogged for stealing apples; (2) as a young officer in the army, he performs a heroic act; and (3) near the end of his military career, he receives a promotion to general. In Reid's scenario, when the man is a young officer, he is conscious of having been flogged as a boy. And when the man becomes a general, he is conscious of having performed his heroic act as a young officer. However, at this later time of becoming a general he no longer recalls receiving that flogging as a boy. Reid goes on to point out that, if memory is what provides continuity of identity, then the young officer is the same person as the boy; and the general is the same person as the young officer. By the transitive laws of logic it therefore follows that the general must be the same person as the boy. So far, so good. But Reid then reminds us, "The general's consciousness does not reach so far back as his floggings; therefore, according to Mr. Locke's doctrine, he is not the person who was flogged. Therefore the general is, and at the same time is not, the same person with him who was flogged at school." In short, Reid has shown that Locke's criteria for personal identity involving introspection and memory lead us to absurd and logically contradictory conclusions. So this account of identity can't be right.

Perhaps we could try to save Locke's theory by amending it slightly to avoid the problem raised by Reid. That is, we might insist that Locke was on the right track with respect to the importance of memory. And what is needed is the less stringent requirement that there must be at least *some* continuity within a person's string of introspective experiences. Thus, while I need not now remember my eighth birthday in order to maintain continuity of personal identity between then and now, what is needed is that I remember yesterday, and that yesterday I remember the day before, and so forth. Locke's amended criteria, then, would be that there exist a chain of memories between my current life now and my life as an eight-year-old.

Admittedly, this amended set of criteria involving memory would avoid the absurd conclusions associated with Reid's illustration. However, there are other scenarios that illustrate problems with even these amended criteria. Suppose that the person in Reid's story suffers from Alzheimer's Disease and that his memories are different from those described by Reid. As a general rule, the man *does* remember his early childhood and being flogged as a boy. However, because Alzheimer's has deprived him of any memories from his adult life, he *does not* remember his heroic act as a young officer. And he may not even remember what happened yesterday. In such a scenario, there is no continuous chain of memories building on one another through time.

In addition, Bruce Banner might get drugged by a bad guy and be so confused for hours that he can't remember much of anything at all, including previous moments of self-awareness. Yet, that doesn't make him a different human being during those hours. He's still Bruce. Something like this actually happened to Spider-Man for a lot longer than just a few hours when Doc Ock once attacked him with a powerful device that gave him temporary amnesia about who he was. It took him quite a while to sort it all out, and yet during that time it was the same superhero, Spider-Man, who was undergoing the amnesia.[1] And so even our amended criteria are not immune to counterexamples.

It's difficult to say whether we can further tweak Locke's memory criteria to account for all possible counterexamples. Some modern philosophers have made such attempts. Yet, all appeals to memory as what constitutes personal identity suffer from a final problem. This problem is one of circularity. Suppose someone has a false memory of working as the starring actor in the original *Adventures of Superman* television show in the 1950s. Perhaps the person is senile and, after watching George Reeves in costume on a rerun, somehow confuses television with his own reality. Or perhaps the person is delusional and thinks he actually is George Reeves. Or maybe the person has been hypnotized at a party or has had a dream in which he seemed to experience wearing the cape in front of the cameras. Although it honestly seems to this person that he starred on this show, seeming to remember something is different from actually remembering something. What's the difference? Obviously, in the case of a genuine memory, the experiences we remember having are the experiences we actually had.

However, a problem looms in this discussion of false and genuine memories. We have seen that the introspective phenomenon of *seeming* to remember something is not sufficient to establish a genuine memory. What more is needed? Well, we must add the further conditions that the experiences the person seems to remember are experiences that once actually occurred and that those experiences belong *to the same person* who is later having this apparent memory. But now our criteria for identifying personhood have become circular. For memory was supposed to provide the conditions for continuity of personal identity. And now, in order to specify what a genuine memory *is*, we must stipulate that it involves a past event that was experienced by the same, identical person who is now doing the remembering. In sum, the appeal to the mental realm of introspection and memory seems not to provide ade-

---

[1] Stan Lee and John Romita, *Amazing Spider-Man*, issues #53–#59.

quate criteria for determining continuity of personal identity. As the judge in the Bruce Banner trial, you must look elsewhere for adequate criteria.

A Causal Account of the Hulk's Identity

The categories of cause and effect are important in science and philosophy. It could be suggested that personal identity doesn't consist in simple physical or mental continuity, but rather is to be understood in terms of a causal account ranging across both physical and mental characteristics. If the big green (or gray) Hulk body and raging Hulk consciousness both arise causally from the body and mind of Bruce Banner in certain ways, then perhaps that is sufficient to constitute personal identity through such radical change.

We live in a world of natural causes and effects. The young, buff Marlon Brando became a huge corpulent loner through food, drink, drugs and other causes that naturally resulted in the radical changes that we all witnessed over time. In fact, human beings generally grow from tiny babies through childhood and into old age by means of certain causal mechanisms involving food, drink, exercise, experience, accident, disease, and many other things. Perhaps the Hulk is the same person as Bruce Banner precisely because the Hulk state of body and mind develops periodically from the normal Banner state of body and mind by means of certain causal mechanisms involving a complex interplay of radiation, danger, and anger. The Hulk is Bruce Banner precisely because it is Banner who "Hulks out" and becomes this monster. Bruce doesn't disappear from existence and get replaced on the same spot with an altogether different being, the Hulk, who then after a time himself disappears and, by some amazing coincidence, is replaced once again by Bruce Banner. Rather, it's just that the same person morphed into different appearances by a complex set of natural, though rare, causal factors.

The problem with such a causal account is that, like the previous theories of personal identity, it allows for strange and counter-intuitive consequences. Suppose that through a complex form of causal interactions—perhaps involving the devices of a mad scientist who attempts to clone Bruce Banner—the body of Bruce were to split into *two* huge rampaging bodies,

each with its own consciousness. These new monstrous creatures would both be causally derived from Bruce. And yet, if
they are indeed two separate creatures capable of wreaking
havoc in two different parts of a city at the same time, it seems
obvious that they could not *both* be the one person, Bruce
Banner. At this point, it can begin to look as if no account of
personal identity can do the job we need it to do without having absurd consequences we know to be false.

Is There No Way to Tell?

Faced with the problems associated with attempts to locate personal identity in either the physical or the mental realm, some
philosophers have questioned whether there exists such a thing
as personal identity. Contemporary philosopher Derek Parfit
notes that we sometimes ask questions about whether an evolving nation or a recently repaired machine is the "same" nation or
machine as in previous times. And Parfit observes, "No one
thinks that in these cases the questions 'Is it the same nation?' or
'Is it the same machine?' must have answers." Parfit's point is that
perhaps it is a mistake to assume there must be a correct answer
to questions involving something's (or someone's) identity.

To illustrate his point, Parfit calls attention to a number of sci-
ence-fiction-like scenarios that are not too different from the
cloning example mentioned in the previous section. In one of
Parfit's scenarios, he has us imagine a case where "my brain is
divided, and each half is housed in a new body." Given medical
discoveries that self-consciousness can arise when only half of a
human's brain is left intact, it is possible in Parfit's example that
both halves of his brain will form centers of self-consciousness.
And each of them may experience some strong form of continuity with the state of consciousness associated with the brain
before its bifurcation. Parfit then asks, "What happens to me?"
He notes that there is no obvious answer to this question. His
own conclusion is that it is most plausible to "suggest that I survive as two different people without implying that I am these
people."

If Parfit is right that it's a mistake to think that people must
always have a single, continuous identity over time, then should
we abandon our search for a criterion for personal identity? We
shouldn't, I think, be too quick to do so. After all, most of us

intuitively believe that there *is* an answer to the question of whether I would be the same person if I had only half my brain, or if part of my brain was somehow transplanted into another body. We may not *know* what the answers are in difficult situations like the one Parfit describes. But this does not mean that there *aren't* ultimately answers to these questions. Just because the truth is difficult to find doesn't mean that it doesn't exist. It may be difficult to find a fan of the recent Hulk movie among long-time Hulk comic-book aficionados, but nonetheless there may be a few out there.

The Hulk's Relational Identity

If we are to defend our intuition that there must be correct answers to questions of personal identity—including the identity of the Hulk and Bruce Banner—and we can't accept any of the accounts we have looked at so far, there is no reason for despair. There is one final place we might look for adequate criteria of personal identity. In my view, this is also the most promising place to look. We find it in people's ongoing personal relationships. Starting with the premise that personhood arises through relationships with other people, the suggestion here is that a person has a continuous identity in virtue of maintaining continuous relationships with other people.

At first glance it may seem very odd indeed to claim that your personal identity exists because others relate in some appropriate way to you. Yet, the oddity of this claim arguably stems from our living in a post-Enlightenment, overly individualistic cultural framework that, perhaps mistakenly, seeks to identify people by their private characteristics. When someone around us asks, "Who is Kathryn?" the answer will typically be: "She's the one who has dark hair, is about 5'6", likes to read *Hulk* and *X-Men* comics, and is a vegetarian." These are all in a sense private attributes. And we tend to assume that a compilation of these kinds of private attributes is what makes you "you."

Though it may initially seem obviously true that your standing as a personal agent *is* indeed a matter of your having such private attributes, perhaps this perception is more a matter of cultural conditioning than the truth of the matter. In ancient and medieval times, your identity as a person was thought of as not so much a matter of your private attributes (for example, what you looked like), but rather more as a matter of the connected set of *relationships* you had with others. It was the nature of your relationships that determined who "you" were.

Granted, you must have certain private attributes—like rationality, self-consciousness, and freedom—in order to be *able* to relate to others. But think for a moment about the attributes that get to the heart of who you are as an enduring person. A person might be loving, generous, faithful, forgiving, and in general self-giving. Or a person might be resentful, stingy, faithless, disloyal, vindictive, and in general self-serving. None of these attributes can be acquired in a vacuum. A person gets these traits in the first place by relating to others in certain specific ways.

There are some uncontroversial examples of relationally constituted entities in our world. A marriage is one of them. A marriage comes into existence and continues through time in virtue of a relationship between two people, as well as in virtue of a larger network of relationships between the couple and an overarching community, and—in the eyes of religious believers—in virtue of even deeper relationships between all of the above and God. On a more naturalistic level, a corporation is a legal entity that exists and continues through time in virtue of a complex network of interacting relationships. So identities based in relationships are not altogether unknown to us in the modern world. Perhaps, in a very deep way, individual personal identity is itself constituted and continued through time in virtue of one or more continuing relationships.

But as philosophers are often quick to point out, there are possible objections that can be raised against any theory. And any relational theory of personal identity is no exception. First, what happens if people fail to relate to you as the same person over time? Does this mean you don't have the same identity over time? You could stop hanging out at the comic shop, stop visiting Internet chat rooms and message boards, change your phone number, move across the country, and sever all your previous relationships with friends, neighbors and co-workers. Would that be the end of you as an individual person and the origin of a literally new person? Surely we don't think so. Second, what about a person who grows up on a deserted island with no other inhabitants to whom she might relate? Does this mean that she doesn't have any identity as a person at all?

Third, what if people relate to you through the lens of their own biases and emotional immaturity? Can others impose on you an identity as a person that you in no way choose or endorse? Again, that just seems wrong.

There is one possible philosophical reply to all three objections. It involves positing or recognizing the existence of a God who consistently relates to every person at all times and whose interpersonal knowledge of each person is in no way distorted. Thus, it can be held that there is a God who creates us as persons and guarantees that our personal identities will endure through time and, in addition, that they will finally reflect our true commitments to others, even if during our earthly lives others temporarily distort our identities as persons. Granted, nontheists may not wish to appeal to God in attempting to address the three objections I've mentioned. But this is indeed a straightforward and powerful way of handling all three.

It also pulls back into the picture a causal element, since the God who relationally creates and sustains us in existence through time does so as the Ultimate Cause of our existence. And with God in the picture, the chief objection to the causal picture alone can be answered. The standard understanding of divine power does not see it as ranging over impossibilities. So not even God could take Bruce Banner and cause him to become identical with each of two numerically distinct monsters at the same time. Since Bruce could not be identical with two beings who were not identical with each other, not even God could bring about the one scenario that created a problem for the causal account.

What Should We Conclude?

As the judge presiding over the Bruce Banner trial, should you rule that Bruce Banner and the Hulk are the same person? I think you should—on the grounds that Bruce and the Hulk have, overall, the same, continuous set of relationships with the people around them. The relationships the Hulk seeks to have with other people seem essentially to be a continuation of those relationships Bruce Banner has already established with them—however incomplete and altered his behavior might be in his transformed state. Indeed, we often find that Bruce will form an intention to relate to these people in a certain way, and the

Hulk's actions will reflect that ongoing intention. For instance, in the 2003 movie, Bruce is told over the phone by his father, David Banner, that steps have been taken to eliminate Betty Ross. Bruce immediately forms the intention to protect Betty and thereby thwart his father's plan. Later in a scene that doubtless caused poodle owners everywhere to have recurring nightmares, we see the Hulk destroy three mutated, blood-thirsty house dogs who have come for Betty.

Similarly, Betty Ross, David Banner, General "Thunderbolt" Ross and others relate to the Hulk as though he is the same person as Bruce Banner. Perhaps they do so because they have seen the form of the Hulk result from a transformation of Bruce's body, and they recognize in the mind of the Hulk some shreds at least of what they know about Bruce. It could be that physical, mental, and causal indicators are used by all of us in rough and ready ways as cues to the identity of others and thus to the appropriateness of relating to them in certain ways. But it still might be the case that these are only cues and clues to the deeper truth that ultimately it is a certain set of relationships that is constitutive of the fundamental identity under question.

Now, whether you as a judge ultimately find Bruce Banner guilty or not of destroying property is another matter. There may be mitigating circumstances or other exculpatory facts in the situation. In most documented appearances of the Hulk, it is others who seem to instigate conflict and make the Hulk go on the run. Perhaps *they* should be on trial for the destruction of property. Still, you cannot excuse Bruce on the grounds that he is not the same person as the Hulk. Bruce Banner is the same person as the Hulk because the two characters have a continuity of relationships with the people around them sufficient for this basic identity to hold true.

18

Identity Crisis: Time Travel and Metaphysics in the DC Multiverse

RICHARD HANLEY

Sir Arthur Conan Doyle wrote the Sherlock Holmes stories in serial form. In a famous oversight, he placed Watson's one and only war wound in the shoulder (in *A Study in Scarlet*) and much later in the leg (*The Sign of Four*). We now call this a continuity error. When Conan Doyle decided to end the series, he had Holmes play nemesis to Moriarty, apparently at the cost of his own life. But the public outcry was so great that Conan Doyle eventually resurrected Holmes, reinterpreting the earlier episode. Both incidents forced the reinterpretation of earlier installments in the serial, to preserve continuity. Let's call such forced reinterpretations *corrections*.

Conan Doyle did not attempt a deliberate correction in the case of the infamous war wound, but others have suggested how to go about it. My favorite is as follows: Watson is the narrator, and surely he knows where his war wound is. He forgot he said it was in the shoulder because he was lying, and he was lying because the real location is too embarrassing to reveal. So it's not in the leg, either. (The wag who gave this interpretation concluded that Watson's wound was probably in the buttocks!)

A century later, we take our serials and their continuity even more seriously. Especially interesting to me is serialization involving multiple authors. Legal aspects aside, there is nothing to stop me from writing another Holmes story, but nothing that mine says will "correct" Conan Doyle's, and yet what is in Conan Doyle's stories definitely affects what is true in mine. Given this asymmetry (and assuming no worldly resurrection of Conan Doyle), I conclude that the *serialization* of Holmes is over and done.

But things are different with comics. Here we have genuine serialization, and the possibility of correction, in spite of later stories being written by different authors. And like any creative opportunity, it is a two-edged sword, to be wielded with care and attention.

The DC Comics Multiverse

The 1940s Golden Age of comics saw the DC universe expand, as two sister companies merged their characters into a single "universe." But then came the post-war comic-book bust, and DC comics limped along with little more than the franchise heroes Batman, Superman, and Wonder Woman. In 1956, the Flash returned—sort of—updated as Barry Allen, who reads comic books about the exploits of Jay Garrick, the original Flash. Franchise heroes likewise were updated—literally—being transplanted into contemporary times, Superman remaining Clark Kent, and Batman remaining Bruce Wayne. The Silver Age had begun.

All this could have been resolved by thinking of Jay Garrick's exploits as a fiction-within-a-fiction. But then, any part of Garrick's world would likewise be fictional. Even this could be resolved: if Superman was part of Barry Allen's world, then he could also appear, temporally displaced, as a fictional character in the Jay Garrick stories (the way London appears, without temporal displacement, in the Holmes stories). DC Comics went for a different resolution, however. In *Flash* #123, Barry Allen (from "Earth-1") ends up in another universe ("Earth-2"), and meets Jay Garrick. One cannot meet merely fictional characters, of course. Earth-2 is populated with Golden Age superheroes, including suitably older versions of Superman and Batman. The DC multiverse is born.

The worlds multiplied as alternative histories proliferated, heroes and anti-heroes routinely jumped from one to the other, and things got pretty hard to follow, especially for relatively new readers. From a continuity point of view, an unfettered proliferation of storylines is deeply unsatisfying: it has the consequence that there is just one correction strategy: postulate yet another world. (Alternatively, the proliferation might remove any further need for correction, if we suppose that the multiverse is more or less complete, and all the worlds are there as needed.) By the

1980s, franchise heroes were again in need of updating. Something had to be done, and in 1985, it was.

Crisis on Infinite Earths: The Story Unfolds

We learn that the multiverse was created inadvertently by the irresponsible actions of an Oan scientist, Krona, who disobeyed a strict rule against investigating the origins of the universe. Somehow, he replaced what was a single universe with a multiverse, and moreover created an extra, anti-matter universe. A powerful evil arose in the latter: the Anti-Monitor. And in a yin-yang plot point, his positive counterpart, the Monitor, came into being as a caretaker of the multiverse.

Equally powerful, the Monitor and the Anti-Monitor were deadlocked for a million years, until they simultaneously rendered each other "immobile and unconscious." After more than nine billion years, on one of the Earths, another brilliant but irresponsible scientist—will they never learn?—ignored the legends, and investigated the origin of the multiverse by messing with antimatter. That couldn't be good, and it wasn't. He inadvertently liberated the Anti-Monitor. Worse still, he destroyed his own universe, thus shifting the balance of cosmic power. The Anti-Monitor becomes more powerful if positive universes are destroyed, so he now has the upper hand on the Monitor. Which brings us to the present . . .

The entire multiverse is under threat. The Anti-Monitor is obliterating whole universes, absorbing more and more power, while the Monitor grows ever weaker. In a Christ-like act of self-sacrifice, he allows himself to be killed in order to save Earth-1 and Earth-2, and their respective universes, creating a sort of pocket multiverse to store them in. His assistant Lyla, as Harbinger, then brings three more universes into it, saving Earth-4, Earth-S, and Earth-X in the process—but only temporarily. The five pocketed universes are merging, and we are told, "When they occupy the same place at the same time . . . they will destroy each other."

Thanks to some more matter-antimatter plot devices, some superheroes penetrate the anti-universe and battle the Anti-Monitor. They destroy a big machine, thus halting the convergence of the worlds in the pocket multiverse, and nearly terminating the Anti-Monitor. But he survives the battle, and Supergirl doesn't.

Then things take a turn for the even worse. Apparently, it's not enough for the evil Anti-Monitor that all (positive matter) life be wiped out. The Spectre reveals the full plan:

> He has fled from this era . . . retreated to the past . . . before life evolved . . . before this Earth was formed! He has traveled to the *very dawn of time itself!* From there he will change the course of all time! No longer will there be positive matter. Only antimatter will prevail! All Earths . . . all universes . . . all *life* will be eliminated.

But the Spectre has his own counter-plan. Superheroes and supervillains are to join forces:

> Half must travel to the beginning of time. The others must go to the planet Oa, where history must be changed.

The supervillains go back in time to Oa, but fail to prevent Krona's experiment. However, the superheroes who travel to the dawn of time have more success. The Spectre intervenes with the Anti-Monitor, and somehow neither the multiverse, nor the Anti-Monitor's preferred version of things, results. The past is changed, in such a way that only a single, positive-matter universe exists.

The remaining superheroes have a final battle with the Anti-Monitor, and destroy him. Then it's time to deal with some personal—and personnel—crises. Each superhero from the dawn of time mission remembers there being a multiverse, but no one else does. And now there is only one Earth, and *three* Supermen (or at least, two Men and one Boy). Superman of Earth-2 remembers his wife Lois, who now—if that's the right word—never existed. The resolution? After the three Super-guys team up, travel to the anti-matter universe, battle the Anti-Monitor, and victory is secured, Superman-2 and Superboy pass up the trip back to the positive side of things. They are taken instead—along with Lois, who, it turns out, doesn't never-exist after all!—to "that other place . . . where . . . there will be no fear . . . only *peace* . . . everlasting peace." This leaves Earth-1's Superman as the one and only Superman, on the one and only Earth, in the one and only (positive matter) universe.

It's a very complicated business all round. Whether or not *Crisis* succeeds on its own terms—whether or not it cleaned up the continuity mess that existed previously—is debatable, but that's not my focus here. The story invokes two metaphysical conjectures dear to my heart: time travel, and multiverse. Let's examine these in turn.

Time Travel and Wishful Thinking

The laws of physics don't rule out the possibility of time travel, and philosophical arguments for the impossibility of time travel don't work. But there are clear constraints on time travel. Probably the best known is that you can't change the past.

The naïve view of time travel thinks of it this way: suppose a disgruntled fan, Joe, builds a time machine in 2020, and returns to the 1984 of his childhood with the intention of preventing *Crisis* from ever being published. Well, he might kill Marv Wolfman (*that'll* teach him to kill off Supergirl!). No Wolfman, no *Crisis*. Joe thereby changes the past: it used to be one way, and now it's a different way. Although Joe-the-child was around in 1984, there was no time-traveling adult Joe in 1984, the first time around. Then, the second time around, 1984 saw the arrival of Joe from the future, and the future is now *different*. Were Joe to return to 2020, *Crisis* would never have been.

But there is a puzzle at the heart of this naïve description. Either Joe returns to the 1984 of his childhood, and is present twice, as man and as boy, or he doesn't. If he returns to the 1984 of his childhood, then it's clear that Wolfman was not killed, and *Crisis* would be published in due course. That's what *happened*, after all. It seems a straightforward contradiction to suppose that one and the same event both happened and yet never happened.

This does not show that time travel is impossible. We must distinguish between changing the past and affecting it. In *Superboy #85* (1960), the story "The Impossible Mission" describes Superboy's attempt to save Abraham Lincoln from assassination. He travels back to the fateful day, and seems to have tracked Lincoln to a hotel room. But "Mr. L." turns out to be not Lincoln but Lex Luthor, who has also traveled back in time, to escape Superman. Luthor thinks Superboy is after him, and immobilizes him with some red Kryptonite. While Superboy is down, Lincoln is assassinated on schedule by the nefarious John Wilkes Booth. When Luthor realizes this, he is distraught.

Why is Luthor so upset? Because he realized that he has helped *make* history. Had Luthor not interfered, Lincoln would have been saved by Superboy. Nothing at all has been *changed*, though—the one and only April 14th, 1865, included not only the killing of Lincoln by Booth, but also the immobilization of Superboy by Luthor, who, unknown to historians, were both present on that date. (Of course, had April 14th not included the immobilization, it wouldn't have included the killing, since Booth would have been stopped and Lincoln would have been saved.) In this respect, the story is coherent.

How different things are in *Crisis*! First, there is but a single universe, and all is hunky-dory. Then, Krona messes it all up, rewriting the history of the cosmos so that there is a multiverse plus an antimatter universe. Then, had the Anti-Monitor been able to have his way, he would have made a second revision to get rid of the multiverse, so that only the antimatter universe would ever have existed. But instead yet another revision is made, restoring things to a single, positive-matter universe. (It's not clear how close to the original version the final edit is: I suppose it has to be different—not including Krona's experiment, for instance—but it is otherwise as things would have gone in the first place, whatever that means here.)

There are two ironies here. First is the obvious analogy between serialization itself and the history of the cosmos: "later" events manage to force the revision of earlier ones. The second is that many writers on time travel have tried to keep storylines coherent precisely by appeal to a multiverse. They have argued that the best way to make sense of time travel, given that you cannot change the past, is to postulate multiple timelines. When Joe kills Wolfman, he prevents the publication of *Crisis* on a timeline different from his native one. So time travelers to the past don't change the world, rather they change worlds.

The *Crisis* writers seem to think you can do even better. When he first hears the Spectre's plan, Earth-1's Superman objects:

> What you're talking about, Spectre, is *changing history*. That can't be done. Lord knows I've tried to.

The Spectre replies:

It can be done, Superman, but only at the *dawn of time.*

The idea seems to be that you can't change one timeline—one history—but you can *eliminate it altogether*, by going back to the very beginning of everything. We shall see whether or not this understanding of a multiverse is coherent. But, coherent or not, is there any reason to *believe* in a multiverse?

More Things in Heaven and Earth?

The notion of a multiverse is not restricted to science fiction and comic books. There are several arguments for the hypothesis that the space-time we occupy is not the only one that exists.

The Everett-Wheeler "many-worlds" interpretation of quantum mechanics (QM) postulates a branching multiverse. When a quantum choice is made, a world literally splits into two; to put it another way, if the quantum choice is between events A and B, then A happens on one branch and B on the other. Two quantum choices produce four branches, four produce eight, and so on. Each timeline is then understood as a unique way of picking a path through the branching structure. The many-worlds interpretation of QM is taken seriously by many physicists, so to the extent that we are committed to QM, we *might* be committed to believing in a multiverse.

A more recent motivation comes from so-called "fine-tuning" arguments. Cosmologists would like to know why the initial conditions of the universe happened to be the way they were. More precisely, there are about twenty quantitative measures of the initial conditions that appear "fine-tuned": had any one of them not been precisely what it was, then a radically different universe would have resulted, one not remotely conducive to life, let alone intelligent life. Many argue that this "fine-tuning" of our actual initial conditions requires special explanation, and a popular suggestion is that it shows that God exists. But even if you think that fine-tuning requires special explanation, there is another explanation that might do: a multiverse. If every way that the initial conditions might have been corresponds to an existent universe, then there's nothing special about *this* one existing.

Even more radical is David Lewis's modal realism. Now we move from physics straight to philosophy. The philosophical study of modality is the study of necessity, possibility, and impossibility. Princeton philosopher David Lewis was, before his death in 2001, one of the foremost investigators of what is meant by these important terms. Lewis argued that the best account of the truth of statements of possibility and necessity—statements like "It was possible for this chapter to be shorter than it actually is"—is one that assumes the existence of a world (or total array of realities) for every way that the actual world might have been. To put it bluntly, it was possible for me to write a shorter chapter than this because in some other world, I did. But Lewis's hypothesized worlds are strictly isolated from each other, with no causal interaction from one to another. If the many-worlds interpretation of quantum mechanics is true, then we inhabit an *actual* multiverse of connected realities. That just means the actual world is far bigger than most folks think it is. But Lewis thought that there are an infinite number of other possible worlds, *in addition to* the actual world, regardless of its size. However big the actual world is, it's but a teensy-weensy part of all that exists.

Now, let's turn back to science. The physicist Max Tegmark likewise has produced a welter of arguments for a multiverse—indeed, for different multiverses. Tegmark thinks that physics gives us reasons in addition to those already laid out for postulating a multiverse. So, although it's not exactly orthodox to believe in a multiverse, there's a lot of such talk going on these days, and it's happening across disciplines. Do any of these hypotheses fit what happens in *Crisis*?

A Multiversity?

The DC multiverse is not the one that Lewis's modal realism hypothesizes, since the DC worlds are not causally isolated. There can be interaction between them. And that is not true of the worlds Lewis postulated. In addition, what physicists think of as the standard branching multiverse picture is likewise ruled out, because in the DC multiverse, non-time travelers are able to interact with different timelines.

A closer fit is the distinctive many-worlds interpretation of quantum mechanics given by physicist David Deutsch. Deutsch believes that experimental results (specifically, the two-slit experiment, in which individual photons produce a wave interference pattern) demonstrate that there are distinct universes interacting with each other at the microscopic level. But something else is available.

I think the multiverse conjecture that fits best is one that explicitly postulates a second time dimension: call it *hypertime*. Anyone who postulates a multiverse to permit time travel without changing the past is committed to hypertime. Look at it this way. If Joe leaves his native timeline in 2020, and arrives in another timeline in "1984," what makes this a *past* time? It's not in his native timeline at all. We can make sense of this only if we impose a *plane* of time on the branching lattice. If "1984" in each timeline is a different time occurring at the same hypertime, then Joe travels back in hypertime, but not time. To make Joe a literal time traveler, we can instead suppose that each "1984" is the same time, occurring at a different hypertime. Either way, it's a coherent picture: Joe can kill Wolfman in 1984 on another timeline, even though he can't do it on this one. The cosmos must be at least five-dimensional, with three spatial and two temporal dimensions.

We're still not quite there, though. *Crisis* tells us:

> In the beginning there were many, a multiversal infinitude . . . the multiverse shuddered . . . in that instant a universe was born. A universe reborn at the dawn of time. What had been many became one.

"In the beginning," "in that instant," and "had been" cannot refer to plain ol' *times*, or this is simply incoherent. So is it an ordering in hypertime? Well, no, that would be incoherent, too. These are references to changes in *hyperhistory*, not plain ol' history—they tell us that what was five-dimensional became different. At a minimum, then, we need to postulate a *six*-dimensional cosmos, with three spatial dimensions and three temporal ones, including, perhaps we should say, *supertime*! A *timeline* or history is a four-dimensional (three spatial, one temporal) path through the cosmos, and it seems that we humans and superheroes alike perceive only four-dimensionally. A hyperhistory is a five-dimensional path, such as a multiverse. And a *superhistory* is a six-dimensional path. There's only one DC superhistory, it seems.

Does Anything Change, or Not?

Although the superhistory postulation renders the DC storyline coherent, it doesn't clearly do justice to it. The problem is that the multiverse, and the antimatter universe, at most *cease* to exist—it's not true that they never existed, except in a rather limited sense. Indeed, it's not clear that they even cease to exist.

Consider the time travel analogy. Joe goes "back" to 1984, and kills Wolfman. The consequence is that there is at least one history in which *Crisis* never exists. But *Crisis* exists all right, both from the four-dimensional perspective of Joe's native history, and from the five-dimensional perspective. The most we can say, then, is that it will *seem* to Joe that he made *Crisis* never exist. It's *as if* he changed history, but all he did was exchange histories, going from one to another.

Now in a superhistory, if that's what *Crisis* describes, it's *as if* our superheroes change hyperhistory, eliminating all trace of the Anti-Monitor. But all they've done is switch from one hyperhistory, that includes the anti-matter universe, to one that doesn't. For all we know, the antimatter universe is alive and well in the not-quite-native hyperhistory.

(Presumably, the native hyperhistory is the original—in supertime—single-universe one. And until Krona's fateful experiment, no one could have detected the difference between time and hypertime...Then again, it could be that there's a lot more to the cosmos than we have so far considered. For instance, it looks as if there's a heaven of sorts, and Wonder Woman apparently ends up on Mount Olympus in one hyperhistory described to us. But if there is a God (if not gods), why doesn't He help out against the Anti-Monitor? Or does He, perhaps, by sacrificing his offspring—the Monitor? Perhaps it's better to ignore the extra metaphysics . . .)

I suspect the writers of typical "past-changing" stories aren't in any way satisfied with a multiverse resolution. What they really seem to envisage time travelers doing is "turning back time" in the sense of *reversing* it. I call this *dynamic change*—instead of bringing about one history in which an actual past event didn't occur, the hypothesis of dynamic change supposes that one can bring it about that *no* history contains that event—and that is an incoherent notion. Similarly, I suspect that the writers of *Crisis* envisaged a story in which, not only is there a hyperhistory in which the multiverse doesn't exist, but also that there is no hyperhistory in which it ever exists. (For instance, we are told that Wonder Woman goes back through time, getting younger and younger until she ceases to exist altogether. Then she is reborn, and has a completely different life.) That, likewise, is incoherent.

Identity in *Crisis?*

There's another difficulty with trying to give a multiverse resolution of a time-travel story, but few if any fans of the hypothesis have noticed it. What exactly is the relation between Superman-1 and Superman-2? Is it strict identity, so that one and the same person is both Superman-1 *and* Superman-2? And if they are not strictly identical, then are they at least cousins of some sort?

It's tempting to immediately say that they are distinct individuals. They are natives of different worlds (we presume), they are different ages, they work for different newspapers, and so on. But then, a similar argument can be made against identifying you as you are now with any individual who was around ten years ago. You're different in all sorts of ways from the past individual we usually identify you with. This is the philosophical problem of *persistence*: how can one and the same thing change its properties over time, and yet persist as *the same thing*? There are two competing accounts. According to *perdurantism*, persistent objects are only ever *partly* present. Just as your head and your butt are (I hope) distinct *spatial* parts of a larger thing that is you, you-now and you-ten-years-ago are distinct *temporal* parts of a larger thing that is you. You are literally a four-dimensional, space-time "worm," made up of a lot of little segments. Those segments can differ from each other, just as (I hope) your head and your butt do.

The alternative account of persistence is *endurantism*: there is strict identity between you-now and you-ten-years ago— indeed, you are all there—wholly present—anytime you are present. There is no space-time worm—it's just you, instanced again, and again, and again. (On the picture of perdurantism, you, the persistent thing, have only one instance, spanning all the times you are alive.) Another way to characterize the difference is that these two views conceive of *change* very differently.

According to the perdurantist, change over time is qualitative difference between different temporal parts of a thing. (It's like the way the scenery changes as you change spatial location.) Endurantist change is when one and the same thing has different properties at different times.

If perdurantism is true, then Superman-1 and Superman-2 are two different space-time worms. They are not the same individual, and do not even overlap—they have no parts in common at all. (Unless I have grossly misunderstood the story, things are not branching with every quantum choice—it seems that branching occurred long ago and stopped. So it's a bit of a mystery why things are so similar in all the branches). The Wolfman that Joe kills in the alternative 1984 is *not* our Wolfman, and if Joe were to meet "himself" as a child, that's not *Joe*.

Perdurantists aggregate temporal parts of individuals—they conceptually put together distinct temporal parts as parts of one ongoing thing—and in principle they can aggregate further. Superman-1 and Superman-2 can be regarded as distinct hyper-temporal parts of a still larger thing—call it *Hyper*Superman! (And distinct HyperSupermen can be regarded as supertemporal parts of SuperHyperSuperman! At least it stops there, given but one Superhistory . . .)

Endurantism, on the other hand, has the resources to identify Superman-1 and Superman-2—if one and the same thing can exist at different times with different properties, why not on different timelines with different properties? Most endurantists whom I know might accept this, but balk at what happens in the DC multiverse, because they would regard it as impossible for Superman to meet himself. (Perhaps this is the explanation of why the five pocketed universes cannot coincide, but then it would also prevent their apparent overlap.) Perdurantists have no difficulty with the storyline in this regard—Superman-1 meeting Superman-2 is no more problematic than you meeting me.

Endurantist Past-Changing?

But suppose an endurantist were to bite the bullet, and grant that Superman-1 and Superman-2 are strictly identical—one and the same individual. Then a fascinating possibility presents itself. If one and the same *thing* can be *very* different over time, or across timelines, then why can't something similar be true of one and the same *timeline*?

Up to now, we have implicitly taken for granted that a multiverse *must* consist of numerically distinct timelines. But perhaps one and the same timeline exists *this way*, in this 1984, and *that way*, in another. This presents us with the possibility of *endurantist* changing of the past. Joe can bring it about that 1984 is not the way that he remembers it, by killing Wolfman, and preventing the existence of *Crisis*.

But even granting the coherence of endurantist past-changing (something I myself find metaphysically distasteful), this doesn't get us *dynamic* change. Joe does not in any measure *erase* the past he remembers. So endurantism, no matter how far we carry it, does not remove the necessity of a six-dimensional cosmos as the setting for *Crisis*. And given that six-dimensional cosmos, nothing in it *changes* in the sense of turning back time. That sort of changing of the past is mere wishful thinking. To close with a quote from Wolfman himself, in reply to the common complaint, "Did you have to kill the Barry Allen Flash?"

> We always liked Barry, so when we were asked to kill him we planted a secret plot device in the story that could bring him back if someone wanted to. Don't look for it; you won't find it—but if you corner me at a convention, and I'm in a good mood, I'll tell you what it is.

Maybe the device is perdurantism: the Flash we see killed isn't really Barry Allen, but a counterpart. Or else it was him, and we'll bring back a counterpart. Or maybe what's at work is endurantism: the Flash we see killed is Barry Allen, all right, but since when did that stop him from surviving on another timeline? This much is certain: once you have the multiverse and its resources, they don't go away, no matter how you write and rewrite the story . . .

19

What's Behind the Mask? The Secret of Secret Identities

TOM MORRIS

> Though manners make, yet apparel shapes.
> —John Florio (1591)

Why did the Lone Ranger wear a mask? Way out in the middle of nowhere, his normal arena of operation, who in the world was going to recognize him? And what did he have to hide? He did only good deeds, he was scrupulously careful not to kill even the worst of his adversaries, and he was widely admired, not only for his actions, but also for his style, and his notoriously impeccable grammar. For whatever reason, he wished to perform his many services for his fellow man in such a way as not to be identifiable if and when he was ever out of costume. Only Tonto knew his real identity, and he wasn't talking, except for all that "Kemo Sabe" stuff ("trusty scout"), which wasn't very helpful.

Of course, Zorro also wore a mask. So did many adventurous heroes in the history of fiction, including that courteous, smooth-talking, dashing swordsman in *The Princess Bride*, and the Spirit, the Phantom, and too many other swashbuckling, colorful characters to possibly list here. It's hard not to have great respect for the success of their efforts at disguise. Every time I've put on one of those little raccoon masks that were apparently so effective for them—you know, the ones that cover the eyes alone and a bit of the nose—I've always been instantly recognized by anyone who even remotely knew me, and then asked repeatedly what I was doing. Outside the worlds of comics, television, and film, those masks seem to work only at Mardi Gras, and most likely nobody there knows you in the first place, and if they do, they're too drunk to see straight anyway, so what's the point?

For the great superheroes, however, there is always a point. To begin to get a sense of what it might be, let's first take a step back from masks and secret identities, and contemplate a more generic phenomenon. It's one that is well known in ordinary life as well as in the comics.

Dual Identities

Think about dual identities for a minute. In the world of super-heroes, dual identities are very common. Here's a short, partial, but fairly representative list of the sorts of dual identities to be found in superhero stories:

The Hero Identity	The Normal Identity
Aquaman	Arthur Curry Orin
Batman	Bruce Wayne
Black Canary	Dinah Drake
Captain America	Steve Rogers
Captain Marvel	Billy Batson
Daredevil	Matt Murdock
Flash	Barry Allen
Green Arrow	Oliver Queen
Green Lantern	Hal Jordan
Hawkman	Carter Hall
The Hulk	Bruce Banner
Invisible Girl	Sue Storm
Iron Man	Anthony Stark
Mr. Fantastic	Reed Richards
Spider-Man	Peter Parker
Superman	Clark Kent
Wonder Woman	Diana Prince
Woody Allen	Allen Stewart Konigsberg

I threw that last one in just to make sure you're paying attention.

As soon as anyone gets superpowers and takes on a mission of dramatic crime fighting or world-saving outside normal channels, he or she always seems to face an immediate and unexpected wardrobe challenge. "What am I going to wear?" And the answer almost inevitably involves some sort of a mask, or a surrounding hood of brightly colored spandex, often with just eye-holes and a mouth opening at least large enough to sip through a straw. Then the next question seems to be: "What am I going to call myself?" Although, after donning the new outfit, some heroes suddenly find themselves too busy to worry about that one, and just get named by innocent bystanders. With the striking costume and new name, a new identity comes into existence. And it's not always about secrets.

Everyone knows who the Invisible Girl is. It's Sue Storm. She doesn't try to hide her real identity. In the same way, everyone knows that Reed Richards is Mr. Fantastic. They don't attempt to use their flashy outfits or catchy new names to mask their true, original identities. For them, the spiffy superhero presentation is more like a team uniform or a mode of dress that says, "I'm on-the-job." In this regard, think of scientists' lab coats, doctors' scrubs, a Marine's fatigues, or that guy at the garage with "Bob" stitched on his grease-stained shirt. There's no secret identity stuff going on here (unless Bob's real name is actually "Frank" or "Charley"—in which case you'd better scrutinize your repair bill a little more carefully). But there is something a little bit like a dual identity captured in each of these cases. Butch Bassham the Marine lieutenant may be a tough, aggressive, and even frightening guy in his full battle regalia, and while performing his duties, he may even get called "Wild Dog" by his compatriots. But he might also be the nicest dad a kid could have, and act as a kind, loving husband at home. When he puts on the uniform, he makes a transition into an alternative role, and to some extent, an alternate identity. This doesn't mean that Butch is a schizophrenic, or a person with multiple personality disorder, or that he has any other sort of psychological pathology. We play different roles in the world, and when one of those roles is very difficult, we often go into a different mode of self-identity and self-presentation in order to perform it well.

Philosophy professors often don tweed sport coats, and carry ratty brief-cases, redolent with hidden wisdom. Your white-coated physician will stand over you adorned with all those official accessories like a stethoscope, hospital name badge, and a bunch of tongue depressors sticking out of her pocket. Many of us have lucky ties, power suits, or some outfit that we put on for special, high-pressure situations. More people than we realize dress to impress, and there are many ways to do so. The amount of life that involves bluffing by appearance can sometimes be a bit scary to contemplate, and quite interesting. And it's relevant to the superheroes.

Batman has always been very honest about his costume. It was designed to strike fear into the hearts of criminals, who, as he often reflected, are "a superstitious and cowardly lot." It was a piece of theater for a purpose. His outfit was meant to effect something in the minds and emotions of his adversaries, something supportive of his mission, giving him perhaps a split-second advantage that might make all the difference to the outcome of an otherwise well-matched fight. For most of the superheroes, the outfit, and the identity that goes with it, is a means to an end. It's a calling card and a tool—a threat to the bad guys that gets them off their game, and a reassurance to the good folks that help has arrived.

I think it's a general rule in our society that women are even more conscious of clothing choices and their effects on those around them than men are. In part, that's because women are simply more conscious of everything than men are. And it's natural to assume that the same holds true in the world of superheroes. In that case, it won't just be guys like Batman who use costuming as a tool. I've always hoped that the most scantily and provocatively clad female superheroes chose their striking costumes for similar reasons and not because they were just outrageous exhibitionists. They knew they could rely on the "gawk factor" to give them an extra split second, or in the case of some bad guys, all the time they could want, to get the edge and win the day. While the bad guy was momentarily frozen, sizing her up, the beautiful and well-displayed female superhero would already be busy taking him down. Now, it could be that this is too generous an assumption, and that it's the comic-book illustrators and their readers who have always been doing the main gawking. But it's preferable to assume the best about both real and fictional characters, whenever possible.

Many athletes use clothing as a tool. You can sometimes see runners on cold days dressed in something like bright red long johns, white gym shorts, and a vibrantly colored jacket trudging down the side of the road. By putting on those special clothes, reserved only for their runs, many of those runners get themselves "up" emotionally for the experience, focusing their minds, and making themselves emotionally ready to take on the elements for miles and miles.[1] The bright colors also help keep them from getting hit by a car. So there is often a dual purpose for such outfits, and it works.

But for most of the superheroes, getting into an outfit isn't just a matter of psychological self-preparation or of public perception. And it isn't just a matter of dual identities—one hat at work and another at home. There is much more at stake than this. For most of the superheroes, a dual identity is primarily about masking. The costume and the superhero persona (from the Latin for "mask," or presentation) keep a secret. The people who see Spider-Man in action are not to know that he's Peter Parker. And the people who see Peter each day are not to know that he's Spider-Man. Attorney Matt Murdock doesn't want people to know he's Daredevil. And Daredevil is just as eager to prevent people from realizing he's the blind lawyer of Hell's Kitchen, Matt Murdock.

Keeping Secrets

This is a small point, but one worth making and highlighting. Secret identities go both ways. When Spider-Man is busy web-slinging and crime-fighting, he doesn't want people to know that he's really the young Peter Parker. And when Peter is at school, he can't allow his mates to know that he's the crime-fighting superhero, Spider-Man. He often wishes they knew, so that he'd get a little more respect. But he realizes that the knowledge of his alternate, crime-fighting identity could put them and him in jeopardy. Secrets are hard for people to keep, especially interesting and even exciting secrets. If any of his friends knew that Peter was a superhero, and let that information slip in the

---

[1] Superheroes, like star athletes, seem to be masters of the strategy of preparation and action outlined by philosopher and psychologist William James in his famous essay, "The Will to Believe," reprinted in many places, including his *Essays on Faith and Morals* (New York: World Publishing, 1962). See also Tom Morris, *True Success* (New York: Putnam, 1994), Chapter 2, and *The Art of Achievement* (Kansas City: Andrews and McMeel, 2002), Part Two, to learn how this works.

hearing of the wrong person or at the wrong time, great danger could result. Villains who can't defeat a superhero in direct battle are always eager to get to their loved ones and friends in order to gain a unique form of leverage. And this could be disastrous for everyone involved. So the secrets seem justified.

However, an ethical problem involving secret identities has crossed the minds of many comic-book readers over the years. Secrecy involves deception, and deception, like outright lying, is considered by most good people to be a bad thing. Superheroes stand for the good, the true, and the just. How then can they justify the deceptions and even blatant lies necessary to create and preserve their secret identities? Honorable conduct seems to be definitive for all the classic superheroes. Therefore, secret identities appear to pose a problem.

First of all, as philosophers we should be careful here. Deception isn't always wrong. We all admire a good quarterback fake in football, or a masterful head fake in basketball that allows the guard to blow by his opponent and get an open shot to the basket. There is a special place for skillful deception in sports. But even that is carefully regulated and very limited. It's one thing for the punter to fake a kick when he really intends to pass the ball, but it's another thing altogether for a lineman to try to hide the fact that he's illegally holding an opponent, or punching him in the face. Not all deception is allowed in sporting contexts. Lying to the referee or umpire might be expected of many players these days, but almost no one off the field, in their more reflective moments, will think it's morally commendable, or even acceptable.[2]

An author can mislead us in the course of his suspense yarn, and we may applaud the deception that surprises us. But if he plagiarizes from another writer and tries to cover it up, that's different. A painter can deceive us with a clever perspective and bring us delight. But if he dupes us when we purchase his work, we won't be amused at all. In sport and in art, skillful deception within the rules is acceptable, but not outside the context legit-

---

[2] On this, see Randolph Feezell, "Baseball, Cheating, and Tradition: Would Kant Cork His Bat?" in Eric Bronson, ed., *Baseball and Philosophy: Thinking Outside the Batter's Box* (Chicago: Open Court, 2004), pp. 109–125. Also, Mark J. Hamilton, "There's No Lying in Baseball (Wink, Wink)," in the same book, pp. 126–138.

imately created by the rules of the activity itself. The question we need to ask is whether there is anywhere in real life, apart from such artificial, special contexts as sport and art, where it's also ethically permissible.

Although we don't talk about it much, the answer is yes. While all developed and sensitive moral traditions condemn lies and deceptions generally, most of them also allow for important, though rare real-life exceptions. In one philosophical way of making the distinction, although a lie may always be in itself a bad thing, judged as to its own nature, it can sometimes, in extreme circumstances, be morally right, or even obligatory. If a lie or a deception is reasonably judged to be necessary for the avoidance of great harm to an innocent person, or is the only thing that will prevent an unnecessary act of killing from taking place, then the lie or deception is typically considered morally permissible and morally justified. We may even sensibly go so far as to offer moral praise to a soldier in wartime, or to a cop on the beat, who is able to disarm a dangerously murderous adversary by deception instead of using extreme force to severely injure or kill him.

The deceptions that superheroes have to engage in to create and preserve their secret identities are likewise typically morally justified, and perhaps can even be morally praiseworthy, rather than being merely acceptable-though-regrettable, in so far as they are reasonably judged necessary to protect innocent people from harm, including prominently those to whom the superheroes bear special obligations, like family members, good friends, civilian co-workers, and significant others. In some circumstances, maintaining a secret identity may be just the thing to do. It can be part of the behavioral repertoire of a good and honorable person involved in extreme situations.[2]

Superman's Interesting Motivation

Many comic-book fans and writers have claimed in recent years that Superman is different from the average superhero with respect to this secret identity issue. Their point is typically that, in other cases, the superhero identity is a secondary, artificially

---

[2] In Chapter 14 of this volume, Christopher Robichaud reflects carefully on what might be some of the limits to this moral justification.

constructed identity, while the original, ordinary civilian identity is the real one, but that for Superman, it's the other way around. Superman is really a super-powered alien. He was not born as Clark Kent but as Kal-El on the distant planet Krypton. He then later took on the ordinary civilian identity of Clark Kent. The Clark Kent persona is then the disguise, and the bright blue tights with their splashy color-coordinated emblem really present us with the actual identity. The mild-mannered awkward reporter guise is just that, a sustained ruse to keep people from knowing where Superman normally works and relaxes when he's not in costume and on duty.

Spider-Man was Peter Parker before being bitten by the spider and gaining his superpowers, with their related second identity. Batman was little Bruce Wayne long before he took on the goals, knowledge, power, skills and couture that created his alternate identity as Batman. Daredevil was the excellent student and nice guy Matt Murdock first, and that particular young man took on his second identity for a purpose. In case after case, we see regular people gaining superpowers and donning a second identity for various reasons that are crucial for the mission they have chosen to assume. The real identity is the civilian one. But Superman is different.

One thing that is interesting about the case of Superman is that, of course, he didn't originally and intentionally devise the cloaking identity of Clark Kent for any specific purpose at all. The Kansas farm couple Jonathan and Martha Kent found him as a small baby abandoned in a space-ship out in their corn field and did what any good Midwesterners would do under similar circumstances—no, they didn't call the *National Enquirer* or set up a roadside attraction, they took him in and gave him their family name. We all know the background story. On the planet Krypton, the scientist Jor-El discovered that his entire world was about to be destroyed. He put his new baby Kal-El into a custom designed space-ship, presumably with an ample supply of toys, sippy-cups, and whatever else was needed, and blasted him into space, hoping that he could survive. The infant made it through the interplanetary journey, somehow crash-landed safely outside the town of Smallville, and was raised by the Kents as their son Clark. With the passing years, when he began to realize that he had superpowers, he knew he should hide this fact from everyone except his parents, and most likely for the reason that if other people knew, they'd all probably likely freak out and do something stupid that would be bad for everyone involved.

So as a young man, and then later as an adult, Clark didn't want people to know he was really Superman. And that can sound precisely like the cases of Matt Murdock and Peter Parker, and so many of the rest—once they realized they had super-powers, they didn't want other people to know. But they already had a core personal identity of a normal sort before gaining those extra powers. With Clark, the powers preceded the developed civilian identity. And his real identity was not that of a human at all. Uniquely, it seems, his superhero identity is his real, core identity.

When Clark moved away from home and went to Metropolis to experience life in the big city and find his destiny, he faced a choice that any of us confront when we go off to college or move to a new part of the country. Who will we be? How will we present ourselves? What image will we cultivate? Of course, our small-town alien farm-boy continued to use the name 'Clark Kent' but also began assiduously to cultivate a special persona involving a meek and mild manner, a social awkwardness, and a skittish sensibility that would remove him as far as possible from any image remotely considered heroic. Otherwise, his phony thick-framed black glasses alone would never likely succeed in keeping people from recognizing him as the Man of Steel, given his identical height, weight, and coloring, along with the awkward fact that he was often seen in the proximity of events involving Superman, yet somehow seemed to disappear during all the excitement, only to be found later by his friends with slightly mussed hair and a question about "What happened while I was gone?" Fortunately for Clark, people in Metropolis are apparently a little slow at connecting the dots.

Why did Superman consciously choose to disguise himself as the newspaper reporter, Clark Kent? First, it clearly served his purposes as a crime-fighter to be in a newsroom, keeping up on all breaking stories and having the opportunity to get out as a roving journalist, ostensibly to cover the news, but actually to make it. And it could be that, at least at first, keeping a secret about who he really was had been undertaken partly to protect his human family and all the good people of the *Daily Planet* from what would otherwise very likely have been various forms of unpleasantness, including the parade of paparazzi and celebrity interviewers who would inevitably camp out on the lawn, the various authorities, promoters, and hucksters who would be bringing requests and urgent demands to his family and friends in order to get some back-door access to him, and especially the very serious potential of kidnappings and deadly reprisals on the part of the frustrated villains he knew he would have to thwart and subdue on a fairly regular basis. But haven't you always suspected that there was more to the story than just this?

Superman, of all the great superheroes, is best positioned to defend or rescue anyone in his inner circle who might be threatened with harm of any kind. With super-senses and super-speed to go with his super-strength, he can track what's going on, get there, and deal with it like no one else. Perhaps part of the secrecy about his identity is meant just to cloak his background in mystery. After all, the less people know about him and his origin, the less access they can have to information that might be compromising to him, such as the fact that he's vulnerable to Kryptonite. Any less-than-omnipotent being has to be on the defensive, and part of any good defense involves guarding information that might give an enemy an advantage. But I suspect there is even more going on than this.

Superman knows he is an alien. He feels like an alien. He is the ultimate outsider. But he has tasted enough of human life and the human condition to feel very attracted to it, and deeply drawn into it. Jonathan and Martha Kent were good and loving parents, and Clark grew up experiencing friendship, sadness, excitement, happiness, hope, and all the normal emotions and relationships of a genuinely human life. At some level, it seems that he wants desperately to be human, or at least to know what it means to be human in the deepest, most intimate possible way. And he understands enough about human reactions to realize that this will not be feasible if he's perceived as being who he really is. He has to fit in. He can't stand out in the way that he would if the whole truth were known about him.

Imagine if a person about your age and demeanor were to walk up to you in a crowded cafeteria, or in a packed fast-food restaurant, and ask if he or she can share an open space at your table. You barely look up, but agree, and the stranger sits down to eat. This intrusion will interrupt and alter your emotional state to some small extent. You'll feel the presence of someone you don't know, and it might make you the slightest bit uncomfortable. But it would be easy to greet the person and start up a conversation, and then after a while, you might feel like you've made a new friend. But let's take this little thought experiment and make a slight change in it. When you glance up at the stranger, you're utterly shocked to see that it's your favorite movie star, or rock star, a person you'd never expect to see in the flesh in your entire life, but whose poster you have on your wall. The emotional reaction is likely to be vastly different. It will be extremely hard for you to act completely natural and feel anywhere near normal in the presence of this individual. That's the difference the "other-ness" of celebrity can make. The seventeenth century philosopher Blaise Pascal (1623–1662) saw that this is all a function of our imaginations, and is not at all due to the other person existing on a different dimension of reality, or being of an alien race.[3]

But now change the story again and let the stranger actually be recognizable as a unique alien being from another planet with superpowers that could save or destroy, heal or kill in an instant. It will be as hard as possible to have a normal, natural conversation with such an individual and to go away with anything other than a major case of the heebie-jeebies. The restaurant would probably empty out as if it were on fire, and the local SWAT team would be outside within minutes, surrounding the place until the federal authorities could arrive. You'd be very unlikely to end up sharing an order of fries and your life stories. If even Batman, a fully human being, in all his dark and menacing power stood over you in a dimly lit parking lot, the mere force of his presence would probably make your heart race and adrenaline pump through your body. Your skin might crawl, you could tremble with fear, and you might even hurl or pass out. In other words, anything remotely resembling a normal relationship would be, at best, quite difficult. Multiply even that a few times and you can get some sense of how hard it would be for a clearly super-powered alien to walk among us in all his other-ness and yet experience ordinary human relationships and, through them, the full emo-

---

[3] Pascal, *Pensées*, translated by A.J. Krailsheimer (London: Penguin, 1966), Section 44, pages 38–42.

tional range of the human condition. If such a being craved this experience, he would have to appear among us so well disguised that he could blend in and be accepted as one of us. That's exactly what I think Superman decided long ago to do. His true identity is indeed that of the Man of Steel, but I suspect that at least an important part of him wishes it were Clark Kent.

In the *Bhagavad-Gita*, the great Hindu holy text, the god-like Ultimate Being Krishna takes on the appearance of an ordinary chariot driver in order to help guide the prominent leader Arjuna at an important juncture in his life. In this identity, Krishna is able to have a casual conversation with Arjuna, and the leader listens to his wisdom. In the Bible, we are told that God the Son, a literally divine being, took on the form of a man, and the fullness of our condition, in order to experience what we experience, suffer what we suffer, and save us from the deepest consequences of our heedlessly selfish ways by transforming us, as one of us, and as more. But the New Testament is full of what theologians call "the messianic secret"—the reluctance of Christ to reveal the fullness of what and who he really is until the people around him are ready to understand and accept it. These themes are reflected in various ways in many of the best Superman narratives over the decades. The greatest guardian, defender, and savior must be one of us, while also being more than us.

Superman doesn't aim to serve the world exactly as the alien Martian Man-Hunter might, or even as Alan Moore's Dr. Manhattan, in all his aloof other-ness, would. He doesn't want to be a nearly Aristotelian God, an unmoved mover of the world, isolated in his own autonomous independence. He craves an existential connection to us. He wants to serve us as really one of us. His secret identity as Clark Kent isn't just a normal superhero ploy, one more tool or weapon in the super-arsenal. It's a crucial part of a real quest to live the human adventure and guard humanity from within. And I can't help but believe that this desire is the result of the love he was given by his human parents, and even by some of his childhood friends. The transformative power of their total acceptance of him and commitment to him has elicited within him a desire to share mutual acceptance and commitment with more of the people of this world.

Switching Identities

Can Superman really become Clark Kent in more than a disguise? I want to say, "Tune in next week to find out," but I can't. We have to settle this here. As almost every superhero says at some point in his career, "This ends now." I'm joking, of course, but only partly. To get a better fix on whether Superman could ever possibly change fundamental identities and in any sense become primarily Clark Kent, let's look for a moment at his iconic counterpart, Batman.

Superman and Batman are the Plato and Aristotle of the comic-book world. Plato is the theoretical philosopher of the Ideal, the other-worldly spiritual thinker who directs our gaze away from the details of this world and focuses us on the heavenly pattern of The Good. Superman is from the heavens, embodies our ideals, and is always committed to The Good, to such an extent that he's often referred to as the superhero Boy Scout. Aristotle, by contrast, is the earthly, this-worldly thinker, interested in the natural sciences and immersed in the practical and the real. He is also thought of as the inventor of logic, but is perhaps best described as one of its primary discoverers and its first masterful expositor. Likewise, Batman is the down-and-dirty, pragmatic, this-worldly superhero who uses whatever is available, but is at the same time a master of applicable science and technology, along with being the supreme detective, an unsurpassable practitioner of logic in all that he does. Superman is the most super-powered superhero. Batman is the most human superhero, having no superpowers at all. Yet Batman is perhaps the only member of the Justice League of America who could take down all the others, including Superman, if they ceased to serve the world properly and went out of control as the destructive forces they are capable of being. Thus, in an odd way, Superman and Batman are counterparts.

We began our discussion of secret identities with the claim of many commentators that Superman is different from all the other dual-identity superheroes in having as his core identity not his civilian persona, but his superhero persona. But he might in the end have one companion sharing that category with him— Batman. Batman did start life as Bruce Wayne, and only later became the Dark Knight. However, this second identity arose not from some sort of tragic accident that mysteriously brought with it superpowers, as in the case of so many superheroes, but rather from years of intentional effort and painful transformation. Bruce Wayne worked at a superheroic level in cultivating his human qualities to their maximal extent. As a result, he has become the perfect specimen, mentally and physically, for one purpose: to keep the promise he made to his dead parents and do all within his power to fight the crime around him. This mission consumes him to the extent that it makes other normal human activities and experiences more difficult, and some almost impossible.[4]

As you track Bruce Wayne over the years, you can see his transition from a wealthy industrialist who seems to dabble in fighting crime on the side to a totally focused and committed crime-fighter who merely uses his persona as the wealthy Bruce Wayne—industrialist, socialite, and playboy—to keep his real life going as a nearly full-time vigilante and self-created superhero. At the start of his dual identity, his core identity was clearly that of Bruce Wayne, and his alternate, secondary identity, taken on for a purpose, was that of Batman. But as it stands now, years down the road, it seems to me that there has been a gradual, surprising transformation such that the core identity may have become that of Batman, and the secondary, alternative identity for special purposes is that of Bruce Wayne. The image of Bruce may have become the real mask at this point. And if this transformation has actually occurred, then Superman isn't the only superhero whose primary identity is that of the powerful costumed crime-fighter. Batman now shares the category.

And of course, our final twist is that if such a transformation has been possible in the case of Bruce Wayne and Batman, why not also in the opposite case of Superman and Clark Kent? That is to say, we might be led to ask: given the motivation and the effort, what's to stop Superman from so altering himself existentially that, ultimately, he becomes at least, in some important sense, really Clark Kent as his core identity? It wouldn't be the strangest thing ever to happen in superhero stories. But it would be among the most subtle and instructive things to occur there.

Actually, I think what we may be led to conclude in both these cases is that a duality has replaced a singularity, but with

---

[4] See Chapter 9 in this volume, exploring the implications of his mission for his ability to form and maintain friendships.

a new, fused unity. What I mean is that Bruce Wayne's identity may have evolved to the extent that he is at least as much Bats as Bruce. Some of Batman's superhero friends may have doubts about the healthiness of this transition, and so they insist on calling him "Bruce" when they are alone with him, away from the ears of the public, almost as if they are calling him back to remember the person he started out as, and the person it might be a little healthier to be, as his core.

Likewise, Mark Waid has persuaded me that it makes sense to see Superman as inwardly embracing his alien otherness as an important part of the path of authenticity and genuineness in his own life.[5] Because of this, if I am right in thinking that so much of him inwardly yearns for more of an identification with human-ness, to the extent that he often wishes he were just Clark Kent, it may be that what results eventually is not a transformation of core identity from Kryptonian to Kansan, but rather a similar blended duality enhancing what would otherwise have been a singular persona merely using a costume—in this case, of a newsman—for special purposes. And, when you think about it, don't many of us see the same sort of transformation occurring in our own lives, when what starts out as a mask, or costume, or a specialized role, becomes more fused to who we really are, so that in the end our core identity grows into something more complex and interesting?

There is a fascinating thing that sometimes happens in the cross-breeding of plants that botanists refer to as "heterosis"—a phenomenon of superior strength that results in some cases of hybridization, where the blended individual that comes into existence can have all the strengths but not all the weaknesses of the two identities that gave it birth. Perhaps Superman and Batman can experience this in their own different ways, as they reap some of the deeper benefits of what we can think of as role integration, or as identity expansion. As the case of Batman shows, it can sometimes be dangerous in personal ways to integrate certain roles into our core identities. But with sufficient care, we can expand our identities in ways that strengthen and deepen us.

Regardless of where we come out on the surprising issue of whether Bruce Wayne could actually become at the deepest lev-

---

[5] See Chapter 1 in this volume.

els Batman, so that, like Superman traditionally, his civilian identity is the real mask, or whether Superman could actually become Clark Kent as his core existential identity, our main conclusion here can be at least that secret identities are no simple matter, and are even more interesting than they might initially have appeared. Likewise, personal identities of any kind are not as straightforward as we might have been tempted to suppose. Our core identities can grow, develop, and take on new elements that either strengthen us, or weaken us.

Costumes, masks, and alternative personae can be used for multiple reasons, they can be ethically employed, they can be very effective, and perhaps they can even be transformative. We all know about stories where undercover cops or secret government agents have lived too long in their alternative identities and have "turned" for the bad. Why can't inner transformation also go the other way around? It could be that taking on the costume and launching out in committed, dutiful action as a masked superhero can really effect an inner change of some sort on at least most of those individuals whose crime-fighting and world-saving escapades have entertained and enlightened us for decades. It could also be that by trying long enough to live as Clark Kent, Superman will actually and deeply become a person that he would never otherwise have been.

A further conclusion would then seem to follow that we ourselves should exercise great care if we are ever tempted to put on bright tights and a mask and call ourselves by a different name. Every mask leaves an impression on the person who wears it. And any mask may eventually become more of a reality than we ever imagined. Who we are is always a matter of how we act. And what we become is the result of the activities we engage in day to day. The great philosopher Aristotle knew it, and so have many other insightful thinkers through the centuries, like Blaise Pascal, and William James (1842–1910).[6] If we could keep this truth in mind throughout all our endeavors, we would be able to exercise a good deal more care in what we become.

---

[6] See Pascal's famous Wager argument in his *Pensées*, available in many English translations. Philosopher and psychologist William James makes remarks relevant to this in many places, including "The Laws of Habit" in *Talks to Teachers on Psychology: And to Students on Some of Life's Ideals* (New York: Holt, 1915).

Wow! It Could Be the Greatest Gathering of Minds in Comic-Book History! Hold on to Your Hats and Get Ready for the Bios of Your Life!

JEFF BRENZEL, from a tower high atop the Ivy League of America, forays forth to fan the flames of fanatical devotion among the awesome alumni of ancient Yale University. In addition to directing the Association of Yale Alumni in its quest for enlightenment and international social super-power, he uses his own mysterious prowess in practical reasoning to protect his pedagogic prodigies in the classroom from the pitfalls put in their paths by pompous pedants both past and present. A protégé of prominent ethicist Alasdair MacIntyre, after a Yale degree and a short, super-powered business career, Jeff holds a Ph.D. in moral philosophy from the University of Notre Dame.

C. STEPHEN EVANS is University Professor of Philosophy and Humanities at Baylor University and is the author of numerous books dealing with philosophy of religion in general and Kierkegaard in particular. He is the husband of Jan Evans, a professor of Spanish at Baylor, and the father of three grown children (Kelley, Lise, and Chaz) who have contributed greatly to his superhero education, one of the few notable gaps in his Yale Ph.D. program long ago. When not writing or teaching, he can usually be found either running or on the golf course (and sometimes even running on the golf course, pretending he's a cross between Flash and Tiger Woods), or otherwise enjoying the wonderful outdoor vistas of Waco, Texas.

RICHARD HANLEY wanted desperately to grow up to be Magnus, Robot Fighter. Alas, the problem of identity stood in his way, and, in the guise of a mild-mannered professional philosopher at the University of Delaware, he instead devoted his life to the pursuit of tenure. He has written on time travel, fiction, science fiction, and ethics, is the author of *The Metaphysics of Star Trek*, and co-edited *The Blackwell Guide to*

267

Philosophy of Language. But his real passion is examining metaphysical theories of identity. He is close to a resolution that will permit him—once he gets the flashing lights working—actually to become Magnus, Robot Fighter. So much for the easy part—"growing up" is proving more difficult.

REBECCA HOUSEL is, by day, a professor of writing and literature in upstate New York, and by night both a mutant superhero and researcher with the University of New South Wales. She has written for *Redbook* magazine and has published the *High Seas* series of five children's novels. She has contributed to *Monty Python and Philosophy* (2006) and is currently working on a two-volume book project on women warriors. Rebecca's cosmic powers enable her to combat the evils of having a teenager while helping upstate New York brain tumor patients through the Phoenix Fund at Gilda's Club, a non-profit organization started by that philosophical warrior-princess to help patients survive and thrive. Rebecca also kicks super-villain butt.

KEVEN KINGHORN is a tutor in philosophy at Oxford University, where he took his doctorate and still refuses to give it back. Friends suspect that Kevin's addiction to comic books has unduly influenced his understanding of the Oxford-Cambridge rivalry. He considers Cambridge University to be his sworn enemy and is convinced that it is the root of all the evil in the world. Kevin was recently banned from high table after repeatedly using meal-time to try to persuade his fellow Oxford dons to form a Justice League to do battle against the Cambridge cohort of super-villains. Unsurprisingly, his efforts only managed to draw strange looks. Kevin was last spotted "Hulking Out" after Oxford lost to Cambridge in the annual boat race last summer.

C. STEPHEN LAYMAN, often bitten by spiders, firmly believes that he has gained a host of special powers from these experiences, but since they are completely undetectable, he continues to serve as Professor of Philosophy at Seattle Pacific University. He is the author of the books *The Shape of the Good* and *The Power of Logic*, along with numerous academic articles in professional journals. After all these years, he is still reluctant to don spandex, although he is nonetheless completely committed to using all his powers for good. Interestingly, he once had a student named "Peter Parker." We're not making this up.

CRAIG LINDAHL-URBEN earned a B.A. in philosophy at Reed College, and somehow realized that a Ph.D. would be superfluous for living a wise and full life. Currently an independent scholar in residence at St. Olaf Collage, he has spent many years in the computer industry, both owning a computer software company, and as an executive for large computer companies. He was formerly Publisher and Editor-in-Chief of a weekly newspaper and, unlike his fictional colleague J. Jonah Jameson, he always hoped that Superman and Spider-Man would drop in. The best he ever got was Jimmy Olsen's third cousin, twice removed.

JEPH LOEB continues to work as a writer-producer in movies and television (with such credits as *Teen Wolf, Commando, Buffy: The Animated Series,* and *Smallville*). He has written some of the most distinctive and important comic books in recent times, including *Daredevil Yellow, Spider-Man Blue, Hulk Gray, Superman For All Seasons, Batman: The Long Halloween, Batman: Dark Victory,* and *Catwoman: When In Rome,* just to mention several of the groundbreaking projects for which he has teamed up with artist Tim Sale, and *Batman: Hush* (in which he quotes Aristotle), done with artist Jim Lee. In 2003, Jeph was awarded an honorary Doctorate of the Arts from the prestigious St. Edward's University in Austin, Texas for his work with making pop-culture icons accessible to children. Not bad for a Jewish kid from New York City who discovered comics at the age of eight and has only looked up in the sky ever since.

MATT MORRIS, boy wonder, discovered comic books and the amazing people who create them when he was thirteen. As an aspiring comic-book creator himself, he carried on a regular correspondence with some of the best writers and artists of the mainstream superhero comics, who sometimes asked him, as a middle-school student, if he was interested in a job. Throughout the years, he has benefited from their belief in his superhuman talents. And now, after an academic career that has taken him from the beach in Wilmington, North Carolina, to Harvard and UNC-Chapel Hill, he continues to love the superheroes and all they represent. Still in his early days as an extraordinarily talented filmmaker, he has been known to respond to the Bat-Signal and go wherever he is needed. He honestly can't believe the total number of otherwise productive hours he has spent in hypothetical ruminations over which superheroes could beat which others in a fight. This book was his idea.

TOM MORRIS remembers an odd-looking truck pulling up beside his car in New Haven, Connecticut, years ago, carrying nuclear waste, right before he suddenly found himself with philosophical powers. This is actually true, although he'd be the last to say, "*Post hoc ergo propter hoc,*"[1] largely because hardly anybody would know what he was say-

---

[1] This is, of course, Latin. It's the name of a famous fallacy and, as a phrase means, "after this, therefore because of this"—in case you were wondering.

ing. He is now, by many estimates, the most active public philosopher on the planet, speaking to more people about the wisdom of the ages than any philosopher since Ralph Waldo Emerson. He regularly brings philosophical insight to hundreds of thousands of people in large meeting rooms and convention centers all over America, and after writing many academic tomes, has authored such popular books as *Making Sense Of It All, True Success, If Aristotle Ran General Motors, Philosophy for Dummies, The Art of Achievement,* and *The Stoic Art of Living.* Forthcoming soon will be *Harry Potter and the Meaning of Life.* This Yale Ph.D. can be reached any time at his virtual Fortress of Solitude through the nearly secret portal, www.MorrisInstitute.com.

DENNIS O'NEIL is an award-winning comics writer and editor. He has also been a journalist, critic, television writer, and novelist. His most recent book is the novelistic adaptation of the new film *Batman Begins.* Renowned for the way in which he introduced social themes into mainstream superhero comics, he also guided Batman from the realm of comedic television back into the role of dark, urban avenger. He has lectured at dozens of universities and, aside from participating in the naval blockade of Cuba, writing for a time under the pseudonym "Sergius O'Shaugnessy," and introducing many revolutionary changes into superhero comics, including once stripping Wonder Woman of her powers and costume, he has led a relatively normal, quiet life.

CHRISTOPHER ROBICHAUD is a Ph.D. candidate in philosophy at M.I.T. He received his B.A. from John Carroll University and his M.A. in philosophy from Texas A&M University. When not thinking very hard about what's really real or playing Koosh with his fellow philosophers, Chris wanders around M.I.T.'s Infinite Corridor, hoping beyond hope that he's at just the right place at just the right time when an experiment goes terribly awry, transforming him from an ordinary philosopher into a superhero of transcendental proportions. If that doesn't happen, he at least hopes to finish his dissertation with what little of his sanity remains intact.

CRAIG ROUSSEAU conceived and drew our original cover art. His superhero comic-book credentials include *Impulse, Batman Beyond,* and issues of *Batman: Gotham Adventures.* He's also known for his contributions to, among many comics, *JLA Adventures 2,* a Max Mercury story in *Flash,* a Captain Marvel narrative in *Adventure Comics,* the great art of the animated *Return of the Joker, Ruule,* as well as for his work used in *Catwoman, Harley Quinn,* and on the Spider-Man-Hulk Christmas Tie. Craig has drawn for Disney, covering such super-powered characters as Britney Spears and the Dixie Chicks. Sharing his sur-

name with one of the great thinkers of the past, Craig is now celebrated for his exciting work in the not-quite-so-philosophical *Harry
Johnson* series. Visit him any time at www.craigrousseau.com.

CHRIS RYALL was always told that no good could come from reading
comic books into adulthood. However, since he managed to find a way
to combine his passions with his livelihood, those voices, largely in his
own head, have quieted down. By day, he works as Editor-in-Chief of
comic-book publisher IDW Publishing, and under cover of night, he
serves as Editor-in-Chief and writer for MoviePoopShoot.com, filmmaker Kevin Smith's acclaimed pop-culture Web site. Chris, his
extremely patient wife, and his cat Fletch live in San Diego, California,
where costumed superheroes can often be seen walking (oddly
enough) down the street.

AEON J. SKOBLE is associate professor of philosophy at Bridgewater
State College, in Massachusetts. He is co-editor of *Political Philosophy:
Essential Selections* (1999), *The Simpsons and Philosophy* (2001) and
Woody Allen and Philosophy (2004) and the author of a forthcoming
work in political philosophy. He writes on moral and political theory
for both scholarly and popular publications, and has also contributed
scintillating essays to recent books on *Seinfeld*, *The Lord of the Rings*,
and baseball. You can tell by his name that he has to be an inter-
galactic visitor. And, sure enough, he came to this planet to fight a
never-ending battle for truth, justice, and the American Way.

J.D. SMITH provided the color for our front cover original art. Super-
colorist Smith, one of the giants of computer coloring, is legendary in
the comics cosmos for his work on the Top Cow titles *Witchblade* and
Tomb Raider, Aspen's *Fathom*, Marvel's *Ultimate Spider-Man*, *Deity*,
and *Dark Angel*, among many other astounding achievements. If Plato
had just had acccess to Photoshop, he might have stopped writing and
become an early version of J.D. Smith: in that alternate universe what
was lost to philosophy would have been gained by art. You can see
what he does so well at www.jdsmithcolor.com.

JAMES B. SOUTH is Chair of the Philosophy Department at Marquette
University in Milwaukee, Wisconsin. He edited *Buffy the Vampire
Slayer and Philosophy* (2003) and is co-editor of the upcoming *James
Bond and Philosophy* (to be published, and not stirred, by Open
Court in 2005). He primarily works in late medieval and renaissance
philosophy, with periodic forays into popular culture (where it's
never too late for a renaissance). James has yet to convince his wife
that Black Canary in fishnets is just as formidable as Nightwing in
kevlar. She has said, however, that she is open to discussing the

possibility and efficacy of Nightwing in fishnets. Since cross-dressing for justice is not within the scope of his chapter, or current interests, he wisely dropped the subject.

CHARLES TALIAFERRO, Professor of Philosophy at St. Olaf College, is the author or editor of seven books, most recently *Evidence and Faith: Philosophy and Religion since the Seventeenth Century* (2005). With the assistance of his brave and faithful dog Tiepolo, Charles is engaged in a never-ending fight against hate and cruelty, not to mention over-priced dog toys. His current project, *Love, Love, Love, and Other Essays* is to be published by Cowley Press in 2006. Charles is such a captivating teacher that, if the real (that is, the comic-book) Peter Parker had ever taken his classes, he would likely have dropped the science like a hot potato and become a philosophy major instead, presumably to the great dismay of his beloved and practical Aunt May.

FELIX TALLON is writing under an assumed name, and is said to be a Ph.D. student at St. Andrews University in Scotland, where he is studying the interplay between theology and the arts. He is also reported to look exactly like a famous British actor who has starred in many major motion pictures, including several prominent romantic comedies. But we call him "Felix," as he instructs. His essay on the movie *Psycho* will be appearing in the forthcoming book in this series, *Hitchcock and Philosophy*. In his spare time he rules the small, Balkan country of Latveria with an iron grip.

MICHAEL THAU spent many years as the classroom guru of aspiring philosophy students at UCLA, and now creates his unique existential temple of wisdom at, appropriately, Temple University. Talking to Mike about much of contemporary academic philosophy is a bit like talking to Batman about crime. As soon as some rooms open up at Arkham Asylum, he is prepared to show a few college professors the door. Holding a Ph.D. in philosophy from Princeton University, Mike is the author of *Consciousness and Cognition* (2002) as well as a number of ground-breaking and thoroughly scintillating essays on these and other suitably abstruse subjects.

SCOTT TIPTON received Mego Spider-Man and Batman action figures from his parents for Christmas in 1976 and, well, the rest is history. A graduate of the University of California, Santa Barbara, Scott is the Associate Editor of the entertainment and pop-culture Web site MoviePoopShoot.com, and writer of its most popular feature, the weekly comics history column, COMICS 101. Scott is also communications director and design consultant for Toynami, a manufacturer of action figures and collectibles based on a variety of popular animated series and films. A lifelong comic and toy collector and self-styled comic-book historian, he takes great pride in continuing to find new ways to profit from a wasted youth.

MARK WAID was born in 1962 in Hueytown, Alabama. He bought his first comic at age four and has never since entertained the notion of *not* buying comics. His writing credits include, among many others, *X-Men*, *Flash*, *JLA*, *Captain America*, the best-seller *Kingdom Come*, *Fantastic Four,* and *Superman*. In all his spare time, he helps keep the planet spinning on its axis. Though he can name only nine presidents, Waid possesses an encyclopedic knowledge of comic-book history and trivia and also serves as DC Comics' unofficial historian. His pride in this accomplishment has dwindled in direct proportion to his age.

JERRY WALLS is a graduate of Houghton, Princeton, Yale, and Notre Dame. He finally realized that the point of graduating is getting a job, and now, since the days of his Ph.D., teaches philosophy at Asbury Theological Seminary, as well as at many other points around the globe. Jerry is the author of several distinguished books on Heaven, Hell, and points in between, and serves as Senior Fellow in the Morris Institute for Human Values, powerfully bringing philosophy into the lives of people throughout our culture. Unlike Captain Marvel, he doesn't need to utter "SHAZAM!" in order to get his powers, and unlike Gomer Pyle, he doesn't go around saying it anyway.

Index